THE PRACTICAL GUIDE FOR

HEALING

DEVELOPMENTAL

TRAUMA

Using the NeuroAffective Relational Model to Address Adverse Childhood Experiences and Resolve Complex Trauma

LAURENCE HELLER, PHD, AND **BRAD J. KAMMER, LMFT, LPCC**

North Atlantic Books
Huichin, unceded Ohlone land
aka Berkeley, California

Published by

North Atlantic Books
Huichin, unceded Ohlone land
aka Berkeley, California

Book illustrations provided courtesy of NARM Training Institute, LLC
Cover image © pavlinec via Getty Images
Cover design by Rob Johnson
Book design by Happenstance Type-O-Rama

Printed in the United States of America

The Practical Guide for Healing Developmental Trauma: Using the NeuroAffective Relational Model to Address Adverse Childhood Experiences and Resolve Complex Trauma is sponsored and published by North Atlantic Books, an educational nonprofit based in the unceded Ohlone land Huichin (*aka* Berkeley, CA) that collaborates with partners to develop cross-cultural perspectives; nurture holistic views of art, science, the humanities, and healing; and seed personal and global transformation by publishing work on the relationship of body, spirit, and nature.

MEDICAL DISCLAIMER: The following information is intended for general information purposes only. Individuals should always see their health care provider before administering any suggestions made in this book. Any application of the material set forth in the following pages is at the reader's discretion and is their sole responsibility.

North Atlantic Books' publications are distributed to the US trade and internationally by Penguin Random House Publisher Services. For further information, visit our website at www.northatlanticbooks.com.

Library of Congress Cataloging-in-Publication Data

Library of Congress Cataloging-in-Publication Data
Names: Heller, Laurence, 1944– author. | Kammer, Brad J., 1972– author.
Title: The practical guide for healing developmental trauma : using the
    neuroaffective relational model to address adverse childhood experiences
    and resolve complex trauma / Laurence Heller, PhD, and Brad J. Kammer,
    LMFT, LPCC.
Description: Berkeley, California : North Atlantic Books, [2022] | Includes
    bibliographical references and index.
Identifiers: LCCN 2021060506 (print) | LCCN 2021060507 (ebook) | ISBN
    9781623174538 (trade paperback) | ISBN 9781623174545 (ebook)
Subjects: LCSH: Psychic trauma in children—Treatment. | Psychological
    child abuse. | Psychotherapy.
Classification: LCC RJ506.P66 H425 2022 (print) | LCC RJ506.P66 (ebook) |
    DDC 618.92/8521—dc23/eng/20220124
LC record available at https://lccn.loc.gov/2021060506
LC ebook record available at https://lccn.loc.gov/2021060507

1 2 3 4 5 6 7 8 9 VERSA 26 25 24 23 22

This book includes recycled material and material from well-managed forests. North Atlantic Books is committed to the protection of our environment. We print on recycled paper whenever possible and partner with printers who strive to use environmentally responsible practices.

Contents

PART III Applying NARM with Clients

Acknowledgments

We both want to acknowledge and thank our editor Shayna Keyles and the North Atlantic Books staff. We are proud to contribute to the mission of North Atlantic Books and have appreciated their guidance and encouragement.

We want to thank our colleagues Stefanie Klein, Marcia Black, Ann Shine Duck, Kelli Klinger, and Sherri Sharkins. They provide steady, heartfelt leadership within the NARM Training Institute and have given invaluable support and guidance in our writing this book. They are outstanding psychotherapists and, even more, wonderful human beings.

We want to express our gratitude for the outstanding team at the NARM Training Institute, who have all helped us fulfill our vision to create a heartful and skillful professional community that can bring this important work into the world. A special thank you to Tori Essex for all the technical help.

Larry

My relationship with Brad goes back more than twenty years. First as his teacher, then when he began assisting me, and more recently as he has become a NARM teacher and the director of training at the NARM Training Institute. When I reconnected with Brad during the first NARM training in Los Angeles, he kept asking me what I experienced at the time as "irritating" questions. It turned out that over time those questions spurred me on to be more concrete about exactly what I was doing in sessions and what I was teaching. For that I'll always be grateful. It turned out that he became one of the quickest people to grasp the deeper structure of the NARM approach.

The creation of this book together about the NARM therapeutic model represents the culmination of those two decades. Brad has an incredible

capacity for not only remembering material that was presented over a long period of time but synthesizing it and structuring it in a way that the reader finds accessible and informative. He is one of the hardest working people I know. His brilliance, heartfulness, and his dedication to this project together have made our collaboration joyful and creative. To you, Brad, my deep and ongoing thanks.

I also want to add my thanks to the NARM trainers in the US and Europe for their long-term support, interest, and encouragement. As well as to all the NARM training assistants in the US and Europe for their dedication and heartfelt support.

I want to thank my life partner, Rachel, for her consistent, loving encouragement.

To my son, Kevin, his partner, Bianca, and my granddaughter, Gretchen—I'm so glad that you're in my life.

Brad

I want to express my deep gratitude for Larry. I feel so fortunate to have had such a gifted and caring mentor, and now partner, to support me throughout my career. I first started out as his student. Some years later, we began teaching together. We quickly realized that we balanced each other and were well-matched creative partners. This partnership led to the creation of the NARM Training Institute, as well as to this book, where we are actualizing our vision to share NARM in a more accessible way with the world. I appreciate Larry trusting me to be a collaborative partner in the evolution of NARM.

When I first met Larry over twenty years ago in a college classroom in Vermont, he introduced me to a whole new way of understanding humanity. He shared with me the tools to heal my own complex trauma, and in so doing, a pathway to reconnecting to my heart. I am deeply grateful for his mentorship, collaboration, compassion, and support.

I would not be where I am if not for the connection and support from Stefanie Klein. Together we have navigated the unchartered territory of running a training institute and have spent countless hours learning, failing,

trying again, growing, and expanding the limits of who we are and what we have to offer. I deeply respect Stefanie's thoughtfulness, caring, humor, and integrity, and I am so very thankful for our teamwork and meaningful friendship.

My relationship with Marcia Black has supported me personally and professionally for nearly twenty years. Together, we have traveled this NARM journey from the beginning, and we have shared rich learning experiences filled with moments of laughter, tears, healing, and growth. In her professional and personal life, she models the humanity of NARM by leading with a spirit of generosity and care. I specifically want to thank Marcia for giving me such a beautiful, quiet space to get away and focus on writing this book.

I have had the great pleasure to work with so many passionate helping professionals within the NARM international community. These incredible folks, passionate about healing complex trauma and supporting post-traumatic growth, have taught me so much and have inspired the writing of this book. I want to especially thank our NARM training assistants, who bring so much compassion and heart to our training community.

I have been so fortunate for over two decades to work as a therapist and teacher with such incredible human beings—individuals, couples, families, groups, and communities that have inspired me. I am thankful to each client and student who, through our relationship, has taught me so much about pain, healing, and humanity.

I want to acknowledge and express gratitude for a few teachers who have influenced and mentored me along my professional journey: Peter Levine, Bonnie Badenoch, Walter Zeichner, Paul Nadel, Tirzah Firestone, and Peter Collins.

I am grateful to family and friends around the world. Though we are living in a fragmented time and don't get to spend as much time together as I would like, whether in person or online, I treasure our moments of connection and love.

Words cannot begin to express my love and gratitude for Koda and Cheyo. It is the joy of my life to be their father. The family experiences we share have inspired and supported my work and have brought so much

connection, meaning, and healing into my life. I have learned how to connect to and share my heart in ways that make me a better person.

Sarah, my soulmate, has a heart that radiates deep love and compassion. We truly have gone beyond our dreams as we have grown this family full of life and love. Sarah has been my companion throughout this writing process, providing such caring guidance and encouragement, while also suggesting possibilities on other ways of communicating these important ideas. She has always understood my passion and supported my journey. I will be forever grateful for our deep connection and sustaining love.

As I reflect on all these meaningful people in my life, I also want to acknowledge why I came into the trauma field in the first place. My culture has been impacted for thousands of years by sustained oppression and trauma. The intergenerational and ongoing trauma that has impacted my lineage, my family of origin, and me cannot be so easily healed. Yet it has inspired me to do what I can to heal myself and support others in their healing. I have dedicated my life to helping people transform trauma. I am grateful for the intergenerational wisdom that has emerged out of my trauma. This wisdom fuels and sustains me, and it supports me with greater understanding, sensitivity, and empathy for any individual, community, or culture suffering from unresolved trauma. *We're all in this together...*

Introduction

This book is written to support personal and collective change.

It is an exciting time to be part of the trauma-informed movement. Over the past decade, awareness of trauma has moved beyond psychology and gone mainstream. Trauma has become a theme for blogs, articles, podcasts, songs, documentaries, movies, and TV shows, as well as a cause for celebrities, politicians, and social movements. A greater understanding of the widespread impact of trauma, especially complex trauma, is upending and revolutionizing mental health and other healthcare and social systems.

While it is daunting, and often heartbreaking, to recognize the impact on individuals, communities, and societies, we believe that a greater understanding of complex trauma—and tools to resolve it—can change our world.

The NeuroAffective Relational Model (NARM) was introduced over a decade ago in the book *Healing Developmental Trauma*.[1] This seminal work continues to remain popular as one of the first books specifically designed to address the emerging field of developmental trauma. Thanks to the adverse childhood experiences (ACEs) study and the new diagnosis of Complex Post-Traumatic Stress Disorder (C-PTSD), the trauma-informed field is growing rapidly. As awareness of complex trauma grows, therapeutic models to address the impact of ACEs and C-PTSD are needed.

NARM is one such model. For the past few years, we—NARM creator Dr. Laurence Heller and training director and senior faculty Brad Kammer—have been focused on building a professional training institute, the NARM Training Institute. Our mission is to evolve and promote

trauma-responsive education, training, and treatment for healing complex trauma. This includes addressing the long-term impact of relational trauma that comes in the form of attachment, developmental, cultural, and inter-generational trauma. We have trained thousands of helping professionals internationally and provide ongoing education, training, consulting, and support to individuals and organizations around the world.

Our intention for this practical guide is to promote greater accessibility to the NARM therapeutic approach. We have done our best to take a comprehensive clinical model that requires years of professional training and present it in a way that supports ease of application. While mental health professionals may find it easier to apply, we have written it in a way that supports application for helping professionals working with the impact of complex trauma. We have written this for those of you who work as doctors, nurses, alternative medical professionals, substance abuse and addiction counselors, bodyworkers, coaches, religious and spiritual counselors, educators, first responders, police officers, social workers, probation and correction officers, policy makers, and anyone else whose work is impacted by complex trauma. Our heartfelt desire is that NARM will support the work you are all doing to heal our world.

Additionally, we wrote this as a practical guide for those of you who are seeking personal healing and growth. While NARM has its foundations in advanced psychological theory, this book provides a pathway to anyone interested in post-traumatic healing and growth. Transforming trauma patterns can lead to decreased suffering, increased hope and resiliency, and greater fulfillment in life. Whether you are a helping professional or an individual interested in healing, we hope that you will be able to use what you learn in this book for your professional and personal development.

NARM is not just a clinical model for resolving complex trauma—it's a blueprint for supporting relational health. By introducing a depth-oriented, somatic-based approach for shifting the psychobiological adaptations to complex trauma, we aim to provide readers with a greater understanding of what is driving human pain and suffering. This relational framework is based on a foundation of heartfulness.

By introducing more individuals and organizations to NARM, we hope to contribute to a less pathologizing, more humane framework for supporting connection, health, and aliveness. While traditional psychological and neuroscientific understanding is consistent with the NARM approach, there is much work to do in bringing greater compassion to the application of psychological and neuroscientific methods.

The Roots of NARM

NARM builds upon the pioneers that came before and draws on a variety of approaches, including models from within Western psychology, as well as non-Western approaches to the human experience. From within Western psychology, NARM follows the lineage of depth-oriented, relationally focused, and somatically informed psychotherapeutic models and has integrated aspects of psychodynamic and somatic approaches. Additionally, we acknowledge and appreciate those theories and theorists who are less well-known, those from outside of traditional psychology, and those whose contributions have been minimized or ignored. We have both participated in learning from different cultural, religious, and spiritual traditions and acknowledge the wellspring of traditional wisdom and healing practices that have inspired and shaped our approach.

Throughout the evolution of NARM, the intention has been to offer a therapy that people would feel is respectful, refined, effective, and transformative. In order to support such an approach, we have integrated a focus on relationship, personality, emotions, and the body that is consistent with the developing understanding of neurobiology. NARM specifically aligns with the growing field of interpersonal neurobiology.

Over the past few decades, at least in the United States, these approaches have been largely eclipsed by cognitive and behavioral models. While these models certainly have a role to play in mental health treatment, there are risks involved with losing depth-oriented approaches.[2] Moving away from depth-oriented models means moving away from understanding the complexity and nuances of the human experience. We see some current psychological

models, while well-intentioned, to be further pathologizing, objectifying, and dehumanizing of individuals who are suffering and desperate for help.

Despite developments in some areas within psychology, we are still profoundly stuck in old paradigms that have outlived their usefulness. The medicalization, and subsequent pathologizing, of human suffering has kept us preoccupied with treating symptoms and diagnoses, as opposed to recognizing root causes and treating the human. NARM advocates a shift away from a disease model to a focus on relational health.

In this chart, we present a few differences between NARM and other therapeutic approaches:

NARM CLINICAL APPROACH *IS NOT*	NARM CLINICAL APPROACH *IS*
Primarily historically focused	Primarily present-moment focused
Focused on trauma stories (content-driven)	Focused on the adaptations to trauma (process-driven)
Regressive (child consciousness focused)	Grounded in here and now (adult consciousness focused)
Cathartic	Containment oriented
Pathologically oriented	Resource oriented
Goal driven	Inquiry driven
Strategically based	Curiosity based
Behaviorally focused	Internal-state focused
Focused on symptom reduction	Focused on shifting underlying patterns that are driving the symptoms
Practitioner driven, with client following their lead	Client driven, with practitioner providing new opportunities for exploration

Bringing a humanistic perspective reinforces that we are not simply treating maladaptive symptoms and behaviors but connecting with a human being. We are not working with objects—we are working with a subject. The subject is an individual's whole Self.

Those who have experience with non-Western healing approaches have pointed out the similarity of NARM to the shamanic perspective on "soul loss," in which the soul fragments in response to a traumatic experience and leads to pain and suffering. The work of "soul retrieval" is to bring these fragmented parts of the soul back together. By reconnecting fragmented inner states—physical sensations, emotions, impulses, behaviors, and thoughts—NARM reinforces a deepened experience of one's subjectivity. When these aspects of the Self are invited back into awareness, they create something greater than the sum of its parts. In this way, NARM is not just about post-traumatic healing, but about transformation of the Self.

This takes us into territory where psychology merges with spirituality. In fact, the Greek root of the word *psychology*, "psyche," originally meant "soul." As we begin to work on the deeper levels of human experience, we need a new way of understanding—and tools for working with—the deeper aspects of the Self. You will notice we capitalize the *S* in *Self*. We are following a long tradition within psychology, as well as various religious and sacred traditions, that uses *Self* to acknowledge the spiritual nature of who we are. This takes us beyond our identity—who we take ourselves to be—into a greater sense of wholeness. In this journey of transformation, there are opportunities for connecting with deeper sources of our aliveness. This is an opportunity for becoming more fully human.

The spiritual journey of post-traumatic growth is reinforced by the phenomenological-based approach of NARM: the emphasis on subjective experience and working in the Now. Other elements from depth and somatic-oriented approaches give us access to aspects of the Self that are deeper than the mind and body. When done proficiently, therapy has the potential for being an embodied, spiritual process of radical healing and transformation.

Although we will be describing transformative states that can happen in people resolving complex trauma—for example, as long-standing personality patterns start quieting, a deeper well of calm and stability emerges—it is beyond the scope of this practical guidebook to provide the transpersonal and spiritual foundations of NARM. We very much look forward to presenting this in a future NARM book.

The Cultural Context of NARM and Its Application

We understand that we are using a very specific perspective in this book for understanding and addressing complex trauma. This perspective is built upon the culture from which we have both been trained, and thus it is grounded in Western psychological thinking. The concepts and terms we use are largely derived from this framework. We have done our best to honor this perspective while at the same time practicing cultural sensitivity and humility and doing our part to evolve the modern discourse around trauma. We recognize that trauma and trauma healing have been around long before Western science began. There are elements from a non-Western orientation integrated into the NeuroAffective Relational Model, but the language we use to describe it has emerged largely out of Western psychology.

Additionally, we recognize that we hold certain biases in writing a book about a clinical model that has deep roots within Western psychology. We are writing this book based on the context in which we work. Although both of us have traveled and lived outside the United States and have had many meaningful interactions with teachers and healers outside the Western framework, we were both trained as clinicians in the United States. We understand that this shapes our perspective. We are also committed to reflecting on and learning more about biases that could unconsciously shape our work. In this book, we have been mindful of doing our best not to perpetuate cultural biases that are contributing to ongoing cultural and systemic trauma. But the reality is that there will be areas that readers will feel we have missed. Please know that it is our intention to continue learning, as well as bringing our learning into the ongoing evolution of NARM.

We are mindful of the limitations of Western psychology and appreciate the complexity of working with people from diverse backgrounds, beliefs, and cultures; we also acknowledge that there are certain psychobiological processes that seem universal. A foundational understanding within NARM, and in this book, is that humans have psychobiological needs for both connection and individuation. These human needs are often viewed as polarities, and even pitted against each other in conflict. For example, some cultures are seen as prioritizing community orientation and others as prioritizing individual orientation. These opposing cultural structures are often described as "collectivistic" and "individualistic" societies, but we view them as a continuum of the human experience. Underlying this continuum between community and individuality are complex psychobiological processes that exist beyond culture. NARM supports the human need for both connection and individuation by recognizing the reciprocal nature of these two aspects of being human.

Although there are universalities about the experience of trauma, there are also many different ways individuals, families, cultures, and nations experience, understand, and address trauma. Some of the NARM organizing principles and clinical skills may need to be adapted to the context in which you work. Familial, religious, and cultural differences must be considered when applying any model emerging from Western psychology, including NARM. So we invite you to adjust this framework accordingly to fit with your specific clients and work setting.

We see ourselves as part of the worldwide emerging trauma-informed movement. We view this as an opportunity to learn from each other as part of the gift of a more interconnected planet. As the leaders of the NARM international community, we are active in ongoing explorations, reflections, and discussions on supporting this new framework for mental health that holds trauma as the roots of individual and collective suffering.

The Larger Context of Complex Trauma

As we will further describe in chapter 1, the trauma field is still early in the process of clearly differentiating between post-traumatic stress disorder

(PTSD) and complex post-traumatic stress disorder (C-PTSD). A distinguishing factor of C-PTSD is the focus on *self-organization*, which refers to a neurodevelopmental and psychobiological process of shaping one's personality and life experience. C-PTSD focuses on three areas of disturbances in self-organization: emotional regulation, self-concept, and relationships.

Even within this understanding of complex trauma, some terms are still being defined, including the differences between developmental and complex trauma. We use *developmental trauma* as a subset of a larger dynamic of *complex trauma*. Whereas *developmental trauma* is based on relational disruptions during childhood that impact the development of a child's sense of Self, *complex trauma* is an umbrella term that also includes later disruptions to one's sense of Self. This can include adult experiences like domestic violence, human trafficking, being imprisoned and tortured, or where escape from a toxic, abusive, or violent situation has not been possible.

One of the major errors of Western society and science over the past few hundred years was to separate the individual from their embeddedness within relationships. For better and for worse, relationships shape us. The field of complex trauma stands on the shoulders of attachment theory, which for the past half century has contributed to a greater understanding within psychology of how attachment relationships impact child development. More recently, however, psychology has been challenged even further to expand beyond just focusing on the parent-child relationship and acknowledge the impact of the extended web of relationships that impact child development.

Complex trauma speaks to the way that relationships between individuals in dominant positions impact individuals in subordinate positions. Traumatic relational dynamics can emerge when more vulnerable individuals must rely on those in power for their survival and well-being. In attachment theory the focus is on the way this plays out between parents and children. But it is important to recognize how this also plays out in larger ways beyond attachment failure in family systems.

Relational trauma also emerges out of the oppression of communities, cultures, and nations. These relational systems of oppression and subjugation create and perpetuate complex trauma. We cannot separate a person's developmental process from the society in which they are raised. There is a

growing movement within mental health that speaks to these larger concerns and seeks to expand inclusion of more culturally informed perspectives and models. Within the trauma field, it is important to identify the historical legacy of brutality, oppression, and generations of complex trauma that has deeply impacted, and continues to impact, vulnerable individuals and cultures.

We are hopeful that a NARM-informed perspective can support those who are working to address complex trauma within family systems, communities, cultures, and nations. While outside the scope of this book, we believe that NARM principles can contribute to larger systemic change. What if healing complex trauma can alter ongoing societal conflicts, violence, war, poverty, and other forms of systemic oppression and trauma? We truly hope that some readers of this book who work in social, political, and humanitarian advocacy may be able to apply these principles in shifting the systems that maintain systemic oppression, inequalities, and long-standing injustice. While this book focuses on supporting individual change, we believe that NARM can also be a major vehicle in promoting social, systemic change.

Agency: A Missing Clinical Piece

We get two main pieces of feedback from those who have taken our professional trainings. The first is appreciation of our focus on the helping professional's own humanity. Many people who have gone through our trainings have told us that they experience increased curiosity, openness, presence, and heartfulness. They often find themselves working with less effort and being easier on themselves, which impacts the way they show up with clients. NARM therapists often tell us how much more effective they feel as clinicians as they learn more about their own emotional and relational dynamics. We will be addressing these themes directly throughout this book.

The other main feedback we receive has to do with the NARM concept of agency. We hear frequently from NARM therapists that agency

is a "game-changer." We have had numerous clients report the same. Agency supports a shift in focus away from specific traumas and toward how we've learned to adapt to early traumatic experiences and how we've carried these adaptations into adulthood. While identifying with childhood trauma often leaves individuals feeling helpless, hopeless, and stuck, embodying a sense of agency supports increased capacity for healing, growth, and change.

Agency is related to a client's *psychobiological capacity*, which describes an individual's capacity to experience and use complex patterns of cognition, behavior, emotions, physiology, and interpersonal engagement. Assessing for agency provides a way of understanding where a client is in their present abilities and meeting them where they are. Understanding how clients are relating to and organizing their life experience is the essence of supporting agency in NARM.

As we will detail in chapter 5, the NARM therapeutic process is set up to foster an increasing sense of agency from the very beginning. Prioritizing agency helps establish relational consent between therapist and client. It ensures that the client is steering the ship of therapy. Ultimately, reinforcing a client's sense of agency provides our clients with a pathway to increasing their psychobiological capacities for living a more fulfilling life.

Overview of This Book

It is not easy to write a practical guidebook on resolving complex trauma. There are no simple answers and no quick fixes when working with complex trauma. Just as there's no easy step-by-step process to a fulfilling relationship or effective parenting, working with complex trauma can't so easily be reduced into simple steps. However, the organizing principles and skills that we introduce throughout this book can help guide your way.

Working with complex trauma is often very challenging. Therapists can get lost in their clients' complex web of symptoms and have difficulty staying organized during sessions. Clients with unresolved complex trauma come into our office with varying degrees of internal disorganization.

They can feel overwhelmed and out of control. It is easy for us as therapists to get pulled into our clients' disorganization. But as soon as we do, we become co-opted by the client's old strategies, which generally leads to both client and therapist feeling stuck. Hopelessness thrives in a therapeutic environment where both client and therapist feel lost or overwhelmed and have difficulty trusting in the possibility of change, healing, and growth.

Therapists face this dilemma every day in their work. When faced with hopelessness, stuckness, and limited possibilities, often what therapists do is *try harder*. Many therapists rely on strategies of efforting and pressuring themselves to make change happen for their clients. This intention for making change happen comes from a well-meaning place, but it has consequences for therapists and clients alike.

The NeuroAffective Relational Model provides a way out of this trap. We will be introducing a framework that supports greater therapeutic and relational effectiveness. We will be outlining in detail the process of understanding and addressing the impact of unresolved developmental trauma. The terrain of early trauma is riddled with complexity. We will be describing the terrain and providing a new way to navigate it.

This therapeutic model calls for a spirit of openness, curiosity, and presence that is very difficult for many of us. We will be providing self-reflective exercises and therapeutic skills to support your integration and application of the NARM approach, but we want to reinforce that learning NARM is not easy. As one of our training participants said to us, "NARM is simple, but not easy." While the basic organizing principles may seem simple, applying them is not easy. It is like trying to teach someone to dance or play trombone out of a book. We believe that to truly learn this model, you must directly experience it. And then you have to practice it consistently until it becomes an embodied process. Only then can you apply it proficiently.

Substantial training, guidance, and practice are required in order to be fully skilled in a model that works with sophisticated psychobiological patterns, internal depth, and the subtleties of the human experience. While we do our best to make this work as accessible as possible for you, we also

acknowledge the limitations. If you are interested in developing greater proficiency in the NARM therapeutic approach, this guidebook can serve as a jumping-off point for further learning and training.

Additionally, learning NARM is difficult for another, more personal reason. NARM invites us to connect with parts of ourselves that may be frightening and from which we have distanced as adaptations to our own early life challenges. This therapeutic approach is not only focused on our clients. It challenges us, as helping professionals, to stay open to our own unresolved trauma patterns as we interact with our clients. The *R* in *NARM* is about the therapeutic relationship, which includes both client and therapist. NARM is an approach based in intersubjectivity. This process invites the possibility of deepening connection to Self and others. As we teach in NARM—and will detail throughout this book—connection is both our deepest desire and greatest fear. While there is great hope in finding a model that can so effectively transform unresolved trauma patterns, we also want to keep in mind the internal obstacles you may encounter as you embark on this healing journey.

Organization of This Book

The way this book is organized mirrors the way we teach the NeuroAffective Relational Model in our professional trainings. NARM isn't just a set of stand-alone skills. The interventions we use to shift the psychobiological patterns of unresolved complex trauma emerge from our understanding of the root cause of complex trauma. Helping professionals must first understand how humans learned to adapt to relational trauma, the psychobiological impacts of these adaptations, and how the symptoms of an individual's suffering reflect an individual's deepest desire for connection.

> The spontaneous movement in all of us is toward connection, health, and aliveness. No matter how withdrawn and isolated we have become, or how serious the trauma we have experienced, on the deepest level, just as a plant spontaneously moves toward sunlight, there is in each of us an impulse moving toward connection and healing. This organismic impulse is the fuel of the NARM approach.[3]

In the first section of this book, "An Overview of the NeuroAffective Relational Model," we lay down the theoretical framework that supports our therapeutic process. The second section, "The NARM Therapeutic Model," is built upon this framework; it would be difficult to be effective therapeutically without first understanding what informs and directs these interventions. Although this material can be complicated and psychologically nuanced, we have done our best to make it accessible and practical. We have tried to present just enough theoretical background to support the effectiveness of your therapeutic application of NARM.

In chapter 1 we outline the current trends within the trauma field. We position NARM within the current trauma-informed movement, provide a basic overview of the current research that supports complex trauma, differentiate between shock and complex trauma, demonstrate why models for addressing developmental and complex trauma are so needed, and introduce how the NeuroAffective Relational Model supports complex trauma healing and post-traumatic growth.

In chapter 2 we introduce the NARM organizing principles. We highlight foundational building blocks that frame and guide the NARM approach, including Connection–Disconnection; Attachment and Separation-Individuation; Fear of Attachment and Relational Loss; the Core Dilemma; Adaptive Survival Styles; Shame, Self-Rejection, and Self-Hatred; Emotional Completion; and Disidentification.

The NARM organizing principles help illuminate the internal conflicts that shape a child's development in the face of complex trauma. The ongoing internal battles—between one's connection to Self and connection to others, between one's authenticity and adaptive survival styles, between one's body, emotions, thoughts, and behaviors—lead to complex psychobiological symptoms. Understanding these internal conflicts and adaptive survival strategies supports us in addressing the complex psychobiological patterns that are now getting in the way of the connection, healing, and growth our clients are seeking. These organizing principles set the stage for understanding how to most effectively use the NARM skills and interventions that will follow.

In the second section of this book, "The NARM Therapeutic Model," building upon the framework from the first section, we present the interventions that we use to work through the patterns of complex trauma.

In chapters 3–6, we introduce the NARM Four Pillars, which are the therapeutic skills that support healing and post-traumatic growth. The NARM approach does not follow a strict protocol. This is not a manualized therapy. The Four Pillars provide a framework for exploring how a client organizes their experience in the here and now and supporting new ways they can relate to themself. These skills promote increasing intersubjectivity in the therapeutic process, which has to do with strengthening a client's capacity for connection to their inner world and to other people.

In chapter 3 we introduce Pillar 1: Clarifying the Therapeutic Contract. This intervention supports the client to set the intention for their healing process. By inviting the client to connect to what they most want for themself out of their work with us, we can begin to support an agency-based process focused on exploration, which allows for a collaborative process built upon client intent and relational consent.

In chapter 4 we describe Pillar 2: Asking Exploratory Questions. This intervention drives the way we engage with clients. This inquiry-driven process supports us, and invites our clients, to reflect on and gather information about their internal process. Specifically, we bring curiosity to what internal obstacles are in our client's way of getting what they most want for themself.

In chapter 5 we discuss Pillar 3: Reinforcing Agency. This intervention supports a client's developing capacity for awareness of the active role they play in relating to their own internal and external difficulties, specifically how they are organizing their internal experience in ways that reinforce old trauma patterns. This agency-oriented process supports the possibility that clients can learn new, more life-affirming ways of relating to themselves.

In chapter 6 we present Pillar 4: Reflecting Psychobiological Shifts. This intervention provides opportunities for clients to notice shifts on all levels of their experience—including the physical, emotional, cognitive, relational, and spiritual. We support clients to connect to and embody changes in their internal experience as they begin relating to themselves in new ways—which reinforces an internal process of integration, organization, and transformation.

In chapter 7 we introduce the NARM Emotional Completion Model. We offer a new perspective on emotions and the role unresolved emotions play in complex trauma, as well as a unique approach to working with affect that allows clients to shift complex trauma patterns. We present an important differentiation between primary and default emotions and how we work with them. We highlight the focus on containment, as opposed to expression or discharge, of emotional responses. The Emotional Completion Model supports connection to primary emotions and embodiment of deep and nourishing emotional states.

In chapter 8 we explain the NARM Relational Model. We outline an interpersonal approach for supporting increased relational effectiveness, focused on the therapist's internal experience, by cultivating internal states of curiosity, presence, and active self-inquiry and the therapeutic skills that emerge from these states. We also present a new model for understanding and using therapist countertransference to support relational healing. This mindful interpersonal approach has profound implications on therapeutic engagement and understanding between therapist and client.

In chapter 9 we outline the NARM Personality Spectrum, a framework that helps therapists recognize where their clients are on a spectrum of psychobiological capacity. We provide an assessment tool to identify and assess ten psychobiological traits that are impacted by complex trauma and shape the organization of the Self. This therapeutic map for assessing self-organization has major implications that guide the therapeutic process, interventions, and prognosis. This also helps therapists have a better understanding of therapeutic alliance and issues of countertransference.

In the third section of this book, "Applying NARM with Clients," we demonstrate NARM in action with real clients through the use of two session transcripts. These transcripts include extensive clinical annotations to help identify the NARM organizing principles and skills in real time.

In chapter 10 Brad demonstrates how he worked with Aiyana in support of her desire to feel worthwhile. Coming from an extensive background of familial, cultural, and intergenerational trauma, Aiyana was able to create a successful adult life for herself before she began to experience a diverse array of psychological and physical symptoms. In this session, Brad

demonstrates how NARM can be used to support shifts in lifelong patterns of self-shaming and self-rejection toward a greater sense of self-acceptance and self-compassion.

In chapter 11 Larry demonstrates how he worked with Rich in support of his desire to have a healthier intimate relationship. Rich is in the process of divorce and recognizing the painful impact of his lifelong relational patterns. In this session, Larry supports Rich in beginning to shift the underlying trauma patterns that have been interfering with the way Rich shows up in relationships.

These two sessions, as well as shorter clinical examples throughout the book, illuminate how the NARM approach is used with real clients. We have changed names and details to protect confidentiality, but all examples are pulled from real client sessions, and we are grateful to our clients for allowing us to share their experiences. These clinical examples demonstrate the way that this deeply relational process can shift long-standing patterns of complex trauma. Clinical transcripts like these are used by students in learning NARM, and we hope that they also can support you in your learning, integration, and application of the NeuroAffective Relational Model.

Helpful Reminders While Reading This Book

Since helping professionals from many diverse fields will be reading and using this book, we have simplified the various terms and refer to the individuals we work with as *clients* and those of us who are helping professionals as *therapists*. We understand that some aspects of the NARM approach will not fit for the specific work you do. We are introducing "pure NARM" in this book, and we encourage you to adjust what you are learning as necessary to support your work. There is no one right way to apply NARM. For those of you who are not helping professionals, we hope you can adapt the principles and skills for your own personal healing process. Our intention is to make NARM accessible to anyone, so we encourage you to use what you can.

This book focuses on application. The therapeutic process we present here is research-informed, relying on well-established scientific and clinical

findings from across different disciplines related to trauma-informed treatment. If you are looking for research on developmental and complex trauma, there is a robust and growing field of trauma research that we encourage you to explore. Our intention for this book is to distill these findings to make them accessible in your work with complex trauma.

We will be using two overlapping terms throughout this book: *developmental trauma* and *complex trauma*. Both are used to describe experiences that disrupt healthy development and impact an individual's sense of Self in the world; a key distinguishing feature is that developmental trauma occurs in childhood while complex trauma can occur over one's lifespan. As you do further research, you will come across other trauma terms. There are significant differences between various forms of trauma and important distinctions to be made between them. In order to support ease of application, we will be using *developmental* and *complex* trauma interchangeably, as we will more clearly describe in chapter 1.

Having worked for many years with parents, and both being parents ourselves, we are sensitive to the way that parents have often been blamed for their children's mental health issues. The reality is that complex trauma is just that—complex. Reducing mental illness to failures of the parents is overly simplistic and generally not helpful. At the same time, we must acknowledge the central role parents do play in supporting the development of their children, and the impact that parental abuse and neglect have on their children's well-being. In an attempt to lessen blame and shame for parents, we rely on more general terms such as *caregivers* and *environmental failure* when referring to the dynamics of childhood trauma. The term *caregivers* offers a wider range for understanding the impact that meaningful adults have on a child's early life. *Environmental failure*, which will be explained more thoroughly throughout the first few chapters, offers a wider range for understanding the impact of various forms of trauma beyond just the relational failures within the family system.

Much of what we will be describing relates to childhood trauma, but this book is geared toward helping adults. While NARM works with children, the approach you will be introduced to here would need to be adapted in order to effectively treat children. Similarly, the therapeutic application

would need adaptation to work effectively with couples, groups, or other unique settings—for example, in settings where clients are mandated to participate. This book lays out the general therapeutic model for one-to-one treatment with adults. We encourage you to adapt it accordingly based on your client population and professional setting.

To support your learning of this material, in each chapter we include self-reflective exercises, similar to ones we use in our professional trainings. The exercises provide direct experience with NARM beyond just theoretical learning, and we invite you to use them as a way to directly experience and embody the NARM process. Many of these exercises are also ones you can share with your clients in their learning and growth.

Lastly, we want to express our gratitude to the many thousands of clients and students we have worked with who have taught us so much. We know that the healing journey of complex trauma is not easy. It takes courage. We have been repeatedly touched by the transformation we continue to see in our clients and students. We are honored, humbled, and inspired to have played a part in their healing as they reclaim their lives. It is our hope and desire that the NeuroAffective Relational Model can similarly support you and your clients.

REFLECTIVE EXERCISE

We want to begin this book by inviting you take time to reflect on your intention for reading this book:

- What are you hoping to learn that could support your professional work?
  - If you did learn this, how might it impact your professional work?
  - What would you most like to happen?
- What are you hoping to learn that could support your personal growth?
  - If you did learn this, how might it impact your personal growth?
  - What would you most like to happen?

PART I

An Overview of the NeuroAffective Relational Model (NARM)

CHAPTER 1

The Trauma-Informed Movement

Unless you fix the trauma ... the hole in the soul ... where the wounds started, you're working at the wrong thing ... I think it could be a game-changer.

OPRAH WINFREY ON *60 MINUTES*, MARCH 11, 2018

The field of trauma is changing. And changing fast. Thanks to groundbreaking research like the adverse childhood experiences (ACEs) study, advances within neuroscience, pioneers in the trauma field including Drs. Judith Herman, Bessel van der Kolk, Allan Schore, Daniel Siegel, Bruce Perry, Rachel Yehuda, and others, and a greater recognition and acceptance of trauma within our society, a paradigm shift in our understanding of trauma is happening now. This emerging understanding of a new category of trauma, Complex Post-Traumatic Stress Disorder, has the potential to revolutionize psychological theory and treatment, as well as have significant impact in other areas of our society.

Since 1980, when post-traumatic stress disorder (PTSD) was first officially recognized by the American Psychiatric Association in the *Diagnostic and Statistical Manual of Mental Disorders* (*DSM-III*), the field of

trauma has been focused on PTSD, or what we will refer to here as *shock trauma*. The PTSD diagnosis describes an individual experiencing or being exposed to a potentially life-threatening event that leads to three categories of symptoms: 1) re-experiencing, including flashbacks and nightmares; 2) avoidance, including detaching from others and self-medicating; and 3) hyperarousal, including hypervigilance, panic, and rage. The *DSM-5*, the most recent version, has updated this diagnosis to include an additional category: 4) negative alterations in cognition and mood, including exaggerated negative beliefs of Self and others and difficulty experiencing positive emotions.[1]

While this understanding of PTSD has been revolutionary within psychology and has brought a recognition of trauma into mainstream culture, a new understanding of trauma is rapidly emerging.

> It is a continuing anomaly that current established guidelines for the treatment of trauma relate to post-traumatic stress disorder (PTSD) and are inadequate to address the many dimensions of complex trauma. The differences between complex (cumulative, interpersonally generated) trauma and "single-incident" trauma (PTSD) are significant. Research also establishes not only that "[t]he majority of people who seek treatment for trauma-related problems have histories of multiple traumas," but that those who experience complex trauma "may react adversely to current, standard PTSD treatments." There is thus a clear and urgent need for clinical guidelines which are directed to treatment of the multifaceted syndrome which is complex trauma.[2]

The NeuroAffective Relational Model (NARM) is one of the first therapeutic models that provides a framework and clinical guidelines specifically designed for the treatment of complex trauma, or as it is now officially referred to as Complex Post-Traumatic Stress Disorder (C-PTSD).[3] While other therapeutic models are adapting their treatment protocols to address adverse childhood experiences and complex trauma, NARM was specifically designed to address the long-term impacts of ACEs and C-PTSD.

To help clarify how NARM may be useful in your work with complex trauma, this chapter presents an overview of the current trauma field, some of the important distinctions between PTSD and C-PTSD, and the

need for new therapeutic models that are specifically designed to work with the complexities of C-PTSD, including addressing attachment, relational, developmental, cultural, and intergenerational trauma, and post-traumatic growth.

The Trauma-Informed Movement

The revolution within psychology we referred to earlier has been called "trauma-informed care." Some prefer to call it "trauma-sensitive" or "trauma-responsive." Over these past forty-plus years, our growing recognition of trauma has significantly changed the way we understand and treat mental health. And beyond the field of psychology, a trauma-informed approach is now being used in healthcare, social services, foster care, education, public policy, addiction treatment, law enforcement, criminal justice, correctional care, military and veteran care, emergency medical services, humanitarian aid, coaching, fitness, yoga, meditation, and religious and spiritual centers. Trauma-informed programs can be applied in so many different settings because of the holistic approach to health and well-being that encompasses the mental, emotional, physical, relational, social, and even spiritual levels of human experience.

Trauma-informed care is a broad set of principles that shapes how services are delivered and how individuals and communities are supported. A few examples: Many substance abuse treatment centers have realized that unless they address the unresolved trauma that underlies addictive behaviors, treatment will have limited effectiveness and patient recidivism will remain high. In the United States, there are strong efforts to bring a more trauma-informed understanding into law enforcement and criminal justice, where a disproportionate rate of individuals who are low-income, from minority groups, or both, often with extensive complex trauma histories, are ending up in prison. In many workplace settings, especially those populated by helping professionals such as social workers, educators, nurses, and other healthcare providers, employee health and well-being have not been prioritized, and there is high risk for exposure to secondary trauma, burnout, and substance

abuse. This is often followed by stressful workers' compensation litigation, stigmatization, and alienation from employers and colleagues. While "mental health days" and self-care reminders are a start, they do not go far enough to address the ways trauma interplays with one's employment.

Perhaps one of the most well-known examples of trauma-informed care was presented in the extraordinary documentary film *Paper Tigers*. Jim Sporleder, a principal for Lincoln Alternative High School in Walla Walla, Washington, where all the "troubled kids" were sent, was facing alarming rates of truancy, substance abuse, teen pregnancy, fights, gang activity, and criminal behavior. Principal Sporleder and his staff were overwhelmed and unsure about what else they could do. One day he was introduced to the cutting-edge research on ACEs and complex trauma, which inspired him to implement a trauma-informed approach at his school instead of the standard focus on test scores and behavioral modification. Recognizing that children with unresolved trauma have difficulty concentrating and learning, and that these and other disruptive behaviors are symptoms of their trauma, Lincoln staff realized that they had to change the ways they taught and interacted with their students. Instead of using strict discipline and punishment to control students' behavior, school staff met students with curiosity, interest, compassion, and acceptance. Replacing detentions and suspensions with check-ins and counseling, Lincoln staff began to acknowledge and address the deeper wounds of trauma that were driving these children's problematic behaviors. As one staff member shared with a student: "I know why you smoke weed, why you smoke meth. I know why you're in fights. You don't want to feel. That's the big challenge—I'm asking you to try feeling for a little bit. Because sometimes when you feel, it guides you in the direction that you should be going and not where you are."[4]

This compassionate, heart-centered approach challenges many traditional educational models by prioritizing student health, well-being, and resiliency. From our perspective, addiction treatment, law enforcement/criminal justice, employment, and education demonstrate incredible potential for changing lives—and changing the health of our society. The trauma-informed

movement is striving to change these often-dehumanizing systems to become more humane, supportive, and life-affirming. The need to address and resolve trauma is a human rights issue.

Both of us have worked for many years as trainers and consultants to guide helping professionals and various organizations toward greater integration of trauma-informed practices. It has been exciting to witness trauma-informed understanding begin permeating our social systems. At the same time, despite "trauma-informed" being added to various existing therapeutic modalities and organizations, there are still major gaps in treatment. In fact, we were inspired to write this book because we feel confident that NARM can play a key role in contributing to the necessary advancement of complex trauma-informed treatment.

The following chart demonstrates the important differences between NARM-based, trauma-informed care and previous ways of addressing client care:

CONVENTIONAL PERSPECTIVE	NARM-BASED, TRAUMA-INFORMED PERSPECTIVE
"What's wrong with you?"	"What happened to you? And how have you adapted to what happened to you?"
Treatment focused on individual symptoms and behaviors	Treatment focused on the whole person, recognizing they are living within families, communities, and systems that impact them
Symptoms/problems are pathological; clients are sick, ill, or bad	Symptoms/problems are survival strategies clients use to deal with unresolved trauma; clients are generally doing the best they can given their circumstances
Use labels to describe client pathology	Humanize clients by describing the impact of trauma on individuals, families, and communities
Helping professionals are the experts providing services to broken survivors	Helping professionals collaborate with clients, supporting agency, choice, and control in the healing process

(continued)

CONVENTIONAL PERSPECTIVE	NARM-BASED, TRAUMA-INFORMED PERSPECTIVE
Goals are defined by helping professionals and focus on symptom reduction	Goals are defined by clients and focus on recovery, self-efficacy, growth, and healing
Help is provided reactively, generally focused on managing crises	Help is provided proactively, generally focused on preventing further crises and strengthening resilience
Treatment aimed at managing or eliminating symptoms and behaviors	Treatment aimed at resolving underlying trauma and supporting greater connection to Self and others

REFLECTIVE EXERCISE

We invite you to take a few moments to reflect on the following questions:

- What did you have to do in order to stay safe in your early environment? For example, did you learn to keep quiet? Did you learn to fight? Did you learn to stay away from potential conflict? What adaptations did you learn to make?

- How did you carry forward the adaptations you made during childhood into your adulthood?

- How might these adaptations now be causing distress in your adult life?

As you reflect on these questions, we invite you to notice what you experience internally in your thoughts, emotions, and body.

I (Brad) had the experience of working within community mental health settings with low-income, underserved, and marginalized clients. Most of the clients were dealing with the impacts of poverty, substance abuse, domestic violence, and child abuse. I worked at an agency that served youth and families on Medi-Cal, the Medicaid-based system of California. The program I worked in was specifically designed for "emotionally disturbed" (ED)

children, which is the official label used to describe these children. The majority of children did not live with their biological parents but lived in foster care or with grandparents, aunts, older siblings, or other extended family members. Most of these children were being raised in chronically unsafe homes within chronically unsafe communities. Many also had to deal with the direct and indirect effects of cultural, intergenerational, and systemic trauma, particularly the Native American and Hispanic children and families who made up a significant percentage of the client population.

Many children, as they got into middle school, started running afoul of the law. Most of the boys I worked with were bouncing in and out of juvenile hall. The chaotic, unpredictable, and unsafe home environments created profound negative impacts on their development. As clinical staff, we were required to diagnose the various symptoms and disorders as outlined in the *DSM*. In meetings, I wouldn't refer to these kids as emotionally disturbed. Instead, I referred to the environments as fundamentally disturbed. It was clear to me that the problem for these children was environmental failure. These children were simply doing the best they could, with whatever resources they had available to them, in order to survive.

For myself, and a number of my caring and compassionate colleagues, it felt wrong to locate the disturbance in the child and not address the adult world that was failing the child. As mental health professionals, we were required to give these children serious diagnoses, knowing that the source of the problem existed in the environmental failure. It felt important to acknowledge that children's behavioral and emotional responses, while often problematic, emerged as ways to adapt to environmental failure. Families, communities, and social systems were failing these children on a daily basis.

Like so many clinicians in our position, we had little choice and were required to give *DSM* diagnoses that would allow these vulnerable children to receive the treatment they so desperately needed. In our clinical meetings, we would agonize over official diagnoses like Attention Deficit Hyperactivity Disorder, Depressive disorders, Anxiety disorders, Obsessive-Compulsive Disorder, Oppositional Defiant Disorder, Conduct Disorder, Reactive Attachment Disorder, and Autistic Spectrum Disorder. To make

matters worse, we knew that most of the children would then receive psychotropic treatment that often led to many intense side effects and possible long-term psychological and physiological effects.

The classification systems that we rely on within mental health have not been grounded in a trauma-informed perspective. If they were, these conversations would look different. If we all worked within trauma-responsive systems, like the staff at Lincoln Alternative High School, we would meet children not as emotionally disturbed or juvenile delinquent, but as human beings whose every waking moment is shaped by the need to regulate the effects of unresolved trauma on their brains and bodies. While the research on adverse childhood experiences and developmental trauma is growing, we still have ways to go. It is our hope that the mental health field will shift toward a trauma-informed diagnostic system, including specific disorders that capture the impacts of complex trauma for children and the long-term impacts on adults.

ACEs: Adverse Childhood Experiences

The human brain is a social organ that is shaped by experience, and that is shaped in order to respond to the experience that you're having. So particularly earlier in life, if you're in a constant state of terror; your brain is shaped to be on alert for danger, and to try to make those terrible feelings go away. In a healthy developmental environment, your brain gets to feel a sense of pleasure, engagement, and exploration. Your brain opens up to learn, to see things, to accumulate information, to form friendships. But if ... you're not touched or seen, whole parts of your brain barely develop; and so you become an adult who is out of it, who cannot connect with other people, who cannot feel a sense of self, a sense of pleasure. If you run into nothing but danger and fear, your brain gets stuck on just protecting itself from danger and fear.

DR. BESSEL VAN DER KOLK, "CHILDHOOD TRAUMA
LEADS TO BRAINS WIRED FOR FEAR" (INTERVIEW),
SIDE EFFECTS PUBLIC MEDIA

In the 1980s, our understanding of adverse childhood experiences (ACEs) emerged from Kaiser Permanente's obesity clinic in San Diego, California.[5] The clinic, geared toward patients who were somewhere between 100 and 600 pounds overweight and wanted to reduce their weight, was seeing great patient results. But there was a problem. Dr. Vincent Felitti, the physician who established this clinic, noticed a concerning trend: despite losing significant weight, over half their patients dropped out of the program before they had completed their weight loss goal. Even more curious, all the patients had been losing weight—not gaining—when they quit the program. Dr. Felitti and his team set about answering the question as to why people who were desperate to lose weight, and who were actively losing weight, sabotaged their mission as they were nearing their goal.

As Dr. Felitti and his team conducted follow-up interviews with as many former participants as they could, they stumbled upon a startling discovery: most of these patients had a history of childhood sexual abuse. Being overweight was not the problem—it was the *solution*. As many participants disclosed, being obese made them feel unattractive and therefore less likely to attract sexual attention. Additionally, eating made them feel better, as it helped them avoid their distressing emotions. As most of us have experienced late at night with a pint of ice cream, eating serves to help shift the neurochemicals of anxiety, pain, and depression and leads to at least temporary moments of pleasure and inner calm. As children, many of these patients had learned that a behavior such as binge eating could be used as a strategy to escape the turmoil of their inner world. When their strategy was removed by their participation in the weight loss program, before they had dealt with the underlying wounds of childhood trauma, they would be left facing overwhelming internal distress. At that point, they would quit the program and return to old behaviors of overeating, which once again serves to protect against their internal distress.

Identifying the roots of trauma underlying behavioral challenges highlights the intractability of self-sabotaging patterns of behavior. Despite how much an individual may want to change, people are deeply invested in their

strategies, even when the strategies have unintended and potentially lethal consequences. This was a huge realization. What if all these "problems" were in fact at one time "solutions" to manage adverse childhood experiences? What if self-harming strategies are still being used by teenagers and adults as ways of managing unresolved trauma? From this perspective, self-sabotaging behaviors begin to make sense. It helps us better understand people's reliance on such harmful behaviors as overeating, overworking, substance use, gambling, cutting, unsafe sex, risky behaviors, physical violence, and criminal activity.

But there is another important lesson here from this ACEs origin story. On some deep, unconscious level, these participants did not feel that they deserved the success of meeting their weight loss goals. When a child experiences early trauma, their developing sense of Self becomes embedded in shame. Whether consciously or unconsciously, so many of our clients do not feel that they deserve good things. They do not experience a sense of self-worth. Therapists may feel confused, frustrated, and stuck with clients who say they want to grow, heal, and feel better and yet seem deeply invested in not growing, healing, and feeling better. Understanding the shame-based sense of Self that emerges out of early trauma may provide a new way of understanding the profound internal conflict that leads people to act against their best interests and damage their lives.

Returning to Dr. Felitti, his curiosity around the self-defeating strategies emerging from childhood trauma led him to connect with Dr. Robert Anda at the Centers for Disease Control and Prevention (CDC), and together they launched the study into how childhood trauma impacts adult health.[6] A survey was later created, consisting of ten questions designed to inquire about different experiences of adversity during one's childhood.[7] For each trauma category that an individual experienced, they receive 1 point, which adds up to their ACEs Score, from 0 to 10. The ACEs study focused on the main categories of early trauma that were consistent across research into adverse childhood experiences:

1. Emotional abuse

2. Physical abuse

3. Sexual abuse

4. Emotional neglect

5. Physical neglect

6. Loss of parent

7. Domestic violence

8. Family member with addiction

9. Family member with depression/mental illness

10. Family member incarcerated

REFLECTIVE EXERCISE

We invite you to calculate your own ACEs Score by responding to the following questions.[8] Give yourself 1 point for each question where you experienced that category of trauma *before your eighteenth birthday.*

1. **Emotional abuse**: Did a parent or other adult often or very often insult, demean, belittle, humiliate, verbally assault, or threaten to physically assault you? _____

2. **Physical abuse**: Did a parent or other adult often or very often grab, slap, push, or hit you? _____

3. **Sexual abuse**: Did a parent, adult, or someone at least five years older than you ever touch your body in a sexual way or attempt or have oral, anal, or vaginal intercourse with you? _____

4. **Emotional neglect**: Did you often or very often feel that no one in your family loved you or thought you were important; or your family did not look out for each other, feel close to each other, and support each other? _____

5. **Physical neglect**: Did you often or very often not have enough to eat, had to wear dirty clothes, had no one to attend to your medical and dental needs, or had no one to protect you? _____

(continued)

6. **Loss of parent**: Were your parents separated or divorced, or did you lose a parent for any reason? _____

7. **Domestic violence**: Did you often or very often witness or hear violence between your parents or other adults where someone was being grabbed, shoved, slapped, hit, kicked, had something thrown at them, sexually attacked, or threatened with a weapon? _____

8. **Family member with addiction**: Did you live with anyone who was a problem drinker or alcoholic, who used illicit drugs, or who was addicted to any other substances? _____

9. **Family member with depression/mental illness**: Did you live with anyone who was depressed or mentally ill, attempted or committed self-harm and/or suicide, or hospitalized for mental illness? _____

10. **Family member incarcerated**: Did you live with anyone who went to prison? _____

    ACEs Score (0–10): _____

Upon completion of your ACEs Score, we invite you to reflect on how your score might relate to your psychological and physical health as an adult.

Some twenty-five years later, this study is now known as the adverse childhood experiences study, or ACEs study. We have adapted the original ACE pyramid to include additional layers of intergenerational, historical, and cultural trauma that directly impact childhood adversity (see image). While the field of developmental trauma has largely focused on the attachment and attunement failures from caregiver to child, it is important to acknowledge that the more general term *environmental failure* helps us capture the additional layers of discrimination, community violence, war, famine—anything that negatively affects healthy child development.

What does the ACEs study show us? It demonstrates that childhood trauma is a central factor leading to the development of mental and physical

illness, as well as social and legal troubles. As a person's ACEs score rises, they have a much higher likelihood of developing all kinds of psychological disorders, such as mood, anxiety, panic, dissociative, eating, sleep, behavioral, and learning disorders—as well as multiple physical diseases such as diabetes, heart disease, strokes, autoimmune disorders, and even cancer. In addition, we see higher rates of substance abuse, domestic violence, child abuse, criminal behavior, attempted suicide, and early mortality. We can no longer ignore the source of so much of our suffering.

Here's the good news. As we're writing this, some politicians and community leaders have begun to weave this understanding of the long-term impacts of childhood trauma into their policy efforts. Many cities around the world have begun to set up ACEs task forces in order to address this under-recognized epidemic. And in 2020 California became

ACEs Pyramid

Early Death

Disease, Disability, & Social Problems

Adoption of Health-Risk Behaviors

Social, Emotional, & Cognitive Impairment

Disrupted Neurodevelopment

Adverse Childhood Experiences

Social Conditions & Cultural Trauma

Intergenerational & Historical Trauma

Epigenetic Mechanisms

Intergenerational Transmission

the first state in the US to begin encouraging healthcare providers to use the ACEs questionnaire as part of any intake and assessment process. This emphasis on creating a wider understanding of complex trauma creates opportunities for early prevention, as well as more effective trauma-responsive intervention for children, families, and communities. It is truly a game-changer.

C-PTSD: Complex Post-Traumatic Stress Disorder

After many years of controversy and resistance, in 1980 the new version of the *DSM* (*DSM-III*) finally included the diagnosis of Post-Traumatic Stress Disorder (PTSD). The PTSD diagnosis challenged the status quo of the *DSM* model, which had relied on traditional psychological understanding that focused on description and categorization of symptoms and disorders. The introduction of PTSD posited a new perspective pointing to a clear etiology (traumatic events) that drives psychological symptoms. Instead of just listing a group of symptoms derived from internal psychopathology, PTSD pointed to events that happened to individuals and the maladaptive ways they were forced to respond. This was a profound shift in perspective for the mental health field, and it has had major implications on the government, military, and other social systems.

Even though it had taken many years for psychology to officially recognize trauma, the field of traumatology, once dismissed, now had ground to stand on.[9] Recognizing the reality of trauma ushered in a new way of talking about patients, and eventually talking to them as well. These trauma-sensitive conversations included less focus on pathology and greater compassion for what individuals had gone through. It opened psychology up to concepts like window of tolerance, resilience, and post-traumatic growth. And it brought new understanding and hope for so many patients who had simply felt crazy, out of control, and desperately hopeless.

At the same time, legitimizing trauma was directly challenging to society. Many people, including psychiatrists and psychologists, did not

want to embrace this new perspective. Even today, there are those who are working to narrow the definition of trauma—and even some still actively denying the reality of trauma. Being trauma-informed means that we acknowledge what people do to other people. It can feel horrifying and overwhelming to acknowledge this reality. It also calls out larger relational and social dynamics that are rooted in objectification, subjugation, and interpersonal violence. It requires individuals and societies to take accountability for their impact on others, which for some can be very challenging.

In the early 1990s, just as the trauma field was gaining acceptance, a groundbreaking book was released that has become a staple in most graduate mental health programs. *Trauma and Recovery*, written by Dr. Judith Herman, profoundly influenced the field of trauma and our larger cultural understanding of trauma. In this book, Dr. Herman presents the history of trauma in Western psychology, a comprehensive understanding of the effects of trauma, and a clinical framework for trauma recovery.

Dr. Herman also challenges the PTSD diagnosis as not going far enough to capture all facets of the trauma spectrum, specifically for those who faced ongoing relational trauma during childhood. She does not shy away from the complex legacy of human violence and cruelty that has impacted so many individuals, families, and communities. In her book, Dr. Herman proposes "A New Diagnosis," a new way of understanding the complexity of trauma that will lead to more effective clinical treatment. She writes:

> The diagnosis of "Post-Traumatic Stress Disorder" ... does not fit accurately enough ... In survivors of prolonged, repeated trauma, the symptom picture is often far more complex. Survivors of abuse in childhood ... develop characteristic personality changes, including deformations of relatedness and identity ... in addition, they are particularly vulnerable to repeated harm, both self-inflicted and at the hands of others. The syndrome that follows upon prolonged, repeated trauma needs its own name. I propose to call it: "Complex Post-Traumatic Stress Disorder."[10]

Dr. Herman goes on to differentiate between type 1 and type 2 traumas. Type 1 single-incident traumas, what we refer to as *shock trauma*, are described by the PTSD diagnosis. Type 2 prolonged, interpersonal traumas, what we refer to as *complex trauma*, are described by the C-PTSD diagnosis (in this book we are including developmental trauma as a subset of C-PTSD because at this time developmental trauma does not have its own separate classification). We will further differentiate between PTSD and C-PTSD in the following section.

Despite the strong argument for a new trauma diagnosis that captures the chronic, repetitive nature of relational trauma, there has been resistance from within traditional and academic psychology. This has major implications for the field of psychology and beyond, as recognition of complex trauma has the potential to impact clinical treatment, insurance coverage, academic research, and public policy. Since 1980, we have still been limited to only working with one trauma diagnosis: PTSD.

That is, until June 2018, when the World Health Organization released their eleventh edition of the *International Classification of Diseases* (*ICD-11*), which officially introduced Complex Post-Traumatic Stress Disorder (C-PTSD) as a mental disorder that requires clinical treatment. The *ICD-11* is scheduled to go into effect worldwide in 2022. Although this is great news to be celebrated, those of us in the United States use the *Diagnostic and Statistical Manual of Mental Disorders (DSM-5)*, and not the *ICD*, for identifying, analyzing, and classifying mental health disorders. The American Psychiatric Association announced that a new edition of the *DSM* will be released in 2022, and regrettably, it will not include any additional diagnoses for complex or developmental trauma. While we don't yet know when the *DSM* will catch up with the *ICD*, we are ready for it and will continue advocating for its inclusion.

Why is this diagnosis so important? Let's start with understanding what the C-PTSD diagnosis covers as introduced in the *ICD-11*. Complex trauma results from chronic, long-term exposure to relational and emotional trauma in which an individual has little or no control—in other words, experiences no self-agency—and from which there is little or no

hope of escape—in other words, experiences helplessness. Relational and emotional trauma lead to profound changes in neurological development and functioning, which causes significant problems in a person's life in such areas as family, relationships, education, and occupation.

Relational and emotional trauma that occur in childhood in response to attachment and environmental failure are generally referred to as *developmental trauma*. A key factor involves a child who is dependent on an adult for their safety and well-being. Relational and emotional trauma can also occur for adults in cases of domestic violence, long-term exposure to torture and other crisis situations, or trafficking and other forms of servitude.

Research suggests that the origins of C-PTSD, or at least the vulnerabilities to later developing C-PTSD, begin in childhood with various forms of environmental failure. Trauma theorists such as Dr. Bessel van der Kolk and others have lobbied the *DSM* subcommittee on trauma for an additional diagnosis to cover ongoing relational and emotional trauma for children that would be referred to as Developmental Trauma Disorder (DTD).[11] This diagnosis aligns with the ACEs research in that it identifies the multiple exposures of trauma that children face that impact various areas of life functioning.

However, because the *DSM-5* subcommittee on trauma rejected inclusion of DTD in the current edition, and has recently announced DTD will not be included in the updated version, at this point in the United States we have only the PTSD diagnosis. Thanks to the *ICD-11*, however, C-PTSD has now officially entered the conversation. C-PTSD is being used as a catch-all for both ongoing interpersonal trauma for children and adults and the impacts of childhood trauma on adults. It is our hope that someday soon, in the United States and around the world, we will have two distinct diagnoses to help support clients: Developmental Trauma Disorder for children and Complex-PTSD for adults.

In the proposed *ICD-11* version, C-PTSD introduces three additional categories of symptoms to the diagnostic requirements for PTSD (mentioned at the outset of this chapter), as seen in the following image.[12]

PTSD and C-PTSD Symptoms

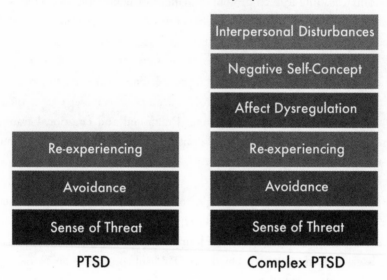

Let's look more closely at these three additional categories, which happen to cover the same three areas of focus in the original book introducing NARM, *Healing Developmental Trauma: How Early Trauma Affects Self-Regulation, Self-Image, and the Capacity for Relationship.*[13]

1. **Affect Dysregulation** describes persistent difficulties in being able to regulate one's emotions, which also includes a larger sense of being out of control of one's body and reactions, or in more extreme cases, dissociating from one's internal physical, emotional, and cognitive states.

2. **Negative Self-Concept** describes persistent difficulties with identity, including negative beliefs about oneself as being shameful, bad, contaminated, dirty, evil, or worthless, or in more extreme cases experiencing a fragmented sense of Self or no sense of Self.

3. **Interpersonal Disturbances** describes persistent difficulties in relationships, including feeling disconnected from and acting out on others in areas such as friendship, intimacy, and parenting, or in more extreme cases, avoiding relationships altogether.

From our perspective, the C-PTSD diagnosis explains so much, filling long-standing holes in traditional understanding. This diagnosis provides a framework for identifying and understanding the suffering that people experience in response to relational and emotional trauma. For children, it helps us understand the root cause of many learning, behavioral, and emotional difficulties; as mentioned earlier, these children are being labeled with other disorders that ignore the underlying trauma. It also speaks to many adolescents and adults who are suffering in profound ways, feeling helpless and powerless, and unable to make meaning of their suffering. The C-PTSD diagnosis has the possibility of providing hope.

Adolescents and adults are also being labeled with disorders that miss the underlying trauma. Instead, they receive clinical diagnoses such as anxiety and mood disorders, sleep and eating disorders, dissociative and psychotic disorders, and personality disorders. These diagnoses and labels fail to capture the full extent of the pervasive impact of childhood trauma on neurodevelopment. The focus on symptoms and behaviors doesn't allow for adequate prevention and treatment of the underlying cause of these disorders. Acknowledging unresolved complex trauma might also help us account for other emotional, behavioral, and social challenges such as substance abuse, domestic violence, child abuse, self-harming, and violent and criminal behavior, as well as the alarming rise in sexually transmitted disease, obesity, and chronic illness. Understanding complex trauma can help us more effectively describe the predictable consequences for children and adults of prolonged exposure to interpersonal, developmental trauma.

Another very important distinction is that the C-PTSD diagnosis focuses on impairments of affect regulation. In NARM we view affect dysregulation through the lens of psychobiological capacity. Based on current neuroscience, the trauma-informed field recognizes the extent to which trauma impacts our neurophysiology, which disrupts an individual's capacity for connection to Self and others. For so many clients, problems with self-regulation lead to issues with eating, sleep, sexuality, and impulse control. Many clients are dealing with other psychobiological symptoms such

as depression, anxiety, panic, numbing, and pain. Additionally, many clients experience difficulty relating to the world, dealing with relational, parental, occupational, and legal challenges. As we begin to see the full scope of these psychobiological symptoms and disorders, we begin to recognize how unresolved complex trauma impacts all areas of our lives. The C-PTSD diagnosis provides a useful framework for supporting more effective treatment by looking beyond the symptoms themselves to the underlying areas of psychobiological disruption.

Recognizing C-PTSD enables us to make a number of significant changes in order to better address the widespread suffering within our society. With a more accurate way of understanding client distress, we can create more effective models that can contribute to the healing of so many individuals, families, and communities in need. Here are just a few areas where more widespread recognition of C-PTSD can be utilized:

- To initiate robust research in order to continue understanding the complex nature of how unresolved trauma impacts the human brain and body.

- To provide a framework for understanding emotional, behavioral, and physical disease.

- To establish more effective treatment protocols based on the consequences of disrupted neurodevelopment.

- To provide early detection and intervention for parents, families, and communities.

- To integrate trauma-informed programs into educational settings for children and adolescents.

- To effectively train the next generation of mental health and other helping professionals.

Ultimately, it is our belief and hope that recognition of C-PTSD helps us broaden, strengthen, and enhance trauma-informed care efforts in multiple areas and fields.

Differentiating PTSD and C-PTSD

All these [DSM] "diagnoses" ignore the most common etiology of these disorders: early trauma and disruptions in the safety of the attachment system. If we were to acknowledge the social realities that give rise to [C-PTSD], we could stop looking for some mysterious biochemical or genetic origin that keeps innumerable research labs in business and start putting our resources into becoming a public health system that focuses on prevention and repair, creating optimal conditions for children and young adults to develop and to thrive.

DR. BESSEL VAN DER KOLK, "THE POLITICS OF MENTAL HEALTH,"
PSYCHOTHERAPY NETWORKER

After relying on the understanding of PTSD for over forty years now, it is a challenge for some to embrace this new understanding of C-PTSD. There are ongoing conversations and debates about whether we truly need this new diagnosis. When the *DSM* committee rejected the Developmental Trauma Disorder, they suggested that the symptoms of developmental trauma overlap with other disorders such as mood, anxiety, and personality disorders. There are mental health professionals who do not believe we need to differentiate shock and complex trauma. Some suggest that therapeutic approaches for PTSD already include elements of working with relational and emotional trauma. They might ask: Why is it clinically important to understand the differences? And what does NARM, a model specifically designed to address complex trauma, offer to our current trauma-informed field?

Certainly there is overlap between PTSD and C-PTSD, but there are also important differences. Recognizing the differences can lead to more effective prevention and intervention.

As a general overview, shock trauma (PTSD) tends to occur in response to one-time events that have a clear beginning and end, often come suddenly and unexpectedly, are out of the ordinary of everyday life, and are immediately life-threatening. This speaks to things like motor vehicle accidents,

physical or sexual attacks, serious injuries, sudden losses, acts of community violence and terrorism, and natural disasters.

Complex trauma (C-PTSD) tends to occur in response to ongoing and repeated events that have no clear beginning or end, are familiar and persistent, are part of one's everyday life, and are not necessarily life-threatening. This speaks to most interpersonal experiences children live with that we have outlined earlier in the ACEs study, ongoing experiences like physical, emotional, or sexual abuse, neglect, witnessing domestic violence, and substance abuse; this is the subset of complex trauma that we refer to as *developmental trauma*. Complex trauma also relates to the ongoing, systemic impacts of relational, cultural, and intergenerational trauma.

Complex trauma does in fact co-occur with experiences of shock trauma, which makes it difficult to differentiate in our clients. Here's an attempt to simplify it: PTSD focuses on experiences of safety, related to life-and-death threat, and the symptoms associated with physiological dysregulation. C-PTSD focuses on experiences of inner security, related to the threat of the Self, and the symptoms associated with psychobiological disorganization.

Two distinguishing features of C-PTSD are early attachment failure and ongoing interpersonal victimization. While these failures from caregivers and environment may have threatened a child's life, they were more than simply one-time traumatic events. These experiences highlight an early environment marked by pervasive threat to the structure of Self. Referred to as the "Bermuda Triangle" of childhood adversity, the toxic combination of impaired caregiving, family violence, and community violence leads to higher rates of complex trauma as children move into adulthood.[14]

Of significant note is that these forms of interpersonal trauma may have more significant impact on adult functioning than one-time, shock-trauma events. This does not discount how impactful those traumatic events are for children but points to a higher likelihood of long-term impact by being raised within, and having to survive, the Bermuda Triangle of caregiver, family, and social failures.

Shock trauma is about mortal threat, imminent danger to one's physical life and immediate safety. The PTSD diagnosis depicts an individual's

experiencing or witnessing a potentially life-threatening experience. Let's look at it through a stimulus-response process. For example, if you are driving a car and see a truck about to hit you (stimulus), you quickly move your car out of the way (response). If we break this down further, we can see that the threatening stimulus (imminent threat of the truck) triggers a fear response activating physiological survival sequences to respond. These survival sequences, generally referred to as fight, flight, and freeze, enable us to respond (move out of the way). This process largely bypasses the cortical areas of our brain and turns on the subcortical areas that allow us to optimize behaviors that are designed to help us survive.

With developmental trauma, experiences of attachment and environmental failure do not simply activate subcortical brain responses of fight, flight, and freeze but involve more complex brain responses that are responsible for the developing organization of the Self. When people experience relational trauma, they are generally not responding to a mortal threat. Instead, they are responding to a threat to the security of one's sense of Self. This has profound impact on the neurodevelopment of children and self-organization. For young children, their sense of Self is dependent on their early environment. They are 100 percent dependent on their caregivers for their survival and well-being. A young child who experiences environmental failure has the lived experience that they themself won't exist without connection and love.

Although shock and complex trauma both relate to survival, they have different implications. Returning to the truck example, when a truck is coming at us, we are not worried about losing the love of the truck. We are in immediate mortal threat and just need to assure our basic survival. But when it is our caregivers "coming at us," we are put in a bind. The caregivers we are fully dependent on for connection and love are at the same time the ones who threaten our sense of safety and security.

While there are certainly elements of fear involved in relational and emotional trauma, the main neurocircuitry in these interpersonal experiences revolves around the psychobiology of shame.[15] Although it is a simplification, in order to support easier application of this complicated material, we will be looking at shock trauma as a response to fear and developmental trauma as a response to shame (see image).

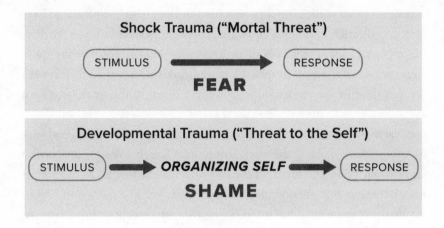

A child's survival depends on their developing a secure sense of Self, which is shaped by secure attachment, consistent attunement, and an environment of safety. Environmental failures thus impact the organization and security of the Self. In order to adapt to early environmental failure, children learn to disconnect from themselves, which leads to profound disorganization of the Self.

As we will see in the next chapter, shame and self-hatred become survival-based mechanisms of disconnection, and they fuel disorganization. Children cannot recognize or tolerate that their environment is failing, because they depend on their environment for survival. Therefore, children are unable to see themselves as a good person in a bad situation. In order to protect against attachment loss and environmental failure, children internalize these failures as their own personal failures: "I must've done something," or "I deserve this," or "I am bad." Children are left with an internal sense of badness. They identify with it. And it becomes part of their identity that they carry into adulthood. For example, many adult victims of abuse and violence blame themselves and are riddled with shame and self-hatred.

Toxic shame begins as an adaptation to adverse childhood experiences. Shame is the mechanism of disconnecting from and attacking the Self. Shame becomes a survival strategy to protect against attachment loss and environmental failure, which are experienced as loss of love in the universe.

When shame occurs early in a child's development, their sense of Self becomes associated with shame. Environmental failure becomes encoded in implicit memory as shame. In NARM we refer to the shame-based identifications that are then carried forward throughout childhood and into adulthood in the form of *adaptive survival styles* (more on this in chapter 2).

Shame has become popularized within psychology and popular culture, and while this has been helpful in normalizing the impacts of shame, these presentations do not usually capture the full picture of the survival-based mechanisms of shame. We view shame as an act of rejecting and hating oneself. Self-rejection and self-hatred emerge out of a child experiencing themself as bad, defective, unlovable. Children blame themselves for environmental failure, even when it is completely irrational from an adult perspective. A child truly believes that they deserve the bad thing that happened to them.

Shame and self-rejection may not sound like a good strategy for assuring connection and love. But to use a graphic example, it is known that if a wild animal gets a limb trapped, they will attempt to chew off their own limb in order to survive. Humans also have an ability to disconnect from essential parts of themselves in order to survive, which is described through the psychological concepts of *splitting, fragmentation*, and *structural dissociation*. While faced with the possibility of loss of connection and love, children will do whatever they can in order to survive, including attacking themselves in profound ways. Shame-based identifications are used to actively reject expressions of one's authentic Self.

Clinically, differentiating between PTSD and C-PTSD leads to important therapeutic considerations. When working with shock trauma, treatment can focus on symptoms fueled by the underlying fear response to a mortal threat. As outlined in the PTSD diagnosis, shock trauma symptoms constellate around physiological dysregulation, which means that effective treatment will work directly with a client's physiology. This lends itself well to therapeutic models that are able to work with physiological regulation—for example, approaches such as Somatic Experiencing, EMDR, neurofeedback, biofeedback, hypnotherapy, bodywork, movement practices, yoga, and meditation.

When working with developmental trauma, treatment can focus on symptoms fueled by the underlying shame response that is triggered in response to a threat to the security of the Self. As outlined in the C-PTSD diagnosis, complex trauma symptoms develop around complex psychobiological disorganization, which means that effective treatment will work with a client's self-organization. This lends itself well to therapeutic models that are able to work "top-down" and "bottom-up," meaning approaches that address the complex interplay of neurobiological systems that lead to disorganized and dysregulated patterns of physiology, emotions, cognitions, behaviors, interpersonal relations, and one's sense of identity. We believe NARM is such a model.

Cultural, Historical, and Intergenerational Trauma

Intergenerational trauma is the transfer of trauma from one generation of survivors to the next. Genocide, colonization, historical oppression, gender oppression, cultural suppression ... structures of pain and violence can and do affect communities, families, parenting techniques, abusive patterns, and coping mechanisms. They affect our relationship with our bodies and ourselves.

TUTU MORA (@TUTU_MORA), INSTAGRAM, NOVEMBER 22, 2019

Attachment failure is at the heart of developmental trauma. However, it is important to recognize the larger context of attachment that includes familial, cultural, and ancestral relationships. These extended relationships create a safety net for caregivers and children. Caregivers are not raising children in a vacuum. When the safety net of extended relationships is impacted by pervasive complex trauma, families and their children suffer. To grasp the enduring nature of complex trauma, in addition to understanding the failures of a child's immediate home environment, we must also understand the larger failures in the child's social environment.

We use the term *environmental failure* to help us capture this larger reality. If you revisit the ACEs pyramid (p. 33), you will see that the first two levels

are "Intergenerational and Historical Trauma" and "Social Conditions and Cultural Trauma." While clearly articulating the features of cultural, historical, and intergenerational trauma is well beyond the scope of this practical guidebook, we cannot discuss working with ACEs and complex trauma without identifying the long-term impact of these forms of systemic trauma.

Environmental failure can be viewed as anything that threatens the security of the Self and impacts healthy child development. Within traditional psychology, this has been viewed through the lens of attachment and focused on the parent-child relationship. For example, within attachment theory, research identifies how parents who as children experienced relatively secure attachment from their caregivers will be much more likely to provide secure attachment for their children. Likewise it identifies how parents who as children experienced insecure or disorganized attachment from their caregivers will be much more likely to provide insecure or disorganized attachment for their children.

Even if caregivers did receive relatively secure parenting when they were children, they could have been, and still may be, impacted by other forms of complex trauma. Focusing solely on the attachment relationship may not fully account for how caregivers are being impacted by ongoing cultural trauma like discrimination, oppression, economic distress, community violence, and war. It may not fully account for how caregivers have been impacted by historical and intergenerational trauma like colonization, forced migration, slavery, and genocide. It may not fully account for how cultural, historical, and intergenerational trauma can be directly transmitted to the child. Although the impact of these kinds of trauma can to some degree be mitigated by the strength of the parental connection, we still should not underestimate the profound impacts that cultural, historical, and intergenerational trauma have on individuals, families, communities, and societies.

Cultural trauma broadly refers to larger environmental failures, including racial, gender, sexual, ethnic, religious, and socioeconomic oppression. These forms of trauma generally impact those who are marginalized by the dominant society and not afforded equal access to basic human rights. Individuals and communities impacted by cultural trauma may internalize patterns of oppression, objectification, and subjugation in order to survive.

Identifying internalized patterns of oppression that lead to profound disorganization helps us understand the ways that individuals must adapt internally in order to survive objectification and subjugation. This also helps us broaden our scope of treatment for complex trauma.

Cultural trauma, which often leads to collective and historical trauma for a group of people, can also lead to the transmission of intergenerational trauma, from one generation to the next. The transmission of trauma across generations has generally been viewed through attachment in the way that caregivers directly impact their children. More recently, the field of epigenetics has begun to demonstrate the gametic and neurobiological pathways of transmission of unresolved trauma across generations.

The experience of intergenerational trauma for children is often one of profound disconnection, disorientation, alienation, apathy, and despair. When ancestral connections are lost, individuals feel lost. For many traditional cultures throughout human history, disconnection from one's ancestral connections meant death. When children, as well as adults, experience severe disconnection from supportive relationships, they face great risks to their well-being and survival. In the face of loss of connection and support, intergenerational trauma can also mimic the implicit encoding of shame-based identifications discussed earlier. A child can be born with the experience that something is profoundly wrong with them, that they are defective, unlovable, hated, and left with a gnawing sense of existential dread. Like all other forms of complex trauma, intergenerational trauma can lead to a loss of subjectivity and an experience of internalized objectification.

Objectification can be defined as an act of disavowing the humanity of another. When a person is denied their independent thoughts, feelings, agency, and self-determination, their sense of Self is profoundly disrupted. They have difficulty experiencing themself as a subject—a real, living human being with their own thoughts, feelings, and needs. Instead, they experience themself as an object—devoid of a sense of independence, agency, and autonomy. Experiencing oneself as an object often leaves individuals feeling profoundly helpless and hopeless.

There is a good argument to be made that most modern societies are based to different degrees on objectification. This can be seen from a more global

perspective in the way most societies currently harm the earth to a more individualized perspective in the way that some individuals use dehumanizing language to describe other people. We see this in social systems as well. Mental health, healthcare, social services, education, criminal justice, and many other social systems use language that reflects objectification. For example, psychology may have moved away from referring to people as lunatics, idiots, imbeciles, and morons, but we still refer to people as a borderline, narcissist, psychopath, and psychotic. While the original intent may have been to describe characteristics within a person, these terms have often been used to dehumanize human beings. The reality is that many social systems have perpetuated objectification, which has led to internalized objectification for individuals and communities.

Being part of the trauma-informed movement, we hope that NARM will be used by therapists and organizations that are committed to making trauma-responsive treatment more accessible despite social disparities and obstacles. These obstacles include the minimization and compartmentalization of trauma itself, something that continues to happen in many healthcare and social systems. The failure to recognize developmental, cultural, historical, and intergenerational trauma is itself a function of the objectification and rejection of subjectivity that create and perpetuate complex trauma. Individuals experiencing profound disconnection have difficulty recognizing the disconnection, thus even the word *trauma* may seem like it does not relate to their experience.

We must also acknowledge that the concept of "post-traumatic stress disorder" does not accurately fit for those individuals and communities experiencing ongoing trauma. For them, there is no "post." Traumatic stress is embedded into every day of their lives. We must acknowledge that individuals, families, and communities dealing with systemic oppression are going to relate to mental health and other social systems differently. There is great risk of using psychological understanding to further pathologize and marginalize already at-risk populations.

Another aspect of the objectification process in complex trauma relates to individuals and systems that are actively perpetuating harm on others. These individuals and systems do not want to acknowledge the impact of their behaviors. When people blame themselves for environmental failures, this lets perpetrators off the hook and does nothing to resolve the

complex trauma patterns that impact everyone involved. This helps explain why societies that have used truth and reconciliation processes after war and genocide have fared better socially than those that have simply "moved on." Trauma, on individual and social levels, needs to be acknowledged and resolved for us all to truly move on.

While this book is not specifically about healing cultural, historical, and intergenerational trauma, we do believe that NARM can be effective in support of such healing. Cultural humility and cultural attunement begin with helping professionals learning to relate to themselves as real human beings, with an increased capacity to relate to the complexity of life experience with openness, curiosity, acceptance, and compassion. Helping professionals can then meet their clients as real human beings with diverse backgrounds and complex life experience, who in many cases are still living within an environment, and dealing with social systems, that created and maintain cultural trauma and objectification. As was beautifully spoken by Brad's friend and peace activist Adar Weinreb, "The path to peace [and healing] is paved through the humanization of the other."[16]

REFLECTIVE EXERCISE

We invite you to reflect on the following questions:

- Can you identify an experience where you felt objectified, dehumanized, or "othered"?

- Can you identify an experience where you may have objectified, dehumanized, or othered another person?

- Can you identify an experience where you felt fully seen for being you—welcoming all aspects of your authentic Self?

- Can you identify an experience where you may have fully seen another person—welcoming all aspects of their authentic Self?

As you reflect on these questions, we invite you to notice what you experience internally in your thoughts, emotions, and body.

Post-Traumatic Growth

In wrapping up this first chapter, we want to introduce the concept of *post-traumatic growth*, which can be understood as an opportunity for transformation through the resolution and healing of trauma. While it's often associated with resiliency, as in the ability to bounce back after life challenges, our perspective of post-traumatic growth encompasses much more.

Post-traumatic growth is not a new understanding. For many thousands of years, Indigenous and traditional cultures have had rituals for how to integrate and transform both personal and collective trauma. Stories and songs that depict the triumph over trauma were shared and passed down as intergenerational wisdom. Tragically, for most modern humans, we have lost connection to this intergenerational wisdom.

Over the past few decades, as our field of trauma has grown, psychology has begun to look at how individuals and communities experience positive change in response to personal and collective adversity. The focus has moved beyond just how individuals and communities can return to normal and now includes how trauma can be used as a vehicle to transform one's life. The five areas of change that post-traumatic growth research generally focuses on are greater appreciation of life, closer relationships with others, increased personal strength, new possibilities in life, and spiritual development.[17]

NARM provides clients with an opportunity for shifting old psychobiological patterns that have kept them from moving toward greater connection, health, and aliveness. It is a psychotherapeutic model that supports greater vitality. Trauma gives us an opportunity to change systems. Whether these are internal systems (within individuals) that are keeping us stuck and sick or external systems (within society) that are leading to social inequities and difficulties, identifying and addressing unresolved trauma allow us to transform complex living systems.

We'd like to share a hopeful story about how a trauma-informed approach can change lives. One of our NARM students (now NARM therapist), Lisa Gillispie, was inspired by her learning and provided her child's school a basic orientation to trauma-informed care. The next year, on the

first day of school, as Lisa was dropping her child off, she walked into the school and saw this sign:

In this school:
- ♥ We are trauma-informed
- ♥ We connect before we correct
- ♥ We stay curious, not furious
- ♥ We understand behavior is communication
- ♥ We believe in co-regulation
- ♥ Kids regulate off the adults in their lives
- ♥ We think "can't", not "won't"
- ♥ We empathize when someone is flipping their lid
- ♥ We believe in restoration, not punishment
- ♥ We believe that relationships buffer stress and build resilience
- ♥ All of us need one another, always
- ♥ Resilience means we see you, we hear you, we are with you

ROCS 2019-2020

Trauma healing has ripple effects. Through one caring parent sharing with her community, this trauma-informed work now has permeated into her child's school. This beautifully demonstrates one way that trauma-responsive models like NARM can be used to support families and transform systems, beyond psychotherapy. While in this book we focus on how to apply NARM therapeutically, we also invite you to reflect on how the principles and skills of the NeuroAffective Relational Model might support broader systemic changes.

REFLECTIVE EXERCISE

We invite you to take a few moments to reflect on how a trauma-informed understanding may support you in your:

- Professional development
- Personal growth
- Family relationships
- Friendships
- Social, political, or environmental work (i.e., work to make the world a better place)

As you reflect on these questions, we invite you to notice what you experience internally in your thoughts, emotions, and body.

CHAPTER 2

NARM Organizing Principles

In a modern world beset by complex trauma and a legacy of suffering, conflict and disconnection, healing trauma can serve as a vehicle for personal and social transformation.

NARM TRAINING MANUAL

The NeuroAffective Relational Model relies on organizing principles that help frame and guide our therapeutic approach. The NARM framework provides a pathway for increased connection between therapist and client, which supports the possibility of increased organization, resolution, and transformation of old trauma patterns for our clients. Using these organizing principles increases the likelihood that effective interventions will be attuned to the specific person sitting in front of us, as opposed to a one-size-fits-all approach.

In this chapter we introduce the NARM organizing principles:

- Connection–Disconnection
- Attachment and Separation/Individuation
- Fear of Attachment and Relational Loss
- The Core Dilemma
- Adaptive Survival Styles
- Shame, Self-Rejection, and Self-Hatred
- Emotional Completion
- Disidentification

Connection–Disconnection

The importance of secure attachment for healthy child development has been well documented. When a young child receives relatively secure attachment from their caregivers, neurobiological mechanisms are activated that support the developing capacity of that child's connection to Self and others. For a very young child, connection to the Self is an unconscious process that has to do with feeling safe to be alive, secure in feeling their right to exist, and feeling loved. Connection to Self is strengthened by a developing capacity to authentically feel, engage, express, and move out into the world. It provides the foundation for a developing capacity for social engagement with caregivers, others, and the world.

Connection is our natural state. It is only when connection becomes a threat that humans must rely on strategies of disconnection to survive. While connection creates the optimal conditions for the healthy development of the Self, disconnection is an adaptive mechanism that helps children deal with trauma.

A particularly devastating failure for children occurs when they experience chronic misattunement by their attachment figures. When this happens, children learn they cannot trust that their basic needs will be met nor that they will feel loved by the adults in their lives. This may happen through neglect, abuse, or failure to meet developmental needs. For children experiencing chronic misattunement, staying connected to their own needs and feelings becomes intolerable and unsustainable. Children are unable to tolerate the distress that occurs in these painful situations. The only strategy they can use to survive is disconnecting from their authentic needs and feelings.

Many young children must also learn to navigate such adverse experiences as neonatal surgeries, domestic violence, parental substance abuse, or being raised in an environment of war, violence, discrimination, poverty, famine, or natural disasters (just to name a few examples). Children have limited capacity to protect themselves against such environmental harm. They rely on early protective mechanisms like dissociation, splitting, and fragmentation—all various forms of disconnection—as attempts to manage the traumatic impact.

As discussed in the previous chapter, the ACEs study and other research on childhood trauma demonstrate the long-term impact that environmental failures have on child development. Although disconnecting from needs and feelings helps children bear unbearable situations, it also creates major obstacles to healthy development. These strategies of disconnection, while life-saving for children, lead to a host of physical, psychological, and behavioral difficulties. As we will be presenting in more depth, we refer to these psychobiological patterns of disconnection as *adaptive survival styles*.

It is important to emphasize that we do not pathologize disconnection. We recognize and respect the strategies of disconnection that children relied on to survive. The framework of the adaptive survival styles helps us recognize the way that these patterns of disconnection, developed during childhood, are now interfering in one's adult life.

Clinically, we track the movement between states of connection and patterns of disconnection with our clients. We will explain this process fully in chapter 6. For now, it is important to clarify that NARM therapists do not make it a goal to eradicate these patterns of disconnection; they also do not make it a goal to get clients into states of connection. The NARM approach supports clients to experience greater agency in relating to these old patterns of disconnection. We know that when our clients no longer need to automatically rely on these strategies of disconnection, they will move organically and spontaneously toward states of connection.

REFLECTIVE EXERCISE

As openly and compassionately as possible, we invite you to take a few moments to reflect on:

- Moments of connection in your life

- Moments of disconnection in your life

As you reflect on connection and disconnection in your life, we invite you to notice what you experience internally in your thoughts, emotions, and body.

Attachment and Separation-Individuation

The "secure base" of attachment supports a child to increasingly move out and explore the world, what Margaret Mahler refers to as "separation-individuation."[1] A child who is provided the basic needs of safety, security, attunement, and caring can begin progressively moving out to explore the world. This begins in very small ways like a baby looking out to the world and engaging with their eyes. Over time this may lead to developmental milestones such as crawling, walking, talking, doing things on their own, being able to leave home for periods of time, and eventually moving into adulthood.

Our biology is wired for both attachment and separation-individuation. Child development is marked by the polarities of attachment and separation-individuation, between life-sustaining relationship with one's caregivers and an increasingly independent, autonomous sense of Self. They are two sides of the same coin. When functioning reciprocally, they both serve in support of the developing Self.

The attachment process emerges from innate mechanisms that support a child's connection with their caregivers. A child's nervous system relies on regulation from their caregivers to lay down the neural networks that create the capacity to experience safety and resiliency. When interpersonal regulation is provided, self-regulation develops. This allows children the secure base from which to move progressively out into the world with a greater sense of trust and confidence.

On the other side of the coin, the separation-individuation process emerges from innate mechanisms that support a child's increasing independence from their caregivers. A child's energetic expansion fuels engagement with the external world and supports them to be more autonomous in relationships. As children grow into adults, the separation-individuation process supports them to engage in relationships where they are not looking at others as objects for fulfilling their needs but can engage with others through more authentic connection, intimacy, and love.

Both attachment and separation-individuation serve to establish a model for a secure sense of Self and a blueprint for healthy adult relationships.

When children grow up in an early environment where their developmental needs for both attachment and separation-individuation are supported, connection with others and with Self mutually reinforce one another. In other words, the more secure the attachment relationship, the greater the capacity a child will develop to feel secure in their autonomy; and the more secure a child's sense of autonomy, the greater the capacity a child will develop to create and maintain secure relationships.

The experience of a secure sense of Self, grounded in healthy attachment and separation-individuation, leads to the ability to tolerate a wide range of internal states, including the sensations of distress that accompany environmental challenges. It also leads to the capacity to hold both frustrating and pleasurable aspects of life experiences simultaneously. This reflects increased psychobiological capacity, or what has traditionally been referred to as *resiliency*.

Embodied adult consciousness is a NARM term that refers to adults who experience themselves not just physically as adults but also psychologically and emotionally. They embody separation-individuation in the sense that they experience themselves as less dependent on others for their sense of self-worth. By so doing, they have greater capacity for authentic relationships. Their behaviors are not driven from adaptive survival strategies but emerge from connection to their authentic needs, feelings, and a sense of agency and self-activation. Being embodied in adult consciousness provides a secure platform to feel connected to Self and others without conflict between the two.

When children grow up in an early environment where their developmental needs for attachment and separation-individuation are not nurtured, it creates an internal conflict between the needs for connection to Self and to others. In other words, the less secure the attachment relationship, the less capacity a child has to feel secure in their autonomy; and the less secure a child's sense of autonomy, the less capacity they have to create and maintain secure relationships.

The experience of an insecure or disorganized sense of Self, built upon disruption in attachment or separation-individuation, leads to problems with self-regulation, affect tolerance, and social engagement (concepts

discussed in chapter 9). It also leads to the inability to hold both frustrating and pleasurable aspects of life experiences simultaneously. This reflects impaired psychobiological capacity, or what has traditionally been referred to as *psychopathology*.

Both as children and as adults, people often have difficulty staying connected to themselves while in relationship with others. We may use the strategy of leaving ourselves to take care of others, which can lead us to feel pressure and inauthenticity in our relationships. Conversely, we may use the strategy of disengaging from others to take care of ourselves, which can lead us to feel lonely and unfulfilled.

In NARM we talk about the *50-50 balance*, which describes a process of continually negotiating our connection to Self and others in the world. It creates a rhythm of engagement between our internal and external worlds: how we become more secure in ourselves *and* more secure in relationships. Reflecting on our 50-50 balance allows us to stay in our adult consciousness while interacting with others because it provides us with an ongoing source of information about our internal reactions in relationship to the world.

REFLECTIVE EXERCISE

For this 50-50 balance exercise, you will need a partner. This exercise is best done silently. We invite you to take time after the exercise to debrief this experience with your partner.

- Start by asking your partner to stand in one place facing you, about ten feet in front of you. Their job is simply to stand there.

- As you stand facing your partner, take time first to just sense your own Self—noticing any sensations, emotions, thoughts, or impulses. Then take time to sense your partner—noticing what it's like to bring them into your attention. Notice the balance between staying connected to yourself and connected with your partner.

- Still facing your partner, find a place in relationship to your partner that feels balanced. Move yourself as needed so you can feel 50 percent

connected to yourself and 50 percent connected to your partner. Mark this spot in your mind.

- Now slowly begin moving backward, away from your partner. When you move ten to twenty feet back, stop, and notice the balance now between staying connected to yourself and your partner. We invite you to take time here, noticing your internal states.

- When you're ready, begin slowly moving forward and past your initial 50-50 spot, until you are right up face-to-face with your partner. Stop, and notice the balance now between staying connected to yourself and your partner. We invite you to take time here, noticing your internal states.

- When you're ready, start slowly moving backward until you find your ideal balance point in relationship to your partner. Please note, this may have changed since the first time you did it, so take time to see where your new balance spot is. Stop when you can experience 50 percent connection to yourself and 50 percent connection to your partner. We invite you to take time here, noticing your internal states.

- If your partner would like a turn, now is the time to switch roles so your partner gets a chance to experience this 50-50 exercise as well.

- Moving into debrief, we invite you to share what this experience was like with your partner, particularly noticing which side of the 50-50 felt more comfortable for you (far away or close up) and how your initial 50-50 spot may have shifted at the end of the exercise.

Fear of Attachment and Relational Loss

When young children are faced with attachment and environmental failures, their survival is threatened. A child experiences an existential threat in response to the reality that their caregivers and environment are unable to support their authentic needs and feelings. Since children are completely

dependent on their caregivers to survive, a child must stay connected to their caregivers no matter what, even if it means disconnecting from themselves.

Early in life, relationship with the caregivers will always trump the relationship to Self. For children, the attachment relationship is life itself. It is the sun that a child's life orbits around. Children cannot survive, and certainly cannot thrive, without adequate attachment. When a young child faces a conflict between Self and attachment, the need for attachment always wins.

When experiencing a threat to the attachment relationship, children are faced with an impossible situation: they need to stay connected to their caregivers, but they also need to stay connected to their authentic Self. This bind pits their relationship to caregivers against their relationship to Self, which reflects a conflict between attachment and separation-individuation.

For children placed in this impossible bind, their impulses toward separation-individuation become an intrinsic threat. In order to solve this impossible bind, a child learns early to shut down their needs for separation-individuation. In so doing, a child begins foreclosing essential aspects of their autonomous Self—including their authentic feelings and needs—as a means to survive. At the root of so much later suffering is the unconscious compulsion to hold on to the attachment relationship at all costs, since the existential fear of losing the attachment relationship is the loss of love itself.

Even if their caregivers are no longer alive, adults continue to experience the bind around protecting against relational loss at the expense of their authentic Self. This deeply embedded fear of attachment loss remains well into adulthood and fuels various strategies people use to protect what they unconsciously experience as abandonment. This can be seen in the ways humans fear what they most want and use self-sabotaging strategies to inhibit separation-individuation, agency, self-activation, and possibilities for love. This conflict between staying connected in a relationship while staying connected to one's authentic Self often shows up for people in their most intimate relationships—with their partners, children, and close friends—and demonstrates the enduring fear of relational loss.

While different cultures emphasize different aspects of attachment and separation-individuation, and it can be viewed through the lens of

polarities, we believe that attachment and separation-individuation are both biological needs. We do not hold these needs to be in opposition to one another. Healthy child development depends on a balance between both. How this balance gets expressed in families and culture is a larger exploration. For the sake of recognizing the challenges our individual clients are dealing with in relation to unresolved developmental trauma, our inquiry focuses on how our client is relating to any potential internal conflict around the themes of attachment (relationship) and separation-individuation (authenticity).

REFLECTIVE EXERCISE

We invite you to take a few moments to reflect on:

- Meaningful relationships in your life and how you have navigated the fear of disconnection and loss. You might first reflect on relationships during childhood and then on relationships you've had as an adult.

- What has been your relationship to the fear of relational loss?

- What strategies did you use to protect against relational loss?

    As you reflect, we invite you to notice what you experience internally in your thoughts, emotions, and body.

The Core Dilemma

When children face this impossible bind between attachment and separation-individuation, they must choose between staying connected to themselves and staying connected to their attachment relationships. As children develop, this *core dilemma* is experienced as a conflict between that which is real within us (authentic Self) and that which we have to do in order to survive (adaptive Self). It leaves children, and later as adults, with the feeling "I can either be my authentic Self or I can be in relationship—but not both."

Many children have profound existential fear that they will lose their attachment relationship if they express their authentic needs and feelings. This generally comes as an implicit message, but in some families and cultural systems, it is delivered explicitly. For example, there is an old English proverb that says, "Children should be seen and not heard." While this could be viewed from the perspective of teaching children how to listen, it could also be viewed as a message to a child to suppress their authentic expression. Particularly in environments where there is threat associated with a child speaking authentically, children learn to disconnect from their own impulses to maintain the sense of connection to the primary attachment figures.

In order to manage the existential threat of relational loss, children learn to reject essential parts of themselves. This may seem counterintuitive from an adult perspective, but through a child's eyes, self-rejection is a protective mechanism used to avoid attachment loss. This survival response of self-rejection becomes wired deep into the brain and body and shapes development.

REFLECTIVE EXERCISE

We invite you to take a few moments to reflect on the following questions:

- What's it like to reflect on your desire for connection and intimacy?

- What's it like to reflect on your fear of connection and intimacy?

- How is it for you to hold both of these sides of the core dilemma?

As you reflect on these questions, we invite you to notice what you experience internally in your thoughts, emotions, and body.

As a way to manage this impossible bind, children develop psychobiological patterns, and associated adaptive strategies, that help assure their survival. We refer to these as *adaptive survival styles*. These childhood survival strategies long outlive their survival necessity and manifest

in adult life as the three symptom categories of C-PTSD (as outlined in chapter 1): affect dysregulation, negative self-concept, and interpersonal disturbances. Additionally, adaptive survival strategies lead to varied psychobiological symptoms such as dissociation, depression, anxiety, eating disorders, sleep disorders, sexual disorders, substance abuse disorders, and personality disorders. Recognizing in our clients their unconscious fear of relational loss, and the subsequent survival adaptations that are driven from this fear, is a key to understanding the origins of many psychological and behavioral disorders, and perhaps even some physiological disorders as well.

Understanding psychobiological symptoms as part of an elaborate survival strategy constellated around the fear of attachment loss and the core dilemma this creates for children helps us understand the stuck and hopeless states our adult clients experience. We use the term *child consciousness* to refer to the experience of being bound to adaptive survival styles that a child internalized as a way to survive early environmental failure. Many adults, despite their physical maturation, are still seeing and relating to the world through the eyes of a child.

When in child consciousness, an adult relates to themself and the world through helplessness, lack of agency, and feeling dependent on others for them to be OK. They experience their lives narrowly and without many options, leading to a limited sense of capacity and resiliency. They feel the regressive need to protect themselves from the threat of relational loss through a variety of strategies of disconnection (which traditionally have been referred to as *defense mechanisms*). Any sense of "growing up" or forward progress may feel like threat to the loyalty to these old survival style patterns.

For individuals with unresolved developmental trauma, any shift toward adult consciousness may pose a threat. This helps us understand why many clients will make short-term gains and then fall right back into old, disruptive patterns. Here are just a few common examples: clients who spent many hours applying for jobs only to not show up for their interviews; clients who were extremely dedicated with diet plans only to gain their weight back; clients who have worked through treatment programs and

achieved sobriety only to return to substance abuse; and clients who spent many months or years dating someone until the relationship moved toward more serious commitment, at which point they suddenly left. *Even states of connection, relaxation, expansion, pleasure, fulfillment, and success can feel threatening.* Understanding the core dilemma helps explain why change and growth can be so challenging.

As NARM therapists, we do not choose sides in our client's core dilemma. We work with clients to create the conditions for all aspects of Self to come back into relationship. We think of it as inviting all parts of who we are to come back to the family table. Much like we may invite once-estranged family members to our holiday meal, we are supporting our clients to invite those parts back that have been disconnected and rejected. We understand that much of the distress and pain our client is currently suffering from has to do with the disconnection from what is most authentic and alive in them.

Throughout the NARM process, we explore these core dilemmas on all levels of the client's experience. We support our clients in learning more about the ways they stay loyal to child consciousness—and support increasing possibility to relate to their needs and emotions from embodied adult consciousness. We explore the psychobiological patterns, strategies, and symptoms that have become obstacles in the way of our clients connecting to what they most want for themselves.

The resolution of these core dilemmas is about learning to be authentic and at the same time be connected with others. The psychological concept of *object constancy* refers to the ability of an individual to feel both love and anger toward a person they are in an intimate relationship with. Holding that emotional complexity is an important capacity for healthy adulthood. For a child experiencing attachment and relational failure, it is simply too threatening to stay connected to themself while staying in connection to their caregivers. Yet for an adult, this relational capacity can feel liberating. New possibilities open up as one shifts from child consciousness into embodied adult consciousness, a process we refer to in NARM as *disidentification* (as we will introduce at the end of this chapter).

Adaptive Survival Styles

As previously described, when a child is raised in a relatively secure environment, their caregivers are able to attune and respond to the child's basic needs and feelings. This supports a child to experience environmental support and love. The following image illustrates the process of a child's needs and emotions being appropriately met by caregivers, which leads to the development of essential psychobiological capacities. These psychobiological capacities create the secure base for a child's development and lead to greater organization of the Self.

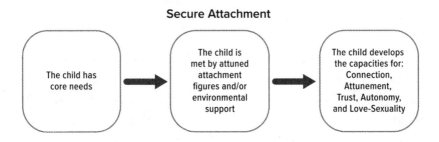

Secure Attachment

The child has core needs → The child is met by attuned attachment figures and/or environmental support → The child develops the capacities for: Connection, Attunement, Trust, Autonomy, and Love-Sexuality

When a child experiences attachment and environmental failures, however, the core dilemma places that child in an impossible bind; they must disconnect from and reject core needs and feelings as a mechanism to survive. This leads to a child experiencing a loss of the possibility for love. Adaptive survival styles are a child's way of making sense of and adapting to the lack of environmental support and loss of love. While these adaptive survival styles help a young child survive the immediate failures in their early environment, they end up creating an insecure foundation for a child's development and generate varying levels of disorganization of the Self. The following image illustrates the process by which patterns of disconnection and compromised capacities lead to the development of adaptive survival styles.

Attachment and Environmental Failure

| The child has core needs | → | The child experiences attachment failure and/or environmental failure | → | In order to survive attachment and/or environmental failure, a child must rely on strategies of disconnection | → | Childhood trauma leads to compromised core capacities | → | The child develops adaptive survival styles: Connection, Attunement, Trust, Autonomy, and Love-Sexuality |

The adaptive survival styles model we use, as outlined in *Healing Developmental Trauma*, describes personality patterns that coalesce around patterns of nervous system dysregulation, distorted emotions, and faulty beliefs a child used to make sense of their early reality.[2] They are false representations of the Self that developed to protect against the threat to the child's authentic Self. These survival styles present as patterns of disconnection the child uses to adapt to environmental failure in an attempt to get love and feel loved. These psychobiological adaptations attempt to resolve the core dilemma for children by providing a way to protect against relational loss through disconnecting from core needs and feelings.

The adaptive survival style framework relies on an understanding of developmental stages and the core needs associated with each stage of early development. Adaptive survival styles developed in response to the failure of a child's environment to meet their core needs at critical stages of development. The psychobiological adaptations originated as strategies of disconnecting from and rejecting their developmental needs and life-sustaining emotions. We will be exploring the impact this has on a person's emotional world in chapter 7; here our focus is on the impact on a child's developmental needs.

The five adaptive survival styles are named after the core need at each developmental stage: *Connection*, *Attunement*, *Trust*, *Autonomy*, and *Love–Sexuality*.

CORE NEED	SELF-REJECTION	CORE DILEMMA
Connection	The child learns to reject their core need for connection to Self and others.	I need connection but can't safely connect.
Attunement	The child learns to reject their core need to experience and communicate needs.	I need attunement but can't safely be attuned to.
Trust	The child learns to reject their core need to trust and depend on others.	I need to be able to trust others but can't safely trust.
Autonomy	The child learns to reject their core need for self-determination and authentic self-expression.	I need to experience my own autonomy but can't safely experience my own autonomy.
Love/Sexuality	The child learns to reject their core need to bring their heart into relationship.	I need to express and receive love but can't safely express nor receive love.

The biological needs are developmental in nature. What a newborn needs for healthy development is different from what a one-year-old needs and what a six-year-old needs. At each developmental stage, core capacities can be disrupted by unresolved developmental trauma, leading to core difficulties for the developing child.

CORE NEED	CORE CAPACITIES	CORE DIFFICULTIES
Connection	To be in touch with our body and emotions	Disconnected from physical and emotional Self
	To be in connection with others	Difficulty relating to others
Attunement	To attune to our needs and emotions	Difficulty knowing what we need
	To recognize, reach out for, and take in physical and emotional nourishment	Feeling our needs do not deserve to be met
Trust	To have healthy dependence	Feeling we cannot depend on anyone but ourselves
	To have healthy interdependence	Feeling we have to control relationships
Autonomy	To set appropriate boundaries	Feeling burdened and pressured
	To say no and set limits	Difficulty saying no directly and setting limits
	To speak our mind without fear, guilt, or shame	
Love/Sexuality	To live with an open heart	Difficulty integrating heart and sexuality
	To integrate a loving relationship with a vital sexuality	Self-esteem based on looks, achievement, and performance

Remember, these patterns of survival adaptation were created as a way to resolve the core dilemma. They are based on a foreclosing of one's authentic Self to protect against attachment loss, which is experienced as the loss of love in the universe. When a child's needs and feelings threaten their caregivers and environment, the only choice is to disconnect from core aspects of the Self. The adaptive survival styles shape the way children, and later as adults, organize, filter, and respond to their life experience.

CORE NEED	SURVIVAL ADAPTATION	STRATEGY USED TO PROTECT AGAINST ATTACHMENT LOSS
Connection	Foreclosing connection Disconnect from body, emotions, and social engagement	Children give up their very sense of existence and disconnect in various ways, such as through dissociation, splitting, and attempting to become invisible.
Attunement	Foreclosing the awareness and expression of personal needs	Children give up their own needs in order to focus on the needs of others, particularly the needs of the caregivers.
Trust	Foreclosing trust Foreclosing healthy interdependence	Children give up their sense of openness and vulnerability and learn to control their environment in various ways, including becoming who the caregivers want them to be.
Autonomy	Foreclosing authentic expression Responding with what they think is expected of them	Children give up a sense of self-determination and direct expressions of independence and authenticity in order not to feel abandoned, invaded, or crushed.
Love/Sexuality	Foreclosing love and heart connection Foreclosing integration of love with sexuality	Children try to avoid rejection by perfecting themselves, hoping that they can win love through performance, achievement, or appearance.

REFLECTIVE EXERCISE

We invite you to take a few moments with each of the adaptive survival styles and notice what you experience internally as you reflect on these questions:

- Connection: Reflect on a time you felt most connected—to yourself, to another person, to a pet, to nature, to God.

- Attunement: Reflect on a time you expressed your needs—and someone responded positively.

- Trust: Reflect on a time you depended on someone—and they came through for you.

- Autonomy: Reflect on a time you stood up for yourself in a relationship— and the other person did not reject you.

- Love-Sexuality: Reflect on a time you reached out with love—and it was reciprocated by another person.

As you reflect on these questions, we invite you to notice what you experience internally in your thoughts, emotions, and body.

Understanding adaptive survival styles helps us in organizing our therapeutic approach. We do not rely primarily on childhood history to help us grasp the complex nature of our clients' issues, nor do we focus primarily on the specific traumas they experienced. We focus on how clients have learned to adapt to these traumatic experiences and how unresolved developmental themes express themselves in clients' present lives. The adaptive survival styles provide a valuable framework to help us understand how clients are organizing their internal experience and relating to their external experience. Clients who have experienced early trauma organize their inner worlds in reaction to their core dilemmas. They develop various cognitive, emotional, behavioral, and relational strategies in reaction to the unresolved impossible binds around connection, attunement, trust, autonomy, and love-sexuality.

The primary focus is not on figuring out what style our clients are. We do not use these survival styles to diagnose, classify, or categorize our clients. We have a saying in NARM: "We do not work with survival styles—we work with humans who identify with survival styles." We recognize that most humans can relate to all the different survival themes to some extent. With our clients, we are exploring the way that survival patterns are expressed moment by moment in the relational process. We use this framework for helping us understand how our clients shape their inner worlds and for helping us organize the therapeutic process.

It is easy for therapists to get lost in the various strategies that clients use. Identifying our clients' core dilemmas, at the root of their survival strategies, allows us to stay on the central thread that leads to resolution of the adaptive survival styles that were constructed to cope with adverse childhood experiences. We acknowledge and respect the various strategies our clients employ, while supporting the possibility that from their adult consciousness clients can relate to themselves free from the fixed identity of the survival styles.

Each one of the survival styles developed as a mechanism of disconnection in order to manage early trauma. The NARM therapeutic approach does not push clients for connection. Instead, we explore the *challenges of reconnection*. We recognize that states of connection will occur when given the right conditions. We explore with our clients what is getting in the way of more authentically connecting to themselves and others.

The process of exploring connection–disconnection is phenomenologically oriented, meaning we work in the here and now with moments of connection and patterns of disconnection. NARM therapists become finely attuned to the various ways clients disconnect from their body and emotions in the present moment. It is important to reflect those moments when clients come back into connection. Old patterns of disconnection dissolve in an atmosphere of curiosity, understanding, and compassion. NARM therapists work in real time toward creating the optimal conditions for reconnection. The therapeutic and relational process of supporting the increasing possibility of reconnection will be outlined throughout this book.

Shame, Self-Rejection, and Self-Hatred

> **REFLECTIVE EXERCISE**
>
> We invite you to take a few moments—with as much self-compassion as possible—to reflect on:
>
> - Some area in your life where you feel self-critical and self-rejecting.
>
> - If one of your clients were struggling with these same feelings, what would you want them to understand?
>
> - What is it that gets in your way of providing this kind of understanding to yourself?

Most clients come into therapy relating to themselves through the strategies of self-shaming, self-rejection, and self-hatred. There is a survival function to these strategies. Recognizing the survival value of these painful strategies helps us be more effective with our clients.

As previously outlined, when faced with attachment and environmental failure early in life, children develop adaptive survival styles based on patterns of disconnection and a rejection of core needs (Connection, Attunement, Trust, Autonomy, and Love-Sexuality). The foreclosure of basic needs is shame-based. For example, if a child's basic needs for being held and nurtured are not being met, the child begins to believe there is something wrong with their need to be held and receive nurturing. No matter what might be happening in the child's environment, a child cannot understand nor tolerate complexity. Shame reduces complex circumstances to simple solutions like "It's all my fault" and "I must deserve this."

There are two important elements in understanding and working with shame, self-hatred, and self-rejection: *primary narcissism* and *splitting*. These concepts were central organizing principles in early psychoanalytical work. We believe that these two psychological concepts continue to be important in helping us address the impact of developmental trauma.

Primary narcissism is a normal state for a child and is different from what we refer to as adult narcissism. *Primary narcissism* simply means that a child cannot experience themself as anything but the center of their own universe. When a child experiences neglect, abuse, or chronic misattunement, they experience it as their fault. The failure is always personal. Simply put, a child cannot experience themself as a good person in a bad situation. By definition, when the environment fails a child, the child believes that they have failed. This brings us to the concept of splitting.

The *splitting* dynamic is part of a larger psychobiological process that relates to how children adapt to environmental failure.[3] When a child has a need, they communicate this need to their environment. When a child is sick, hungry, or cold, needs to be changed, or is otherwise in distress, they will communicate the need and the resulting distress to their caregiver to the best of their ability, given their developmental capacities. For preverbal children, the communication will be emotional and behavioral. Attuned caregivers will acknowledge the child's distress by being attuned to the emotional and behavioral cues. Upon recognition of the child's emotional responses, attuned caregivers will then look for the cause of the child's distress. When there is environmental attunement, the need is addressed, and the child settles.

However, when there is chronic neglect, abuse, or significant misattunement, and the child's basic needs are not being met, the child activates a protest response, which serves as an urgent communication to their environment. For example, a child may start crying, screaming, grabbing, pulling, or hitting. These protest responses are sympathetically dominant nervous system reactions designed to evoke an attuned response from the environment. If the child's protest is still not attended to, there may be an even stronger energetic activation of arousal and protest as a further attempt to get the need met. The protest can quickly turn into anger and even rage.

When these powerful energies of anger toward the caregivers emerge, it puts the child in a bind, because acting aggressively or even feeling strong aggression toward their caregivers threatens the attachment relationship. In order to protect the attachment relationship, children learn to disconnect from, split off, and redirect the anger toward themselves. This helps us

recognize the survival value inherent in turning anger against oneself, seen from a child's perspective—for example, the child who gets stomachaches or self-harms in various ways.

REFLECTIVE EXERCISE

We invite you to take a few moments to reflect on:

- Your relationship to anger.
- What is the scariest thing for you about feeling anger toward someone you love?

There are two sources of relational threat for the child as they begin to feel anger and rage toward their caregivers. One source is external and the other is internal. The external threat comes when the caregivers react to the child's anger with even greater anger. The shaken baby syndrome is an example of this dynamic. The internal threat comes with the energy of anger itself. The child is unable to simultaneously hold both anger and love toward their caregivers. Feeling intense anger at a caregiver, in the child's world, threatens the love and attachment relationship. To manage the anger at their caregivers, the child resorts to splitting. The child splits the image of the caregiver into the good caregiver and the bad caregiver, and the image of themself into the good child and the bad child.

Due to the nature of primary narcissism, children who experience early trauma will always blame themselves for whatever bad happened in their early lives: "My parents are not bad—I am bad." This is a shame-based survival strategy. For the child, to see the caregivers as unable to give love is far more catastrophic than it is to feel that they themself are somehow wrong or unlovable. Put simply, it is better to be the unlovable child of loving caregivers than the lovable child of caregivers who are not capable of loving. A three-month-old baby cannot say to themself, "My parents are under a lot of stress with finances, paying the bills, dealing

with family issues, and that's why they go out and get drunk and come home fighting and be scary to us children. This isn't about me, it's about their troubles." Even if a young child could think this way, it would be too much for a child to experience that their caregivers are unable to meet their needs for safety, security, and well-being. For a child in this situation, it is better to feel that they have done something wrong—and therefore there is hope they can fix it—rather than accept the helplessness that feels like annihilation and death.

Shame-based identifications emerge as an important survival function in response to primary narcissism and splitting, in that children internalize environmental failure and make the failure their own. Children survive by taking responsibility for the failure and by identifying with it, even though clearly this failure does not belong to the child. These distortions in identity shape our sense of who we are, who others are, and how the world is. Shame-based identifications are held in the body as well, in the form of patterns of tension and collapse that impact the muscles, organs, and other physiological systems. The developing identity distortions and physiological dysregulation form as mechanisms of disconnection in response to environmental failure as a way to protect a child's authentic Self—their needs, feelings, and heart. Therefore, shame-based identifications drive the adaptive survival styles, as seen in the following chart.

ADAPTIVE SURVIVAL STYLE	SHAME-BASED IDENTIFICATION
Connection	Feel shame at existing, feeling, and connecting
Attunement	Feel shame when experiencing and communicating their needs
Trust	Feel shame when feeling dependent, vulnerable, or weak
Autonomy	Feel shame at their impulses toward self-determination, autonomy, and independence
Love/Sexuality	Feel shame about sharing their heart and relational intimacy

This process of personalizing and internalizing environmental failures leaves a child with the sense, and later the belief, that they are at fault. When a young child starts off life feeling profoundly defective—believing in their bones that "I am bad," "I am defective," "I am unlovable," and "I deserve bad things"—these shame-based identifications become the building blocks of a compromised sense of Self.

In addition to shame-based identification, there are pride-based counter-identifications that develop as well. The pride-based counter-identifications emerge as strategies of compensating for the toxic shame of feeling bad, unlovable, and defective by developing false qualities of the Self. In fact, in some psychological models, pride-based counter-identifications are referred to as the "false self." A child attempts to project how they want to feel about themself or be seen by the world. For example, a child who feels small and weak inside may project out into the world that they are big and strong. These strategies of compensation help a child manage their internal pain by attempting to turn suffering into a virtue. Just as shame-based identifications do not represent one's "real self," neither do pride-based counter-identifications. They are both rooted in shame, self-rejection, and hatred directed against the authentic Self.

As our adult clients are strongly invested in shame-based identifications and pride-based counter-identifications, change does not come easy. Therapeutically, we see that strategies of disconnection, including shame, self-judgment, and self-criticism, emerge strongly for clients when they are moving into new territory within themselves. Often it is when clients are on the cusp of feeling something very significant, including possibilities for greater connection, expansion, and reorganization, that they will start attacking themselves and shutting down.

For example, an adult client who was experiencing anxiety and tension started to feel settling in her body upon acknowledging that she feels angry toward her father because of how he treated her during childhood. She then quickly moved into rationalizing her father's behaviors, saying that she understands why he would attack her and her siblings due to all the work and financial stress he had to keep the family together. She then moved quickly into self-criticism, saying how selfish and ungrateful she is as a

daughter for having anger toward him. She also began judging herself by going over all the things she has said to him out of anger. As the therapist checked in with her, she reported an increased sense of anxiety and tension in her body.

This example demonstrates how one's authentic feelings (anger), and the associated internal states reflecting greater connection (settling), can be experienced as threatening, and how shame and self-rejection (selfish and ungrateful), and the associated internal states reflecting disconnection (anxiety and tension), can be used to sabotage healing and growth. These psychobiological strategies of disconnection are being used to protect the adaptive survival styles and against the threat of relational loss.

In NARM we do not view shame, self-rejection, and self-hatred as emotions but as psychobiological processes, or strategies, of disconnecting from one's authentic Self. We do not work directly with these strategies but instead explore what unresolved emotions may be underneath them. In the previous example, anger seemed to be emerging as a core emotion beneath the self-criticism, anxiety, and tension. As we will discuss in the next section on emotional completion, working with authentic emotions is a pathway for resolving complex trauma patterns.

Emotional Completion

The broader the range of emotions that a child experiences, the broader will be the emotional range of the Self that develops.

JOSEPH LEDOUX,
"THE SELF AND THE BRAIN," *PROSPECT* MAGAZINE

NARM is a therapeutic model heavily informed by attachment theory and interpersonal neurobiology. These psychological fields both focus on the neurobiological process of relational connection, particularly between children and their caregivers. The vehicle for relational connection is emotion.

Humans are wired for emotional connection. Emotions shape our internal world. Emotions are the building blocks of the Self. People who are able to stay connected to their emotions will be informed by the full spectrum of emotions. There are no "good" or "bad" emotions. Emotions such as anger, grief, and fear coexist with other emotions such as love, joy, and gratitude. A person's ability to experience a full range of emotions reflects their capacity for affect regulation and affect tolerance.

Learning to disconnect from one's internal world—including one's needs and emotions—is a byproduct of complex trauma. Tragically for children who experience early trauma, their capacity to experience a wide range of human emotions becomes disrupted. These individuals learn to run away from their emotions. Clients may not want, or may feel unable, to answer questions about their emotions. They are unable to stay connected to and be informed by their emotional responses. In fact, they often feel in conflict with their emotions and use various strategies to avoid or disconnect from their emotions. This process of repressing emotions may lead people to view emotions as either good or bad. Many clients will relate to their emotions as bad, representing a lifetime of pain, distress, and hopelessness. Seen from this perspective, they will do whatever they can to avoid "negative" emotions, including all sorts of acting-in and acting-out behaviors. With a limited ability to experience their full range of authentic emotions, these clients move through adulthood with significant deficits in affect regulation and affect tolerance.

Most often clients are not aware of what they truly feel. Most children are not raised in environments where they are modeled appropriate ways to reflect on and relate to their internal experience. As adults, they likely have ongoing challenges in reflecting on and relating to their internal experience. They may be aware of the symptoms that are causing distress, but in terms of what they truly feel, they are largely unaware. In fact, many people are using significant life energy fighting very hard to not feel their authentic emotions.

The adaptive survival styles, and their associated strategies, reinforce patterns of disconnection, as people distance themselves from their authentic emotions. The emotional completion process begins when people stop running from themselves and start psychobiologically owning their emotions.

(What follows is a basic introduction to the Emotional Completion Model; in chapter 7 we will provide more details about the emotional completion process.)

The first step in the NARM Emotional Completion Model is about supporting the possibility that clients can become increasingly present to their authentic emotions, what we refer to in NARM as *primary emotions*. As we support our clients to be present to their primary emotions, clients do not have to run from themselves and limit their lives in such extreme ways. Remember, clients are not just disconnected; they are also actively rejecting their internal states. This process of emotional repression—disconnection from and rejection of one's primary emotions—impacts how clients relate to themselves and those they are in relationship with, and it has profound implications on human functioning and well-being.[4]

Once our client is able to be present to a primary emotion, we invite reflection on the implicit intention in that emotion. There is an implicit intention in every emotion. Emotional responses serve as both messages to the environment and a message to the Self. NARM therapists use the following questions to guide their inquiry: *What message is the emotion attempting to convey? What is the underlying intention in this emotional response? What is the emotion trying to accomplish?* For children, expressing emotion is a way of communicating to others about their basic needs. For adults, emotions reinforce connection to one's authentic Self.

Identifying the intention of one's emotion gives a context for understanding that the emotional response is in fact an empowering process, an attempt to communicate something genuine and important. This process serves as an antidote to child consciousness, where the client's belief is that their emotions are bad and that they deserve to be treated this way. As clients connect to the intention of their primary emotions, they embody a different emotional sense: that their emotions are valid and that they don't deserve to be treated this way. The Emotional Completion Model uses adult consciousness to confront and transform these unresolved emotional dynamics left over from childhood trauma.

This last clinical step of the Emotional Completion Model is about how we support clients to be present to and contain the life energy inherent in

the emotion. Completion does not imply that these emotions are finished or go away. In fact, it's quite the opposite. As clients are able to connect to their primary emotions and what they are trying to affect, emotional energy that has been bound up in old adaptive survival style patterns becomes available to fuel their life. This builds greater capacity for experiencing the full range of one's emotional world.

Many psychotherapeutic models recognize the potential benefits of releasing trapped emotional energy and have focused on expression of emotions as a way to help relieve clients' distress. Earlier psychotherapeutic models were often quite cathartic, oriented toward discharging high arousal states of unexpressed emotion. What we have found is that if we explore emotions and encourage emotional expression without working with what is driving these emotional responses, it can lead to regression and disorganization. In NARM we do not focus on discharge, abreaction, or cathartic expression. From our perspective, more emotionally cathartic approaches are good at helping clients express emotions but not necessarily good at helping contain and integrate emotions. The NARM approach supports clients toward greater internal organization, which we are referring to here as a process of *emotional containment.*

The process of supporting emotional containment often leads to greater access to one's life energy. Clients may begin to experience an enhanced capacity for inner states of aliveness, pleasure, creativity, play, gratitude, compassion, and intimacy. As individuals reconnect to their heart and emotions, love for Self and others becomes foundational.

The emotional completion process is a central element in healing developmental trauma. As clients are able to stay present to their primary emotions, recognize the intention of these emotions, and integrate the life energy inherent in these emotional states, they are giving themselves what they never received: they are developing capacity for object constancy and earned secure attachment. No longer meeting the world from child consciousness, preoccupied with trying to get their developmental needs met, clients can come more fully into the present and become more deeply rooted in embodied adult consciousness. From this place of increased psychobiological capacity, core expressions of the life force that had been bound in survival strategies can now be used for more authentic, nurturing connection to Self and others.

Disidentification

Survival styles and their corresponding identifications are held together by unresolved affect. As clients build greater capacity to be present to, tolerate, and integrate unresolved affects through the process of emotional completion, their outdated identifications begin dissolving. The core dilemma between their survival need to protect the attachment relationship at the expense of their authentic Self becomes less compelling as clients deepen into embodied, adult consciousness. As identifications soften, this leads to an increasing sense of separation-individuation, agency, and self-activation. We refer to this process as *disidentification*.

The disidentification process facilitates *increasing psychobiological capacity*, which describes the way clients experience greater organization, increased resilience, and improved life functioning. Many clients have shared with us that they are surprised at how different they feel after NARM sessions. They report feeling stronger and more whole than they were before NARM therapy.

While most clients expect symptom relief out of the therapeutic process, few expect to find such profound change. Clients are often not aware that their symptoms emerge from deeper patterns of identity (also referred to within psychology as *personality* or *character*). These symptoms are the surface expression of deeply held, largely unconscious patterns of disconnection, disorganization, and distortions of the Self (viewed in NARM through the *adaptive survival styles* framework). As psychologist Dr. Jonathan Shedler writes, "The patient needs the clinician to grasp something psychologically systemic about who they are, not just what disorders they have, [as] meaningful and lasting change generally comes not from focusing on symptoms, but on the personality patterns that underlie them."[5] In this way, using NARM to shift personality patterns shaped by the systemic impact of unresolved developmental trauma becomes an opportunity for profound healing, post-traumatic growth, and personal transformation.

However, it is not always so easy. Real inner work threatens one's identity. The more a person invests in personal growth, the more they challenge what they have taken to be their identity and who they believe themself to

be. We cannot underestimate the survival power of identity. Identity develops out of one's most important attachment relationships, including family and culture. Therefore, people take their identities very seriously. Life-and-death seriously. Even when adults are no longer fully emotionally dependent on others for their survival, as they start to challenge their identities, it often provokes a deeply held existential fear: the fear of relational loss.

Without understanding the map that we have laid out in this chapter, it is easy for therapists to get lost in addressing the strategies and symptoms without directly addressing the underlying psychobiological patterns. In NARM we view the various symptoms, strategies, and reactions that create distress as emerging from the underlying core dilemmas, survival style patterns, and identifications. Working with these deeper layers of identity—the "psychologically systemic" nature of one's suffering—continually informs the NARM approach.

The irony is that even though identity seems so solid when we are in it, it is actually not solid at all. If it were so solid, we would not have to hold on to it so tightly. As clients begin to experience disidentification and realize the limitations of who they have taken themselves to be, change can happen more quickly than they may anticipate.

While some people may experience initial resistance to shifting their relationship to Self, as well as their relationship to their family and culture, they may be surprised to realize unexpected benefits. With disidentification often comes increasing freedom to connect with their families and cultures without their past feelings of unresolved anger, guilt, and hurt. The more connected they feel to their authentic Self, the less they feel dependent on their families and cultures for their internal security, allowing them to enjoy their families and cultures in new and surprising ways.

As internal conflicts quiet down and adaptive survival styles dissolve, individuals become less symptomatic. Clients often experience profound psychobiological shifts as the life energy used to bind identifications in the form of physiological patterns and symptoms becomes freed up. This often leads to states of expansion, spaciousness, lightness, fluidity, flow, and joy. Clients learn to play again, to laugh at themselves, and to experience pleasure and intimacy. They begin relating to themselves through increasing compassion.

They develop greater capacity to face internal and external difficulties. As they embody a sense of increasing internal freedom, people begin experiencing themselves, their relationships, their history, and their life in a whole new way.

REFLECTIVE EXERCISE

We invite you to take a few moments to reflect on:

- An experience in your life where you showed up in a more authentic way than you have in the past.

- As you reflect on this, what are you noticing about your quality of presence and sense of aliveness?

The overall intention in NARM is to support the possibility of increasing internal freedom. Embodying adult consciousness provides the opportunity to become less and less dependent on the environment for one's inner well-being. This has to do with increasing freedom to trust in oneself. Instead of being caught in internal conflicts—their core dilemmas—people can move out into the world with greater confidence, ease, and flow.

As the process of disidentification begins, however, the initial state a person experiences is not usually freedom. Often the initial experience is a sense of emptiness or loneliness, which can be difficult to stay present with. The loneliness can harken back to early in life when children felt completely alone. This experience was associated with the terror of attachment loss. Most children never learned how to deal with the loss of connection; instead, they just adapted in order to manage it. Even as adults, people use all sorts of strategies to avoid relational loss and the loneliness that they fear. Many people therefore will choose identifications and suffering over the experience of emptiness and loneliness.

Disidentification ➡ Loneliness ➡ Freedom

Loneliness can be experienced as both frightening and liberating. When in child consciousness, adults may still experience the loneliness as terrifying. These clients often rely on adaptive survival strategies to manage and limit their lives. When in adult consciousness, adults may experience the loneliness as relief, expansion, and increasing freedom. These clients often report an increased sense of internal space and depth in which to meet the world.

We track cycles of connection–disconnection in the service of disidentification. As identifications dissolve, people often experience increasing states of connection: expansion, freedom, hope, strength, and aliveness. One way we resource our clients is to reflect to them when they are able to stay in states of connection for longer periods of time. As people experience greater internal organization, they feel less compelled by old strategies of disconnection. Instead of relying on adaptive survival strategies to control their lives, they experience increasing agency and choice.

Self-acceptance, compassion, and kindness function as solvents for old identifications. The glue that binds the identifications is shame. When individuals push away and reject parts of themselves, they reinforce the shame. As individuals learn to accept their humanness, and the complexity of being human on this planet, that's when change happens.

Self-Hatred ➡ Self-Acceptance

Self-acceptance is not something a person can just tell themself to do. It comes as their preoccupation with internal noise of the survival styles quiets down. Accessing deeper levels of Self allows people to experience increasingly quiet places within themselves. People keep themselves preoccupied and busy so that there is no time for quiet connection with Self. While people crave change, and relief from their suffering, they also fear slowing down and reconnecting.

NARM therapists seek to cultivate quiet within themselves even when clients' strategies are noisy and create distraction. This helps therapists not

get lost in their clients' reactivity. The less noise within ourselves, the more present we can be with our client, which enhances the intersubjective space.

Although strategies of disconnection are strong for us all, we are never truly disconnected from what is most alive and authentic in ourselves. In adapting to developmental trauma, we lose awareness of that deep connection. As we work through our survival strategies, our old identifications, and other internal obstacles, we become increasingly aware of the deep sense of connection that has always been there. It is from this place we can experience a greater sense of aliveness and the possibility of ever-increasing internal freedom.

REFLECTIVE EXERCISE

We invite you to take a few moments to reflect on:

- A time you felt particularly quiet inside.
- A time you felt particularly connected to your heart.
- A time you felt particularly alive.
- What are you noticing now as you reflect on these internal states?

PART II

The NARM
Therapeutic Model

CHAPTER 3

Pillar 1: Clarifying the Therapeutic Contract

Be mindful of intention. Intention is the seed that creates our future.
JACK KORNFIELD (@JACKKORNFIELD), TWITTER, MAY 26, 2011

When working with unresolved complex trauma, the therapeutic process can quickly become disorganized, unwieldy, and overwhelming for both client and therapist. NARM provides a way for creating greater organization in the therapeutic process. We do this through Pillar 1: Clarifying the Therapeutic Contract. In this chapter, we introduce how to support clients to identify and connect with what it is they want out of the therapeutic process, and from there, how to use the client's intention to establish an organizing thread for each session, creating long-term continuity in the therapy process.

This first pillar may sound elementary, but it has been surprising to us how many therapists do not know what their clients truly want for themselves in the therapeutic process. Think of going to an auto mechanic, dropping your car keys on the counter, and saying, "Fix it!" The mechanic would not possibly have the time to go through all the systems of the car to figure out what's truly going on. And yet that's what therapists are doing with their clients on a daily basis. Therapists

may end up following stories, focusing on symptoms, and taking over responsibility for the therapeutic process without any central organizing thread. This is not a useful therapeutic strategy for many reasons that we will elaborate on.

Pillar 1 is about creating a collaborative working relationship where the client provides the fuel of the therapeutic process. When therapists, often with the best of intentions, define and dictate the therapeutic process without fully understanding what it is that is driving the client, a client may experience significant misattunement. Many clients project great authority onto therapists and feel expected to go along with whatever treatment goals and process the therapist provides. Some clients want to take care of their therapist and try to meet the therapist's needs. Other clients will fight to be heard. When there is therapeutic misattunement, clients will respond with compliance, resistance, or cycling between both.

As a way to create more optimal conditions for therapeutic attunement, the NARM therapeutic process starts by encouraging a client's agency from the very beginning. Clarifying the therapeutic contract supports this process by seeking clarity on why the client has come to see a therapist and what they want out of therapy. It is important not to underestimate the power of this question: *What is it that you want for yourself?*

REFLECTIVE EXERCISE

We invite you to take a moment to bring to mind one of your clients.

- Why are they coming to see you for professional help?

- Imagine that you asked them this question: "What is it that you'd like for yourself from our work together? You don't have to worry about it being possible or realistic." How do you imagine they may answer you (in their own words)?

- This exercise invites you to reflect on your client's deepest intention for themself.

Clarifying a client's intention for therapeutic change is about creating an organizing thread for the therapeutic process. We refer to this as the *red thread* in NARM, the through line that helps shape and organize the exploratory process. Clients with complex trauma present with a variety of symptoms, self-defeating behaviors, fragmented narratives, and, overall, a disorganized sense of Self. The complexity of multiple symptoms, behaviors, and stories, sometimes all happening at once, can create confusion and overwhelm for both client and therapist and conceal what the client most wants for themself.

Most therapists, like most caring caregivers, when faced with their client's distress, often work very hard to attune to and help their client. But how does the therapist know what kind of help the client truly needs? Pillar 1 allows the therapist to explore beyond their client's distress to understand what the client most wants for themself. It is the first step toward learning to effort less with clients. Instead of the therapist setting the agenda and outcome, what the client wants for themself provides a compass that orients us to where they want to go. We can then use the client's intention as a way of staying on track throughout the work. Whenever we feel we are getting off track, lost, or confused, we can simply return to the therapeutic contract.

The word *contract* might make you think of a formal legal document like a rental agreement. We use *contract* in the spirit of its original meaning, "to draw together." Clarifying the client's intention for the therapeutic process draws together the therapist's attention with the client's inner world. It is a working agreement between client and therapist. It informs the therapist as to where the focus of treatment will be.

REFLECTIVE EXERCISE

We invite you to reflect on:

* Something you may be struggling with in your own life—for example, working too much, fighting with your partner, or having difficulty saying no and setting boundaries.

(continued)

- See if you're able to clarify an intention for yourself. For example, "I would like to work less," "I would like to stop fighting with my partner," or "I would like to set stronger boundaries in my life."

- We invite you to take a few moments to notice how it is to simply state this intention for yourself.

While this skill gives therapists the opportunity to take less responsibility for the therapeutic process and work less hard, it is not always simple to apply. The client's level of self-awareness and internal organization influences the ease with which the therapeutic contract is formulated. For some clients, the contracting question itself—*what is it that you want for yourself?*—may feel threatening. Clients may not know how to respond. Some clients may actively resist clarifying their intention by reciting symptoms and problems, give the therapist what they think the therapist wants to hear, or get anxious, agitated, or even adversarial. Other clients will move into storytelling, just keep talking, and never identify why they are in therapy. It is often the case that the more disorganized the client's internal world, the more the client will be challenged in clarifying their intention.

The reality is that this person went to great lengths to get into therapy. They had to find you somehow, contact you, schedule time, organize payment or health insurance, travel to get to your office, locate your office, sit in the waiting area, and then finally meet you with the expectation that they will openly share themself with a stranger. Why are they going through all this trouble? What is it that is motivating them? When a client puts themself through all these steps, there is always something they are wanting, even if they have a hard time recognizing what it is.

The contracting process is really about inquiring into our client's "heart's desire," inviting them to reflect on and connect to their deepest wish for themself. This opens a door for clients to explore beyond the symptoms of distress that brought them into therapy, and into what they are truly wishing and striving for.

Sometimes what our clients are wishing and striving for is unrealistic. That is a fine place to start. We may even ask them, "What would be the optimal outcome from this session, even if it's not realistic?" This gives us a window into their internal "operating system," their self-organization. Identifying and formulating their stated desire is an expression of their agency. Our task is to help the client clarify this desire and explore what's in the way of them actualizing what it is that they say they want for themselves. It is important to remember the core dilemma, and that what a client wants for themself is only one side of the story. The other side of the story involves the learned internal obstacles getting in the way of them actualizing what they most want for themselves.

Beginning in the contracting process (Pillar 1), and then moving into asking exploratory questions (Pillar 2), we are guided by curiosity in our client's internal process. Specifically, we are interested in what's getting in the way of what our clients say they most want for themselves. We begin organizing our understanding of our client's internal obstacles, which in NARM we refer to as the *working hypothesis*. The working hypothesis, which we will describe further in chapter 4, begins forming as soon as we meet our clients and inquire about their intention for being in therapy.

Clients generally come into therapy with presenting problems that focus on specific symptoms and a general sense of despair. They are often experiencing hopelessness, helplessness, and desperation. They are largely unaware of the mechanics of their suffering, which includes the internal obstacles in the way of what they most want for themselves. The contracting process begins to shine a light on how these internal obstacles are being driven by the adaptive strategies they have used to manage life. Using the framework of the five adaptive survival styles, we can begin to see how the contracting process can facilitate conditions for healing from the very beginning.

- **Connection:** The contracting process invites clients identified with Connection survival style themes to show up in an atmosphere of safety and consent. The use of contracting emphasizes the therapist's attention, interest, and concern about truly understanding the client. Contracting provides an opportunity to shift old relational patterns of feeling completely alone. This process of intersubjectivity supports

a shift away from objectification toward subjectification. Clients are invited to be active collaborators with their therapist, which provides a sense of control over the therapeutic process.

- **Attunement:** The contracting process invites clients identified with Attunement survival style themes to check in with and express their needs and feelings. From the very beginning, this process provides an opportunity to shift old relational patterns of feeling that they cannot express their needs and feelings. Contracting helps clients feel seen and heard—by their therapist but also themselves. They are invited, welcomed, and encouraged to reflect on their authentic needs and wishes.

- **Trust:** The contracting process gives clients identified with Trust survival style themes the power to set their own course for therapy. The collaborative nature of contracting provides an opportunity to shift old relational patterns where they felt they had to control others in order to feel safe. They are welcomed to modulate their level of openness and vulnerability according to their own sense of comfort and trust.

- **Autonomy:** The contracting process encourages clients identified with Autonomy survival style themes to share their authentic Self in an environment of openness, understanding, and respect. Inviting the client to determine their intention and goals for therapy provides an opportunity to shift old relational patterns of having to control against other people's agendas.

- **Love-Sexuality:** The contracting process supports clients identified with Love-Sexuality survival style themes with a sense of not having to be perfect to be accepted and loved. Contracting provides an opportunity to shift old relational patterns where they felt pressure of having to perform and achieve. Clients are welcomed to share from a more open-hearted and intimate place.

As seen through the adaptive survival styles, the seemingly simple intervention of clarifying the therapeutic contract can set the stage for clients connecting in new ways to themselves and their lives.

Another important element of Pillar 1 is that the therapeutic contract can serve as a safeguard to help buffer therapists against bias. The process of clarifying the contract can support cultural competence. Therapists and clients may have different experiences and opinions relating to culture, race, ability, age, gender, sexuality, politics, religion, spirituality, and a host of other personal matters. As NARM therapists, we do not hold any particular position about our clients' experience. There is great complexity in their experience, far beyond what we can truly comprehend, so instead of trying to figure out the right thing for our clients, we bring curiosity to how our clients are relating to their experience and what it is that they want for themselves. We use clarifying the therapeutic contract to assure that our clients are "steering the ship" of therapy.

NARM is client-focused, in the sense that our therapeutic stance is to learn from our clients, not to dictate to them nor to impose an agenda we hold. Therapy is guided by the client's intention and desire. We are inviting and encouraging their developing capacity for self-determination, even when they want us to take sides, provide suggestions, or give advice. As clients are working with complex personal issues, we hold the perspective that it is up to them what they do with what they are learning in therapy. As we will present in the following section, we use the contracting process as an intervention to reflect on what their intention is for themselves related to the dynamic they are exploring. We hold trust in our clients' agency, which fuels the Pillar 1 process.

Pillar 1 in Practice

Our first intervention is to clarify the therapeutic contract. From the outset of the therapeutic process, and at the beginning of each therapy session, we invite agency and establish relational consent by inquiring around the client's intention. Together, therapist and client agree to move into exploration of what the client wants for themselves and what internal obstacles might be getting in their way.

Notice how we highlight "internal obstacles" when discussing the contracting process. Of course, every client is facing some level of external obstacles. If clients are coming to therapy in an attempt to change external circumstances—whether with their family, friends, employment, or larger social and political difficulties—therapy is not generally the right place for them to create the necessary external change. However, we can address how clients are being impacted by and relating to external difficulties. If a client states an intention that relates to an external challenge, we invite inquiry into how they are being impacted by it and what they would like for themself differently in relation to it. While therapists cannot generally change a client's external experience, we can support internal change, with the hope that a client's increasing internal capacities may lead to new possibilities for creating external change.

We want to start simple with contracting. We want to use language that is clear and concise. We might start with something like: "What would you like for yourself out of our time together today?" Or "What would be the optimal outcome of our work together?" Therapy sessions can get complicated very quickly, so it's best to start simple. Here's a basic example of a NARM therapist inviting their new client to share their intention for therapy.

THERAPIST: I always like to start with inviting you to share with me what you'd most like to get from our session together today.
CLIENT: Yes, thank you. For so long now, I've been feeling a lot of shame. So if I could get some help in being with that differently, it'd be great.
THERAPIST: Help in relationship to the shame?
CLIENT: Yes. I am so self-critical. Everything I do feels bad and wrong. It's hard. I think if I can be kinder to myself, my life will feel so much better.
THERAPIST: So the help would be around being kinder to yourself?
CLIENT: Yes, I think that would make a huge difference in my life.
THERAPIST: Well, I'd be glad to explore with you what this shame is about and what is getting in the way of you being kinder to yourself.
CLIENT: Great.

This client was able to state what they wanted—to "be kinder to myself." The therapist also heard that the client wanted help in being with shame.

The therapist reflected to the client what they were hearing that the client wanted for themself in order to assure that the therapist and client are on the same page before moving forward. The contract was established when they agreed to explore together "what this shame is about" and how shame and not being kinder to themself impacts their life, including whatever external difficulties they are experiencing.

However, clients might not answer the intention question so directly. Some clients will identify goals but not intentions. Some clients will start telling stories or reciting symptoms. And other clients may get frustrated and demand, "You're the therapist, you tell me!" These challenges are a normal part of the contracting process. Many therapists are surprised to find that even "high-functioning" clients often have difficulty initially answering this question around intention.

Some clients, especially new clients, are confused by the question itself. The most common response is "I don't know." It is challenging for therapists when a client responds in this way. Clients may present as passive, unclear, unsure, or desperate for you to lead. It may be tempting for a therapist to take over and set the agenda. In these moments, it is important not to stray from the focus on what the client really wants for themself. The client has come to a therapist for a reason. They may not be aware of that reason in the moment. But there is the possibility of increasing agency when the client begins to reflect on their authentic desire for themself. We do not want to disrupt this opportunity for a client to connect to their agency. The contracting process supports the client to take an active role in their therapy. In these situations, patience and persistence are needed to stay curious and not default into problem solving, which actually takes over functions from the client.

How do we know when there is a solid therapeutic contract? Before the agreement is set, things might seem unclear, fragmented, and disorganized, but when a clear understanding around the client's intention is reached, the client or therapist (or both) may experience a somatic or energetic shift. The client may report experiencing an internal shift, such as feeling greater clarity or grounding. The therapist may observe or sense into a psychobiological shift within the client, such as feeling a landing or settling. NARM

therapists often refer to this as "kerplunk," a moment of connection where things come together and align.

REFLECTIVE EXERCISE

We invite you to take a few moments to bring to mind a decision that you have faced—perhaps choosing between two different events, two purchase options, or two job opportunities.

- Reflect on the decision you made.

- How did you know to make that decision?

- What was it that you experienced as you clarified what you chose?

If possible, you may even put yourself back to your making the decision and noticing what you become aware of in your body, emotions, or thoughts.

The important point to remember is that if the contracting process does not feel easy and smooth, it does not mean you are doing something wrong. While clarifying the client's intention may seem easy, the process with some clients can be quite complex. It takes time. It is essential not to pressure yourself, or your clients. If you do find yourself pressuring or judging yourself, we invite you to reflect on your own reactions, as they are most likely inhibiting therapeutic progress and creating further stress for you.

An interesting phenomenon happens as we get more practiced with starting off our sessions with the contracting questions. A lot of clients begin to anticipate the invitation. They will come into sessions having already reflected on the question. For example, a client might say: "I know you're going to ask me what it is that I want to get out of the session today. I was thinking about it as I was in your waiting room, and what I'm really wanting is…" We take this as a positive sign that the client may be bringing greater curiosity to their internal experience, even outside the therapy sessions.

Typically, most clients will initially answer the contracting question with a behavioral goal or by telling us what they *don't* want. Examples of behavioral goals might be: "I want to stop overeating" or "I want to get along with my partner better." Examples of what they don't want might be: "I don't want to be anxious" or "I don't want to be so angry." NARM is not a goal-oriented process and is not primarily focused on behavioral change. It is focused on the exploration of the psychobiological obstacles that interfere with what a client wants for themselves. With this perspective in mind, we would respond to one of our client's goal-oriented statements with something like "I'm happy to explore with you what your anxiety is about," "I'm happy to explore what's driving your anger," "I'm happy to explore what your overeating is about," or "I'm happy to explore what might be getting in the way of you getting along better with your partner."

As you can see, we are shifting behavioral goals into invitations for internal exploration. We know this runs counter to many current therapeutic approaches and treatment plans. We hold the perspective that as clients learn to relate in new ways to whatever obstacles they are experiencing, the desired change tends to occur organically. We know from many years of clinical experience that when some clients primarily have behavioral goals, their therapy process feels unfulfilled. They often end up feeling fundamentally missed, which can lead to feeling frustrated and resistant. The NARM approach creates an alternative pathway to therapeutic change. As Carl Rogers says, "The curious paradox is that when I accept myself just as I am, then I can change."[1]

There are several other challenges with behavioral contracts, and one is that, as therapists, we cannot guarantee that we can make change happen. Purely behavioral goals can be a setup for therapeutic failure. A client might have an unconscious strategy of self-sabotage, where they set unrealistic goals for themselves that they can't meet, and then they blame themself, or others, for their failure. For example, a client says to their therapist, "I need help completing this project." We cannot guarantee that our work together will achieve this behavioral goal, but we can agree to explore what is in their way of completing the project, something they say they want to do and yet are not doing.

Another challenge that comes up with behavioral contracts is that we never truly know what is best for clients in these complex situations. In NARM we don't want to take sides. For example, a client says to their therapist that their relationship is joyless and they want to leave their marriage. Perhaps it is better that they leave their spouse, but perhaps not. There are so many factors involved. We are not the ones to judge what's the right decision for them. Instead of agreeing to work toward a behavioral goal, we might inquire what they imagine it would bring for them in their life if they did leave their marriage. We can explore how they relate to the goals and not agree to the goals themselves. Ultimately, we trust that as a client establishes greater connection to their authentic Self, they will get clearer on what is right for them and do what is best for them given the circumstances involved.

Although it might take time, patience, and persistence, the contracting process draws out the client's intention and provides a way for the therapist to guide the therapeutic process. While NARM is a client-driven approach, NARM therapists are not passive. We are managing the sessions, including using specific interventions based on the client's intention and our working hypothesis. Clarifying the therapeutic contract is an incredibly useful resource for us as therapists. If therapy starts going off track, if the client wants us to take over the process, if the client gets upset by something, or if we ourselves get confused and lost, we can simply return to their original intention.

For example, a client and therapist agreed to explore what is in the way of the client feeling greater intimacy in their relationship. Later in the session, the client was talking about an ongoing pattern of conflict they are experiencing in their relationship: "He says that I avoid him. I just get lost online and he gets frustrated with me, saying that I'm avoiding him. His frustration with me makes me angry, and then I do really end up avoiding him. I just don't want to deal with him." This may be an example of a good time to refer back to the contract: "I hear that you're recognizing this conflict with your partner, which you react to by avoiding him. But when we talked about what you want from therapy, you said that you wanted to feel greater intimacy in your relationship. I wonder how avoiding him fits with

your wish for greater intimacy?" Instead of trying to interpret, convince, provide skills, cheerlead, or take over the reins of therapy in any other way, we are managing the session by gently confronting them with how avoiding their partner is inconsistent with their original intention.

At times the initial attempt to clarify a contract may feel very general or vague. A client may say something like "I just want to be better!" This gives us only a minimal understanding of what they truly want for themself, so we would begin to clarify what this means for them exactly and what it would bring for them if they were able to "be better." Other times our clarification with a client might feel circular or like we are getting into a power struggle with them. While it is useful to at least attempt to clarify further around the client's intention, there are times we might just decide to start very simply with something like: "Would you be open to continue exploring what might be getting in the way of you 'being better'? Does this sound like an OK place for us to start?"

Even if you do start with a more general intention like this, built into the NARM process is what we refer to as *recontracting*. The process of recontracting relates to the way the therapist continues to clarify the working agreement throughout the course of therapy. For example, the previous client started by wanting to "be better," and suppose that now they are talking about wanting to feel more at peace within. The therapist might say, "At the beginning of our session, you said you just wanted to be better. And now you've been exploring how to feel more at peace within. Would you like us to continue exploring what might be getting in the way of feeling more at peace with yourself?"

Sometimes in the middle of a session we discover that what the client really wants is not what we had agreed to in the initial contract. When this happens, we can simply recontract and develop a new agreement that is more aligned with their emerging intention. For example, let's say the client initially said they wanted to work on their anxiety, and then later in the session they are talking about their anger toward their husband. We may say, "I know that initially you said you wanted to address your anxiety, but now I hear you focusing on your anger toward your husband. Would it be more helpful at this time for us to explore what's happening with your

anger toward your husband?" And if the client says yes, that would be more helpful, you could follow up with, "What would be your ideal outcome from exploring this dynamic with your husband? It doesn't even have to be realistic, but what might be on the other side for you?" This invitation keeps the focus on the client's intention.

Now let's say in this example the client says, "No, I want to continue focusing on my anxiety because it's causing me so many problems." We don't argue or try to convince our clients that we believe there is a better path; instead, we bring curiosity to how the topic they have raised (anger toward their husband) might be connected to their original intention (less anxiety). The inquiry-oriented interventions we use as part of Pillar 2 will be covered in the next chapter.

We do want to be mindful with recontracting, because sometimes you are exactly where you need to be in therapy, but the client may begin using a strategy to move away from the central thread. Having a solid contract gives therapists permission to be more challenging in order to help clients stay on the thread. For example, a therapist might say: "You said before that you wanted to explore the relationship between your anxiety and anger toward your husband, and now you are sharing all these concerns you have about your child's school and what to do about it. Would it be OK for us to bookmark what's happening with your child's school and stay with exploring the relationship between your anxiety and the anger toward your husband?"

Or at times we might even use the contract as a form of therapeutic confrontation: "You say you want to explore your anger toward your husband, but every time we begin exploring this dynamic you change the subject. I'm curious about that." Therapeutic confrontation is really just staying attuned to the client's intention. While we are always open to recontracting if necessary, we also want to be sure that we are not colluding with a strategy to avoid what is emerging for them.

If the therapist forgets what it was that the client originally said they wanted for themselves, the therapist can always just check back in with the client. When therapists feel foggy or unsure, they often pressure themselves to remember, to figure it out, or even just to start using interventions

because they don't know what else to do. As NARM therapists, we make it easy for ourselves and would say to our client something like, "We've covered a lot of ground; however I'm unclear what it is exactly you'd like for yourself at this point?" Or perhaps something as simple as, "Can you please remind me what you originally said you wanted for yourself?"

Some therapists worry that this will be perceived as us not listening or caring. We have found that most clients appreciate being checked in with. Remember, many clients have never received this level of attunement. In fact, most are used to feeling overlooked and misunderstood. When the therapist takes time to inquire about the client's inner world, it is often experienced as a deeper level of attunement and care. Additionally, clients may simply be at a different place than they were at the beginning of the session. Recontracting demonstrates interest in where the client is now. It also provides ongoing opportunities for the client to bring curiosity to their intention, which may lead to new insights.

We imagine that some of you at this point are reflecting on your clients and thinking that we're making this sound easy. Sure, clarifying the therapeutic contract might work well for a few clients, but what about the clients who don't want to answer? Using the framework of the five adaptive survival styles, we can understand how the contracting process can be difficult depending on the challenges of each particular survival style:

- **Connection:** Because of the client's core dilemma about not feeling safe to show up and connect with others, an invitation to communicate what they want in the intimate setting of therapy could lead them to feel unsafe and suspicious. Clients may respond by being evasive, or even noncommunicative, about what they want out of the therapeutic process.

- **Attunement:** Because of the client's core dilemma about not feeling safe to identify and express their needs, an invitation to state their needs for therapy could lead them to feel ashamed for being needy. Clients may respond by denying or minimizing the impact of their distress. They might expect the therapist to define the direction of the therapeutic process.

- **Trust:** Because of the client's core dilemma about not trusting in others nor wanting to feel dependent on anyone else, the action of simply sitting in front of a therapist can be extremely challenging. Clients may not want to be authentic or share any vulnerability due to their fear of being criticized, controlled, or humiliated. They may not respond to the invitation to set a therapeutic intention, which may be experienced as weakness. Instead, they may focus their attention on how they can get the upper hand in the therapeutic process.

- **Autonomy:** Because of the client's core dilemma about not wanting to be controlled by other people's agendas, they may perceive that the therapist is wanting something specific from them, so they may worry about providing the wrong answer or may respond by withholding what they are truly feeling. They often confuse an intention with a goal, putting pressure on themself and the therapist to make something happen, to "fix them."

- **Love-Sexuality:** Because of the client's core dilemma about not feeling perfect and sharing their "messy" heart feelings, being in therapy is admitting that they are not put together in the way they might want to see themself or present themself to the world. Clarifying their intention for therapy challenges them to acknowledge their imperfection. Clients may respond by giving polished answers, which does more to conceal than clarify their heart's desire.

We address these challenges in different ways depending on the specific client, their capacity, the level of their disorganization, and the relationship we've established. For example, contracting is generally more challenging during a first session than many sessions later. But despite whatever challenges you may have in contracting, remember what we wrote earlier about the great lengths this person went through to get into your office. There is something that motivated them to seek out therapy. There is something they want for themself. We might reflect, "You've told me you don't like me asking you this question about what it is that you'd want for yourself out of our time together here, but I am aware that you came to me for a reason. I am unable to help you if we're not able to clarify your reason. I understand

it may feel hard, but this question is important for both of us to know how to proceed."

One note here: when you are working with mandated clients, whether that means by court order, employer, family, or spouse, the contracting process may look different. Pillar 1 is much easier with clients who voluntarily chose to come to therapy. If the client is mandated, it doesn't mean that the contracting process won't work, but there will be a bind about their intention for being there. They may say they don't really want to be in therapy but they need to satisfy their court, work, or family requirements. It is best to name the bind explicitly. For example, when contracting with a client coming in at the request of their spouse, we may say, "I understand that you don't want to be here. But it does seem important to you to make this marriage work. So I'd be glad to explore with you your part in why it is not working."

If a mandated client is willing to try to meet the requirements laid out to them, they will usually, begrudgingly, say they do need to address these issues for them to get what they want. This is the beginning of a contract. For example:

THERAPIST: What would you like for yourself out of our work together?

CLIENT: Well, my wife made me come.

THERAPIST: Why did she make you come?

CLIENT: She says I have anger issues and need anger management.

THERAPIST: What about you—do you think you need anger management?

CLIENT: If I want to keep my family I do. She left with the kids and is staying with her sister.

THERAPIST: And that's why you're here?

CLIENT: Yes. I don't believe in therapy, but she says unless I learn to control my anger, I can't keep my family. Do you think you can help me with my anger issues?

THERAPIST: What do you hope might come out of working on your anger issues?

CLIENT: I'd have my family back.

THERAPIST: Well, I can't guarantee that you'll get your family back, but I heard you say that you need to learn to control your anger for that to happen.

CLIENT: Yes, I need to stop yelling at her and the kids. Then she'll come back.

THERAPIST: I know you said you don't believe in therapy, but are you willing to work on your anger with me? If so, I'd be happy to explore your anger issues. My hope is that this will help you with your family.

CLIENT: All right, I'll give it a shot. I'll do whatever I need to do to get them back.

Even though the client reported not believing in therapy and only coming to therapy because his wife made him, there is still an underlying intention that he is willing to work toward. The client agreed to a therapeutic contract, however reluctantly, and now the therapist has a working agreement and a thread to organize the session.

Clarifying the therapeutic contract is a relational process, and no matter how compliant or resistant the client is, consent is essential. Before moving forward with a working agreement, we must be sure that we are on the same page with our client. This helps prevent misattunement, bias, and acting out from client or therapist. If a client does not give their explicit consent about their focus for moving forward, we do not move into exploration and processing. We continue clarifying their intention until we've landed upon a working agreement that they consent to. Our focus is on building a collaborative partnership from the very beginning.

Ultimately, it is an ethical issue if we continue working with clients but don't know what we're working on or haven't received consent. Our ethical responsibility is to provide clients with the best standard of care; patient autonomy, choice, informed understanding of risks, and a discussion of appropriate treatment alternatives are all part of assuring that we are meeting our ethical requirements. If we start moving forward in treatment without knowing what the client truly wants for themself or having their consent, even with the best of intentions, we may be enacting a harmful relational dynamic.

Remember that while we start the therapy process with contracting, it is an ongoing process throughout the therapy. When first learning NARM, many therapists expect they should have a working agreement right away, which may put pressure on themselves and their clients. There

are times when it does happen quickly and easily. But often the contracting process takes time and patience. It is important that the therapist not give up on its significance. New NARM therapists at times give up too easily, reporting that the client did not answer their question no matter how many different ways they asked it. We remind them that the questions themselves are an invitation for clients to connect to themselves in a new way. As long as the therapist is asking from an open and nonpressured place, the contracting process is an ongoing invitation toward greater self-awareness.

Finally, many new NARM therapists will turn contracting into a goal-oriented process, with the belief that NARM therapy doesn't start until they get a contract. We remind them that contracting is itself a powerful intervention. It supports a deepening into the client's increased connection to themself. A person's intentions for themself unfolds and evolves. Pillar 1 is a process of self-discovery that we're offering our clients. It's more than just reducing symptom distress; it's an invitation to come home to oneself. In this process, clients have an incredible healing opportunity to reconnect to their heart's desire.

The Therapeutic Process of Pillar 1

So how do you start applying Pillar 1?

1. Ask your client what it is that they want (their intention).

    THERAPIST: What would you like for yourself out of our time together?

    CLIENT: I want to be more comfortable in social situations.

2. Gather information about their intention.

    THERAPIST: All social situations? Or are there some social situations where you are more comfortable?

    CLIENT: It is pretty much all social situations but particularly large groups.

3. Reflect back the client's intention, turning it into an exploration, and check in for consent on this working agreement.

THERAPIST: I'd be happy to explore what might be getting in the way of you feeling more comfortable in social situations and particularly large groups. Does this sound OK for us to explore together?

CLIENT: Yes, sounds great.

Remember, if a client wants you to join them in a behaviorally oriented contract, this puts you in a bind. When clients say they want something but are not able to do it, we recognize that there is more than one side to their story. If we agree to set up a behavioral plan in order to help them meet their stated goal, we are ignoring the other side of them that may want to resist this stated goal. We want to explore with them all sides of this dynamic, including what is in their way of doing what they say they want do to. While we cannot guarantee that such exploration will automatically lead to their stated goal, we can provide them with support and guidance toward greater understanding of a very complex internal struggle they are having that is causing distress. For example:

CLIENT: I just need a kick in the ass to complete these job applications.

THERAPIST: I'm not in the ass-kicking business, but what I can do is explore what is getting in your way of getting these job applications completed.

CLIENT: What's getting in the way is my laziness.

THERAPIST: Would it be OK to hold off for the moment on explanations, and see if we're able to explore more about this pattern?

CLIENT: If it's going to lead me to get these applications completed, I am all in.

THERAPIST: I'm not able to guarantee that you'll complete these applications, but I am curious; let's say you were able to complete these applications—what do you imagine that might bring for you?

CLIENT: Well first, maybe I'd get a new job. But also I'd feel more hopeful, like I was actually doing something for myself and not just waiting for my boss to fire me.

THERAPIST: So completing these job applications might give you the sense that you are doing something for yourself?

CLIENT: Yes, doing something productive and positive for myself besides just rotting in this damn job.

THERAPIST: OK, I'm happy to continue exploring what's getting in your way of doing something productive and positive for yourself, specifically completing these job applications. Hopefully our exploration will give you a better sense to know what you need for yourself. Does this sound like a good place for us to start?

CLIENT: Yes, sounds like a good place to start.

Notice what the therapist does not do here: they do not become goal-oriented by creating a strategic plan to help this client complete their job applications. The therapist does not take sides nor set an agenda. The therapist also does not accept a simple explanation like "my laziness." The therapist wants to better understand how their client is relating to their symptom and their entire inner world. The therapist recognizes the dilemma, in that the client states that they want to complete their job applications while they are not doing so. If the therapist agrees to work with the client on meeting their goal of completing the applications without understanding the obstacles in the way of completing their goal, they are walking into a trap. These traps can be seen as therapeutic enactments between client and therapist that generally lead to stuckness and power struggles within the therapeutic process.[2] In order to avoid the enactment, the therapist stays present, curious, and interested in both sides of the dilemma and begins inquiry into the underlying dynamics that are maintaining the client's symptom and distress. We trust that as the client is able to stay more present to their internal struggles, they begin to build greater psychobiological capacity, which leads them to make more authentic, empowered decisions for themself.

In this clinical example, notice how the therapist also explores more than just symptom reduction and behavioral change. Initially the therapist agrees to "explore what is getting in your way of getting these job applications completed." This is a good starting point, but generally we are inquiring with our clients around internal states, not just behavioral change. Notice how the therapist then asks, "Let's say you were able to complete these applications—what do you imagine that might bring for you?" When the therapist asks what this behavioral change might bring for

them, this invites the client to reflect on what they are really wanting. The client responds with their desired intention: "I'd feel more hopeful, like I was actually doing something ... productive and positive for myself." This points to an internal state that underlies and supports behavioral change.

While there are other ways NARM therapists may phrase this invitation around the intention for internal states, the key thing to remember here is that when clients report wanting behavioral change and symptom reduction, we want to inquire about what this will bring them internally. "If you're able to reduce your anxiety, even if it's not realistic, what might be the optimal outcome?" Or "If you're able to stop being so reactive in relationships, how might you hope this impacts your life?" We help clients distinguish the internal states that we as humans seek—such as confidence, compassion, or the capacity to love or speak up for yourself—from the behavioral strategies we have developed simply to manage the best we can.

Sample Language for Pillar 1

NARM LANGUAGE EXAMPLES OF CLARIFYING THE THERAPEUTIC CONTRACT

- NARM language examples of setting up the therapeutic contract:
    - What would you like for yourself today?
    - What would you like for yourself in your session with me?
    - What would you most like to get out of our therapy together?
    - What would be the optimal outcome for our work together? It doesn't even have to be realistic.
- At times, clients have difficulty stating an intention but can easily identify a symptom they want changed. In response to the client saying, "I've got anxiety [or any symptom] and I'd like to get rid of it," you might offer:
    - I'd be willing to explore what your anxiety is about.

- I can't guarantee we'll be able to get rid of your anxiety today, but I'm happy to continue exploring with you what might be in your way of feeling less anxious.

- Recontracting when things get murky (for you or the client)

  - I'm unclear, please remind me what it is that you want to get out of this session?

  - You said earlier you wanted to explore anxiety [or any symptom], now I'm hearing you talk about anger [or any new topic].

  - You said earlier that you wanted to explore your self-judgment and what's getting in the way of you feeling more at ease within yourself, and now I'm hearing you talk about your grief. Which would you like to explore first?

Therapeutic Shortcuts for Pillar 1

- The client sets their intention for the work—*what is it that the client truly wants for themself?*

- The client's intention does not have to be realistic; in fact, we may want to invite reflection on what is their optimal outcome or heart's desire.

- We want to be mindful not to take over responsibility for the client—remembering that it is not our goals but the client's intention that fuels therapeutic change.

- It is essential that consent is established with the client around their intention before moving forward into deeper exploration.

- Contracting sets the collaborative tone of NARM therapy.

- Central to the collaborative nature of Pillar 1 is treating the client like an equal partner in the therapeutic process.

- We want to emphasize that the client is the expert in their own inner world.

- The therapist stays open and curious as to how the client is organizing their inner world.

- The therapist relates to contracting as an exploration-oriented process, not a goal-oriented process.

- The therapist does not pressure themself or clients to "get a contract."

- Therapy does not start after the contract is established; the contracting process itself is an important element of the healing process.

- It is useful to reflect on the initial contract throughout sessions, and particularly at the end of the session.

- Whenever it is needed, the therapist and client can always recontract.

Practice Exercise for Pillar 1

With a client—or a friend or peer first if you prefer—we invite you to follow these steps:

1. Ask opening questions inviting your client to reflect on their intention.

   For example: "What would you like for yourself today out of our session together?"

2. Gather information about their intention.

   For example: Let's say they said they want to feel more confident. You can ask questions like "When you say 'more confident,' can you give me more of a sense of what this would look like?"

3. Reflect back the client's intention, turning it into an exploration, and see if they're on board with this working agreement.

   For example: "I hear you would like to be more confident in many different situations. I would be happy to explore what might be in your way of having more confidence. How does that sound to you?"

Please stop here for now (until you have learned the other three Pillars). We invite you to ask your client how this was to clarify their intention. Notice also how it felt for you to be clarifying their intention. Of course, like learning any new skill, this might feel awkward, silly, or contrived— remember to practice staying present, curious, and open to new learning. We know this might take time to integrate smoothly into the way you work. But we have trained enough therapists now to feel confident that once this skill becomes woven into how you practice, you will find yourself working less hard, finding greater clarity in sessions, and having greater organization in the overall process of therapy.

CHAPTER 4

Pillar 2: Asking Exploratory Questions

I have no special talents. I am only passionately curious.
ALBERT EINSTEIN, LETTER TO CARL SEELIG, MARCH 11, 1952

Curiosity fuels the NARM approach. An active inquiry process helps clients move closer in connection to themselves. We use Pillar 2: Asking Exploratory Questions to support both therapist and client in gaining a greater understanding for how clients organize their inner worlds. Most clients have spent their lives running away from their inner worlds, which causes lasting patterns of disconnection, disorganization, and ultimately suffering. In this chapter, we provide guidance on how to use exploratory questions in a supportive way that helps connect clients with disconnected parts of themselves, thereby giving them an opportunity for greater organization and freedom from suffering.

The power of meeting another human being with true curiosity—fueling deep intersubjectivity between therapist and client—is central to relational healing. It could be argued that most therapists are already proficient with using curiosity and inquiry in their therapeutic work. However, it is our perspective that most therapists, themselves meeting the world through their own adaptive survival strategies, have their own internal challenges with curiosity and inquiry.

In the English language, the expression "curiosity killed the cat" is used to warn of the risk of exploration. Many children are indoctrinated early through their family, society, religion, and education to replace being curious with knowing. Most adult educational and training programs do the same. Albert Einstein highly valued curiosity and expressed his concerns that curiosity can survive formal education systems: "The important thing is not to stop questioning. Curiosity has its own reason for existing. One cannot help but be in awe when he contemplates the mysteries of eternity, of life, of the marvelous structure of reality.... Never lose a holy curiosity."[1] Regrettably, many people have become habituated to meeting uncertainty, novelty, and difference with fear. People cling to what they take to be knowledge as a way to manage the fear of the unknown.

Knowledge is certainly important to inform psychological treatment, but curiosity is the lifeblood of the interpersonal work of psychotherapy. Yet the trend in modern American psychotherapy is clear. The push for treatments that emphasize symptom reduction has impacted the field of depth-oriented treatment. Manualized approaches have replaced emotional, somatic, and other relationally oriented approaches. This is not to say that curiosity and the therapeutic relationship do not play a role in many other therapeutic approaches, but we do believe that the overreliance on standardized protocols creates a mechanistic therapeutic process, which distances therapists from the depth-oriented, interpersonal connection that curiosity facilitates.

Transcendent human experiences that Einstein alluded to, like aliveness, spirituality, and love, are difficult to measure. They don't fit well in modern psychological and scientific theory. There is a tendency to try to reduce complexity. We see curiosity as a pathway for supporting nuance within complexity. It allows us to exist, and delight in, the full spectrum of human experience. It frees us from having to figure anything out and instead supports us to have a direct, lived experience.

Pillar 2: Asking Exploratory Questions is the therapeutic vehicle for discovery. This is a deeply interpersonal process, grounded in the NARM Relational Model (which we will cover in chapter 8). We support therapists to be curious about their clients' inner worlds—how clients organize and

relate to their life experience. We also support therapists to be curious about their own internal process as they sit with clients. This focus on inquiry into both the client and therapist's internal experience creates a process of intersubjectivity, something that sadly many people did not receive growing up from their caregivers. Throughout one's life, many clients have never had anyone truly express interest in and the capacity to stay present to their inner world, which has created significant relational misattunement. Curiosity supports empathy and relational attunement, which in turn support a deeper sense of connection to Self and others.

Why is curiosity such an important aspect of healing complex trauma? As discussed previously, modern psychology stresses the importance of a child being raised in an environment of security. A key ingredient of secure attachment is the caregivers having an interest in the child's inner world. Many new parents experience profound awe and reverence when they are first connecting with their newborn child, a deep curiosity as to who this being is and what kind of support they will need to have a healthy life. Secure attachment is built upon authentic empathy, which emerges as caregivers recognize the uniqueness of their child and meet them with curiosity, openness, and interest.

Many children are not raised in such environments; their caregivers focus instead on the child's behaviors, performance, goals, and results, which can lead to a child feeling fundamentally unseen. It is a form of objectification when adults focus solely on correcting a child's behavior. This lack of empathy gives the child a sense that no one has interest in who they are underneath the behaviors.

There are two significant consequences to a child feeling such rejection. First is their hopelessness, despair, and pain from experiencing this level of misattunement. Second is how a child personalizes and internalizes this experience of misattunement. The environmental failure is experienced by the child as their personal failure. Tragically, a child then learns to treat themself in ways that they were treated. If a child's openness and curiosity are minimized, unsupported, or attacked, they learn to do that to themself.

Chronically misattuned connection from caregivers leads to transactional relationships as children learn to adapt to the expectations of the adults in

their world and, later in life, as they learn to manage complex interpersonal situations. Adult relationships are often transactional in the sense that one person is trying to get something out of the other person. Like a game of chess, these relationships can feel like navigating a set of strategies. As children and as adults, people are rarely met by another with openness, curiosity, and interest. It is our perspective that we are living in a time of a collective failure of empathy. It is heartbreaking for us to watch humans losing curious and empathic engagement with themselves, others, and life itself.

REFLECTIVE EXERCISE

We invite you to take five minutes to simply *be curious.*

- Give yourself permission to follow your curiosity—whether this means to be curious about something in your environment, about exploring something outside your present environment (like going outside), or about focusing internally and being curious about your body sensations, emotions, images, or thoughts.

- We invite you to notice how easy or difficult this might be for you to shift into a space of being open and curious.

- We also invite you to notice how this exercise feels overall.

Many clients report feeling profoundly missed in relationships. Despite our best intentions, clients can and do feel profoundly missed by therapists as well. By bringing curiosity, openness, and interest into the therapeutic relationship, we are supporting clients in finding curiosity, openness, and interest into their own inner worlds, which is where they develop the capacity to regulate and organize themselves in ways that bring about the change they are seeking.

Inquiry-based interventions might bring up images of the Rogerian approach or motivational interviewing. While there is overlap with how other therapeutic approaches use exploratory questions, the inquiry we

use in NARM is a relational, embodied, and agency-oriented process. As we will outline, the questions we ask are relational in the sense that they emerge out of the collaborative process of clarifying our client's intention for themself in being in therapy (Pillar 1). The inquiry then helps reset the power dynamics between therapist and client as we refrain from interpreting their experiences, telling them what they are experiencing, or being prescriptive about their process. Instead, we invite clients to join us in an open exploration. This is an embodied process in the sense that our exploration includes all levels of an individual's experience, emphasizing the internal shifts that are often felt in the body (Pillar 4: Reflecting Psychobiological Shifts, which we will detail in chapter 6).

Agency is a central aspect of NARM inquiry. Pillar 2 is an agency-oriented process in the sense that it invites and activates a new relationship to oneself. Learning to ask exploratory questions is a key step toward helping clients understand, organize, and transform their inner worlds. We are curious about what role the client has in their own distress. Adult clients with unresolved developmental trauma tend to externalize difficulties—"things are happening to me from out there"—and miss what is going on inside themselves. This tendency is clearly seen in clients with greater internal disorganization. But most of us can relate to becoming externally focused when we are experiencing distress. Of course, there are always external circumstances creating distress, but as we will discuss in the next chapter, we differentiate between "what is" (external reality) and "what we do with what is" (agency and internal self-organization).

We recognize that our clients experience themselves and the world through deeply embedded adaptive survival strategies, which are not so easily surrendered. These same survival strategies are now causing distress, and we want to begin supporting other ways clients can relate to their internal worlds that are not based in old survival patterns. By meeting our clients with curiosity—and not trying to figure it all out, give them advice, do the work for them, or take sides in their internal conflicts—we are in a better position to support them connecting to their own sense of agency. We use therapeutic interventions, such as inquiry, that reinforce an increasing sense of agency and embodied adult consciousness.

This process of exploration is in service of *disidentification*. As introduced in chapter 2, disidentification is the process of a person bringing a quality of mindfulness to their consciousness, taking their thoughts and reactions less seriously, not presuming that what they feel is truth, recognizing they aren't defined by who they've taken themselves to be, and ultimately, dissolving their adaptive survival styles. As these old patterns of identity distortion and physiological dysregulation begin to quiet down, people begin seeing themselves less through the filters of their survival style identifications. This helps clients shift out of child consciousness into adult consciousness. Through inquiry, clients receive support and guidance to connect with what's real for them in the here and now.

Pillar 2 in Practice

We progressively support our client to become the expert of their inner world. Our task is to learn about how they organize their inner world. Our expertise emerges out of how we ask more informed questions, helping our clients become better connected with their own inner experience. Questions are used to explore what the client's part is in the dynamics that they are struggling with and that have brought them into therapy. We bring curiosity to how clients are getting in their own way of what they want for themselves.

The NARM inquiry process provides therapists with a vehicle for deepening our connection to what may be going on for our clients. Just as curiosity and interest in a child's inner world supports caregivers to join their children in engaging in mutual, collaborative discovery, NARM provides the optimal conditions for relational exploration with clients. These optimal conditions include the use of relational skills such as attunement, tracking, mirroring, and resonance. Asking exploratory questions goes beyond just the questions we ask. It includes the presence of the therapist, as well as the way of engaging with our clients, that helps clients discover themselves in a new way.

Exploratory questions are built upon the client's intention for being in therapy (Pillar 1). The questions we use invite reflection into what it is that the client wants for themself, as well as whatever might be keeping these

dynamics and symptoms stuck. We don't use questions to try and get our clients somewhere. Remember, NARM is not a goal-oriented process; it is an exploratory-oriented process that relies on true inquiry. Many therapists struggle with staying in exploration. Therapists may report feeling anxious to "get somewhere" or that they are lost and don't know what else to ask. As we remind our students, "You're only lost if you're trying to get somewhere."

We are not asking questions to get specific answers. We know this might sound counterintuitive, but inquiry itself is a healing intervention. "Inquiry for the sake of inquiry" means that we are asking questions to support a self-inquiry process for the client, which builds the capacity for self-reflection. From this perspective, everything is an "answer." If we ask a question and the client goes quiet and doesn't say a word, that's an answer. If the client has a somatic or emotional reaction, that's an answer. If the client screams at us, that's an answer. On our end as therapists, questions help us learn more about how our clients are organizing their inner experience, including the way they receive and respond to the questions themselves.

When asking questions, it is best to use simple language. Questions that are too complicated, or that use too many words, may direct the client to become too intellectual about the question and their answer. These kinds of questions can lead clients to disconnect from their embodied, emotional, and relational experience in the present moment. Consider the wording of this question: "Why do you think you have those thoughts about feeling inferior, and how might those thoughts be causing the reactions you are having toward your boss?" This question is asking about something very important. But notice the difference in how we might ask it from a NARM perspective: "What do you become aware of as you notice the thoughts and reactions you have in relation to your boss?" Or even simpler, "What's it like to reflect on these reactions?" The intention here is to not get lost in the details. It is easy for therapists to get lost in their clients' stories, focused on the content, and drawn into clients' behavioral choices. In the first example, the therapist asked the client to *think about* their experience. In the NARM example, the therapist invited the client to *relate to* their experience. This agency-oriented question focuses on the psychobiological patterns that are organizing present experience and shaping the client's

stories and behaviors. Simple, direct, and clear questions support a client to engage with their present experience with greater curiosity and agency.

A client's answers to our questions begin to shape and inform our therapeutic working hypothesis, which shapes and informs our therapeutic interventions. As we are asking our client questions, we are forming a tentative understanding about the internal conflicts that are creating obstacles in the way of what the client most wants for themself. This begins during the contracting process (Pillar 1) as we begin reflecting on our client's core dilemma. For example, if a client is feeling lonely and isolated and wants to have greater intimacy in their life, we can begin to hypothesize that there is likely to be profound ambivalence around connection. The client may desperately want connection (greater intimacy) while at the same time desperately want to avoid it (which leaves them feeling lonely and isolated). This working hypothesis, oriented around the client's intention, helps organize the session. For this client, we may bring attention to material that relates to the theme of connection and not get lost in attending to peripheral material that doesn't directly relate to this core theme.

Here's an example of how a therapist might use the working hypothesis to inform questions that address their client's core dilemma around connection. In working with a client's relationship to their social anxiety, we might inquire, "So you're acknowledging that there's this inner conflict in you: part of you that you said is desperate to show up in your life, and another part of you that feels it's safer to avoid showing up in your life. What's it like to notice what goes on in your experience right now as we acknowledge that there's both sides here?"

Here's another example of how a therapist invited a client's self-reflection on the core dilemma as a way to begin addressing the client's distress around connection in relationships:

CLIENT: I want to be in relationships with others, a friend, maybe even a romantic partner. But I feel like an alien. I'm always an outsider in every situation.
THERAPIST: I wonder, might there be any benefit to being an outsider in social situations?
CLIENT: I don't think so! It's painful! But let me think about it.
THERAPIST: Take your time.

CLIENT: Well, I know that relationships come to an end, and this is so painful. I prefer to be alone and do things on my own. It just feels safer. So I suppose feeling outside of relationships does protect me from that pain.

THERAPIST: So you always feel like an outsider, an alien, and yet you prefer to be alone.

CLIENT: Yes. I want to connect, and yet I don't want to connect. It's crazy-making!

The client themself named their core dilemma. They want to connect and yet don't want to connect. This is experienced as an impossible bind for clients, in this case revolving around Connection survival style themes: this client longs for connection and yet connection feels threatening.

As a way of addressing this core dilemma, the therapist invited curiosity around the "benefit" of this client's experience of themself as an outsider. Instead of choosing sides in this dilemma—for example, working with the client on social skills that would support them to reach out for connection—the therapist went in the other direction. The therapist inquired as to the survival wisdom of staying disconnected from relationships. The client was able to name a survival strategy of disconnecting from relationships: preferring to do things alone and staying outside of social situations. Despite their desire for being in relationship with others, they also have an investment in protecting themself against the possibility of relational loss.

We can hypothesize that these strategies of disconnection emerged early in this client's life as a way to avoid the pain around attachment loss, the loss of connection in their early environment. People carry these survival strategies into adulthood and now relate unconsciously to their lives through the core dilemma. The survival strategies of staying outside of relationships and preferring to be alone made sense for the child attempting to manage early trauma around connection. Now these strategies are obstacles in the way of what the adult client most wants, which is to connect in relationships, and cause the client such emotional pain that they seek out therapy.

THERAPIST: How is it in this moment to recognize that part of you wants to connect, and yet part of you doesn't want to connect?

CLIENT: Well, it's been painful. And frustrating, because it's always been like this.

THERAPIST: I understand. And how is it in this moment to be present to both your desire for connection and your preference to be alone?

CLIENT: You know, as I hear you say it back to me now, it doesn't feel like it's such a conflict.

THERAPIST: It doesn't feel like such a conflict? What feels different about it in this moment?

CLIENT: I know that not all relationships are drama or end painfully. I really enjoy being with my friend Toni, and if it ever does start getting to be dramatic, I can take space. I know that even if that happens, we can stay connected. In this moment, I also feel that if the relationship does end, I would be able to handle it.

THERAPIST: So how is it to recognize that you can connect and also disconnect when you want to? That they don't have to always be in conflict?

CLIENT: It feels very grounding. I feel like it opens up new possibilities, like I wasn't seeing something before that feels possible now.

As this client was able to stay present to both sides of their core dilemma—their desire for and fear of connection—they were able to begin shifting old adaptive strategies and move toward the possibility of experiencing greater connection with Self and others.

The working hypothesis can be useful in working with the various choice points we encounter during therapy. Clients with complex trauma often present with many stories, associations, strategies, and symptoms, and the sessions can feel disorganized and fragmented. Identifying the core dilemma as it emerges from the contracting and inquiry process can provide structure to the therapeutic process. In the previous clinical example, the therapist stayed focused on the client's intention for relationships, which introduced their core dilemma around connection. The questions asked were then focused on the client's relationship to the internal conflict around connection.

Future chapters will explain other factors that influence the working hypothesis, such as the client's psychobiological capacity, the role of shame

as an adaptive survival strategy, unresolved needs and emotions, and the therapist's capacity for self-inquiry. Remember, the working hypothesis is cultivated through curiosity and openness to the client's internal world— and not through interpretations, which can be distorted by the therapist's unconscious biases and countertransference reactions. Therapists hold the working hypothesis in a way that does not simplify the client's experience but encourages the therapist and client to be present with increasing complexity, nuance, and depth.

It is important to state that we do not hold to our working hypothesis as absolute truth. We hold what we are learning with humility and openness. We are tentative in any conclusions we draw and are willing to be wrong, learn, and adjust our engagement and interventions. This process mimics an essential ingredient of secure attachment. During childhood, the capacity of caregivers to openly inquire into the experience of their children is essential for supporting attunement, empathy, and optimal developmental. The working hypothesis in NARM is a process of supporting intersubjectivity.

Exploratory questions emerge out of the working hypothesis to foster increasing intersubjectivity. We use exploratory questions to break down complex patterns, so that the client can gain greater awareness into how they are organizing their internal experience and relating to themself and the world. These questions also help us better understand how our clients are relating to their life experiences, particularly those that are causing them distress and bringing them into therapy.

We use two main interventions to ask exploratory questions: *deconstruction of experience* and *drilling down*.

Deconstruction of experience refers to when the therapist invites the client to focus on one specific experience that is emblematic of their difficulty. This gives the therapist direct access in real time to the larger pattern that has been driving the client's distress. The therapist starts to deconstruct this pattern by inquiring into their present-moment somatic, emotional, and cognitive experience of this dynamic. We often use deconstruction of experience after clarifying the client's intention (Pillar 1).

For example, a client has been experiencing anxiety, and their intention is that they want to feel less anxious in their life. The therapist received consent around the working agreement "I'd be happy to explore what's in the way of you feeling less anxious." The therapist might ask the client for a specific experience where they were feeling anxious. This is usually quite easy for clients to pick from the list of experiences that have been affecting them. In this example, the client shared an experience at work: "I was at work yesterday and my boss was watching me, waiting for me to mess up again. I had to hand in my report by the end of the day, and I just knew it wasn't going to be good enough for her." The specific situation itself is not our focus—we're looking at the underlying pattern that is emblematic of a larger process driving the client's anxiety. The therapist might choose to explore how they were relating to their belief that their boss was watching them and waiting for them to mess up again.

THERAPIST: What happens when you have the belief that your boss is watching you, waiting for you to mess up?

CLIENT: I feel so anxious. I'm sure I messed up the report.

THERAPIST: So as you imagine her waiting for you to mess up, you feel anxious?

CLIENT: Yes! She's sitting there thinking how crappy I am at my job.

THERAPIST: As you imagine her sitting there and you believe you know what she is thinking, what are you noticing internally?

CLIENT: I feel edgy inside. I just want to leave.

THERAPIST: So you are feeling anxious and edgy inside, and then you want to leave. Are there any emotions besides feeling anxious you are aware of?

CLIENT: Yes, I hate her! I am angry.

The inquiry-based intervention of deconstruction of experience is an opportunity to slow down and elucidate often very complex *psychodynamic* elements that may otherwise be unconscious and automatic. This psychodynamic material gives us important clues on how to address these adaptive survival patterns. A major clue for us in this example is that underneath the client's anxiety and projection is anger (we will discuss how to work with the Emotional Completion Model in chapter 7). If we stay on an abstract or

theoretical level with clients, such as talking about anxiety in general here, we can reinforce intellectualization, which in turn creates disconnection. Inviting a deliberate, refined way of engaging with these complex dynamics allows clients to have an experience of embodied connection to their inner landscape.

We can also go in the other direction, where we start with an experience of a time that they did not have this feeling. Sometimes this question can be harder to answer, although most clients are able to come up with an opposite experience, even if it felt like an anomaly.

THERAPIST: Can you share an experience you've had recently when you felt less anxious?

CLIENT: I was at work and my boss was out of town for a business meeting, leaving just me and my colleagues who I get along with. The office was so quiet. I noticed that for the first time in a long time I was able to breathe easier and I felt relaxed.

THERAPIST: What was it about your boss being gone that may have led you to being able to breathe easier and feel more relaxed?

CLIENT: She wasn't sitting there thinking how crappy I am at my job.

THERAPIST: And when you imagine her sitting there thinking how crappy you are at your job, what happens for you?

CLIENT: My body tenses up. I feel edgy and anxious.

THERAPIST: And as you notice your body tensing up, feeling edgy and anxious, are there any emotions that you are aware of?

CLIENT: I don't know, I'm unsure what to do. But maybe frustrated?

THERAPIST: So as you imagine her sitting there thinking how crappy you are at your job, you're not sure, but maybe you feel frustrated?

CLIENT: No, I know. I am definitely frustrated!

Notice how the therapist deconstructs this experience where the client felt less anxious. This is another example of how we are working to unravel a complex pattern of beliefs, emotions, and sensations in response to a specific dynamic. The therapist uses questions to inquire into this larger pattern of distress that the client named as anxiety and that they agreed to explore together throughout this session ("I'd be happy to explore what's in the way of you feeling less anxious").

Using this intervention of deconstruction helps us understand how specific experiences are representative of larger, unconscious patterns of distress that are disrupting clients' lives and bringing them into therapy. In both example scenarios, inquiry supports the client to begin to own their projections and connect to unresolved anger ("I am angry" and "I am definitely frustrated!"). Further exploration is needed to explore this relationship between their recurring anxiety and their tendency to project, as well as helping them integrate unresolved anger.

REFLECTIVE EXERCISE

We invite you to reflect on:

- A challenging theme in your life. For example, perhaps an area where you often feel unsupported, ignored, or easily triggered.

- Once you've chosen your theme, pick a specific experience where this theme emerged. For example, if you often feel unsupported, let's say you were recently planning a party with several friends and ended up feeling left with having to do all the work.

- Reflecting on this specific example, see if you can notice what happens in your thoughts, emotions, and body sensations.

- Particularly focus on how you are relating to this experience now in the present moment.

- Are you criticizing yourself?

- Do you feel embarrassed?

- Do you wish you could've handled it differently?

- Do you feel self-compassion and understanding?

We invite you to notice how you are in relationship in the present moment to this specific experience and the overall theme.

Drilling down—the other main intervention we use for asking exploratory questions—is a process of gathering more information on all levels of experience via inquiring about the details of whatever is being shared by the client. The easiest example of this is when clients use words like *it*, *that*, or certain euphemisms. For example, a client says: "It just sucks." We would inquire: "What's the 'it' that sucks?" Another example, a client says: "I just can't get over that." We would inquire: "What is it exactly that you can't get over?" An example of a client using a euphemism, in talking about the conflict in their marriage: "I may have to be moving on." And we may respond with: "When you say 'moving on,' what are you referring to?"

Let's say a client has been feeling depressed and hopeless, and their intention is to feel joy again.

CLIENT: The shades have been pulled for so long, I can barely see any light.
THERAPIST: When you say "the shades have been pulled" and you "can barely see any light," what do you mean by this exactly?
CLIENT: It just feels bleak.
THERAPIST: What's the "it" that feels bleak?
CLIENT: I guess the "it" is my life.
THERAPIST: So your life feels bleak?
CLIENT: Yes, bleak.
THERAPIST: Do you have any other words that you might use to describe this bleak feeling?
CLIENT: Sad. I feel really sad.

Notice how the therapist does not assume to understand what the client is expressing. The therapist meets the client with openness and curiosity and continues asking questions supporting greater understanding. Communication can conceal more than reveal, so we want to support clients in the process of gaining greater clarity, refinement, and acuity of their internal experience.

REFLECTIVE EXERCISE

We invite you to reflect on:

- Something that you have been frustrated by or recently complained about to a partner, friend, or therapist. For example, it might be your work, your relationship, or a political or social issue.

- We invite you to reflect on what it is exactly that you are frustrated about.

- Notice the language you use to describe your frustration.

- Try to pinpoint the focus of your frustration.

- As you are able to gain greater clarity on the source of your frustration, see if you can gather any other information about this dynamic.

- We encourage you to bring open curiosity to this issue, even if you have reflected on it many times before.

We invite you to see what new information might emerge for you now as you practice curiosity and self-inquiry.

The inquiry process is not focused on historical material but on an individual's present experience. As a phenomenological model, NARM relies on inquiry into direct experience and the nature of one's consciousness. However, there are times when we do want to get information from our client's history that will help us understand and contextualize how the client is organizing their experience in their adult life.

Returning to the client who felt depressed and hopeless, we may want to learn more about how long these feelings have been going on and if there were any immediate or proximal triggers for this symptom—for example, a recent death or loss in their life. This information will provide us with valuable information that helps with context for the client's present experience. As we explore, we learn about the associations clients have for themselves that may be contributing to their present symptoms.

Generally, as we work in the present with clients, developmental material will surface. This may emerge explicitly, for example, "My childhood home life was abusive," or it may emerge implicitly, for example, "Every time I am around authority figures I feel anxious." One of the challenges is how much information is enough but not so much that we get lost in the client's adaptive strategies.

One strategy that clients use is focusing on personal history as a way to avoid agency. For example, a client who is presently dealing with anger issues in their relationship may start telling stories about their childhood abuse and say they cannot control their anger because they grew up in a home with adults always raging. The client's association of their present-day anger to their history is not determinative, however, since the client's two siblings do not presently have anger issues. While a client's narrative is always important, we do not see the story as the place for change. We see the client's present relationship to their experiences as the vehicle for healing and growth.

Clients who have experienced NARM have shared with us that the focus of inquiry into the details of their present experience, and not on their past, has felt liberating. As one client said, "Not focusing on my familiar story allowed me to make space for something new to happen. The story was no longer in my way of connecting to new experience. While it used to feel scary, now it feels freeing to meet the world with 'beginner's mind.'"

Using the past to orient to our present and future is a common experience. When there is unresolved complex trauma, the way we relate to our past will impact the way we relate to our present and future. Narratives are strong in the context of unresolved shame and pride-based identifications. Working in the present moment, using inquiry from a phenomenological orientation, allows us to explore underneath the layers of adaptive survival strategies.

NARM inquiry is not behaviorally oriented. One of the challenges in working primarily with behaviors is that the same external behavior can be driven from different places internally. For example, in the United States it is common to meet people who are thinking of moving 3,000 miles to get away from their parents. This behavior can be driven from child consciousness or adult consciousness. When in child consciousness, behaviors are

driven from a web of survival style identifications and strategies; when in adult consciousness, behaviors emerge from connection to one's authentic needs, feelings, and a sense of agency and self-activation.

As a way of not getting entangled in child consciousness strategies, the questions we use focus on what is driving behaviors. For example, if we are working with a client whose intention is to get clear on if they should move across country to get away from their family, we inquire into the intention, not the behaviors. We might ask: "If you imagine yourself living 3,000 miles away from your family, what do you see for yourself there? What is your hoped-for outcome in doing this?" These questions can begin to shed light on the client's relationship to the behavior. Instead of working directly with the behaviors, we are holding trust that as the client is supported to reconnect to themself with curiosity and presence, within a relationship of understanding and compassion, they will develop increasing capacity to make choices that will lead to a more optimal life for themself.

The last key point we want to emphasize is that even though we use various kinds of questions as part of the process, there are no "right" questions in NARM. We want to move away from putting pressure on ourselves to get the right question. Instead, we hold the spirit of "inquiry for the sake of inquiry." This spirit of inquiry supports intersubjectivity, which is the opposite of experiencing life through objectification. *Intersubjectivity* is the recognition of one's inner humanity, from which one can then relate to another's inner humanity. Similar to the spirit of the *namaste* greeting used widely on the Indian subcontinent, it expresses an interpersonal recognition of the sacred in each other.

A fundamental building block of intersubjectivity is inquiry. The process of inquiry is driven by curiosity, openness, and interest. These ways of relating to oneself serve as antidotes to relating to oneself through self-shaming, self-rejection, and self-hatred. Curiosity expresses the desire to learn and grow. The process of inquiry enhances attunement, leading to deeper connection to Self and others. In support of intersubjectivity and deepening connection, we encourage you to freely practice curiosity and not worry about "getting it right."

The Therapeutic Process of Pillar 2

So how do you start applying Pillar 2?

- Deconstruction of Experience

  THERAPIST: I am happy to explore together what's in your way of feeling less isolated and more connected. How does this sound? [This is Pillar 1: Clarifying the Therapeutic Contract, which sets the stage for the next phase of inquiry.]

  CLIENT: It sounds right.

  THERAPIST: OK, so you mentioned a couple examples already of feeling isolated and disconnected, and sometimes it's helpful to take one specific example where you're feeling this way so we can better understand the dynamics involved. For example, have you noticed being in an experience where you wanted to feel more connected but were struggling to do so?

  CLIENT: Yes, just last week at work when my colleague started to cry in front of me. I wanted to reach out to her, to comfort her, to share in that grieving process with her. And yet instead I felt myself distancing. I shut down and stayed disconnected.

  THERAPIST: So you felt the longing to reach out, but then the behavior was more about distancing?

  CLIENT: Correct.

  THERAPIST: OK. And what do you make of that now as we're sitting here?

  CLIENT: It sucks.

At this point, we may shift into drilling down to begin understanding what it is exactly that "sucks" for the client.

- Drilling Down

  THERAPIST: You said "it sucks." What's the "it" that sucks?

  CLIENT: The desire to connect, and yet being alone, isolated.

  THERAPIST: Your desire to connect and yet feeling alone and isolated sucks?

CLIENT: Yes! And, it also sucks because I didn't even realize this until you pointed it out to me. Before it was just automatic.

THERAPIST: When you say "automatic," what do you mean exactly?

CLIENT: Not aware of these feelings, of this pattern.

THERAPIST: So it sucks not only to have the feelings but also not be aware of them?

CLIENT: Yes. I was completely oblivious, completely blind to it.

THERAPIST: So what brought you into therapy?

CLIENT: The desire for connectedness. I want to learn how to connect.

THERAPIST: So you did recognize it on your own at some point?

CLIENT: Yeah, but just out of sheer desperation, if that's the right word.

THERAPIST: You mentioned earlier being in a lot of pain.

CLIENT: Yes.

THERAPIST: Was the pain related to your desire for connectedness?

CLIENT: Yes, absolutely.

THERAPIST: So you said you came to therapy out of sheer desperation, but you also said you have this desire to learn how to connect?

CLIENT: Now that I'm thinking about it, I guess it wasn't so automatic. It's pretty clear that I have a desire to connect. I'm sick of feeling so isolated.

THERAPIST: How is it now to notice you are no longer blind to this desire to connect and the feelings of being alone and isolated?

CLIENT: It's actually kind of cool. Just by recognizing this I feel a little less alone and a bit more at ease.

Notice how we stay focused on truly understanding what our clients mean. We don't assume we understand what they are expressing. We invite deepening into curiosity and self-inquiry. In this example, by deconstructing an experience in which the theme of isolation and disconnection is present, and by drilling down into deeper layers of understanding how the client is organizing and relating to this experience, we are supporting new possibilities for the client. In this example the client begins to shift in how they've been relating to themself through self-shaming, self-rejection, and self-hatred, moving toward greater curiosity, self-reflection, and ultimately self-acceptance and self-compassion.

Sample Language for Pillar 2

NARM LANGUAGE EXAMPLES OF ASKING EXPLORATORY QUESTIONS

- What do you notice internally when you say those words?

- And when you talk about that situation, what's your experience right now?

- What's it like as you stay present to what you are experiencing internally right now?

- Is there anything else that you can say about this feeling?

- What happens for you when you reflect on this experience?

- What happens when you talk about that?

- When you say those words, I'm wondering what comes up for you?

- What's it like to give yourself permission to feel that?

- What's it like for you when you take that in?

- You talked about one side of this dilemma—are there other sides?

- You said you're feeling both anger and love—how is it to hold both of these feelings?

- What's it like to be present with both of these feelings?

- What emotion might be there for you?

- What's the emotion about?

- What are you experiencing overall right now?

NARM LANGUAGE EXAMPLES OF DECONSTRUCTION OF EXPERIENCE

- Can you think of a specific incident when you had this reaction, so we can look at it in greater detail?

- Do you have a recent example of when this came up?

- Is that feeling of impatience coming up for you right now with me?

- You said you have difficulty being clear with your feelings, but you just shared very clearly with me—what's it like to notice that?

- If you saw someone treating your child the way your [mother/father] treated you, what might you feel about that?

- So from this adult perspective can you see what this protective impulse is about?

- What is the meaning that you took out of that experience about yourself and the world?

NARM LANGUAGE EXAMPLES OF DRILLING DOWN

- When you say "it," what is the "it" you are referring to?

- What do you mean exactly by that?

- Can you clarify for me what you mean?

- I notice that you just gave me a thought, but I asked, "What is it that you are feeling about this?"

- Do you know what the sadness [or any feeling or experience] is about?

- Are there any words that come with the emotions?

- And what's the scariest thing for you about this situation?

- When you say you're feeling shame, what are the shaming messages you are giving to yourself right now?

- I'm wondering, are there any more elements to the vulnerability?

- What is your worst fear here?

- How might it have helped you to shut down and go away in the face of conflict?

Therapeutic Shortcuts for Pillar 2

- Our exploration follows the thread of the session which is informed by the therapeutic contract (Pillar 1).

- NARM inquiry is driven by deep curiosity of the client's inner world.

- Our working hypothesis reflects our intention to truly understand how our clients are organizing their internal experience.

- Our questions are primarily focused on what's happening in the present moment, in the here and now.

- We are focused on process and not specifically on content.

- We are focused on the way the client relates to themself and not specifically the narrative they have for themself.

- Our inquiry focuses on what is surfacing in the therapeutic relationship moment by moment.

- We try to use simple, concise language, as too many words and too complex thoughts can take clients out of their present experience.

- All information becomes valuable information for us to be curious about.

Practice Exercise for Pillar 2

With a client—or with a friend or peer first if you prefer—follow these steps (we'd suggest you set a time limit of five minutes for this first practice):

1. Ask your client/friend to choose a theme that they'd like to have more clarity with or are struggling with in their present life.

   THERAPIST: I'm going to invite you to choose an area in your life where you may be struggling.

2. As therapist, simply be curious and ask questions. If the client answered the previous question with "work," here are some examples of questions we may ask here:

   - What is it about work that has been such a struggle?

   - How long have you been struggling at work?

   - You say your boss is bothering you—what specifically is your boss doing that is bothering you?

   - What do you do with your boss's criticisms?

3. See if you're able to meet your client/friend with curiosity from an embodied, heartful place—noticing your internal experience.

Even though you may already feel you are good at bringing inquiry into your relationships, it can be illuminating to observe how it is to just isolate the practice of basic inquiry with another person. Many people begin to notice how hard they work with their clients, trying to figure things out, analyzing, and striving to be helpful and supportive, as opposed to simply staying present in openness, curiosity, and interest. Meeting our clients with open inquiry is an essential practice in becoming a more effective NARM therapist.

CHAPTER 5

Pillar 3: Reinforcing Agency

The real voyage of discovery consists not in seeking new landscapes but in having new eyes.

MARCEL PROUST, LA PRISONNIÈRE

One of the challenging aspects of writing a book that attempts to describe the organizing principles of a living, psychobiological process in its wholeness is that much of what we're writing about lives within a felt, embodied experience. There may not be a concept more alive and defined by the lived experience—and less clarified by written explanation—than self-agency (otherwise referred to in this book as *agency*). In order to try and capture its aliveness, we have included a section in this chapter that shares quotes from clients of NARM about their felt experience of the process of agency (please see "Agency in Its Lived Experience"). In this chapter, we detail the fundamental principles of agency and how to begin applying it as a tool for healing complex trauma.

Before we discuss the framework for how we work with personal agency, we must first introduce *structuralization*. A concept related to self-organization, structuralization refers to the way children internalize their early life experience and form "internal working models" that shape the developing Self. "In psychoanalytic phenomenology, personality development refers to the structuralization of personal experience."[1] Although earlier psychological models theorized that this structuralization process

occurs through the interplay of intrapsychic structures, we now have a better understanding of the specific experience-dependent neural circuits that drive neurodevelopment. Seen through the lens of attachment and the ACEs research, children who experience relational and environmental support have a better chance to develop a cohesive, coherent, and stable sense of Self, whereas children who experience relational and environmental failures have a higher likelihood of developing a fragmented, incoherent, and unstable sense of Self.

When a child moves into adulthood without having developed a stable sense of Self, their core psychobiological capacities become disorganized, leading to disturbances in self-organization and deficits in health and well-being (more on this in chapter 9). One essential psychobiological capacity that becomes impaired is agency. People who experienced attachment and environmental failures in their early life learned to blame, attack, and hate themselves. They internalize the environmental failure in the form of shame-based identifications, and thus the internal working model of their sense of Self becomes organized around shame. As adults, their self-organization becomes associated with a negative self-concept and is strongly identified with child consciousness. Therefore, people with unresolved complex trauma tend to have difficulty listening to themselves, knowing themselves, and regulating themselves. They may feel profoundly hopeless and helpless. They are more reactive to life experience, including having difficulties in relationships, social situations, and work settings.

For a person who lacks an embodied sense of agency, the adult world may feel terrifying and brutalizing. Clients will report that they feel overwhelmed and have little hope for change. Using agency interventions to address patterns of disorganization and fragmentation is a key aspect in strengthening self-esteem and self-efficacy. Agency is used with clients to promote connection (adult consciousness) and decrease the strategies of disconnection (child consciousness). They gain the opportunity to relate to themselves with greater acceptance, care, and compassion. Reinforcing agency helps clients develop increasing psychobiological capacities, including the ability to listen to and regulate themself, which leads to a more organized and cohesive self-structure.

The NARM therapeutic process is based on understanding, identifying, and reinforcing agency. Pillar 3 helps individuals connect to their part in any emotional or relational difficulties that they are experiencing. Agency involves seeing that what one has taken to be reality is being shaped by unconscious identifications and strategies that they developed to manage early adverse experiences. Reinforcing agency is about supporting clients to have greater awareness and clarity about the present ways they are relating to themselves and others. Agency is a critical feature of self-concept and self-esteem and relates to a sense of ownership regarding one's life. A client who was feeling into greater agency expressed it as "I am the one living my life."

Agency comes from a Latin word meaning "to act" and is often used to describe external action. However, we see the therapeutic power of agency lying in the internal action. It involves a person's intentions—that which drives their actions—and how these impact the person and those around them. Agency relates to viewing people as more than simply reactors and passive participants in their own lives—they are complex human beings who are influencing their own physical, emotional, behavioral, and relational experiences. Albert Bandura's definition of human agency is illuminative: "People are self-organizing, proactive, self-reflecting, and self-regulating, not just reactive organisms shaped and shepherded by environmental events or inner forces."[2]

NARM does not focus on traumatic experiences themselves but on the adaptations individuals have made in response to traumatic experience. Adaptation reflects how children have internalized the experience of environmental failure and how they carry those shame-based identifications and strategies forward into adult life as adaptive survival styles.

Agency provides a way of understanding how childhood experience relates to symptoms in adulthood. Agency serves as the bridge between child consciousness and adult consciousness. Agency is the link between early history and current experience, between our past wounds and present symptoms. As clients begin to gain greater awareness of these unconscious adaptive patterns and how they lead to symptoms, we begin to support new ways that clients can relate to themselves and the world. As clients begin relating to their past experience from adult consciousness, they begin to experience that it's not what happened to them in the past that drives their

current symptoms, but it's about how these adaptive survival patterns have been carried forward into adult life. In this process, they begin to experience and embody an increased sense of agency.

Agency can be viewed not just as a therapeutic skill but also as a function of mental health. In Margaret Mahler's groundbreaking work on separation-individuation, she used the term "psychological birth" to describe the process of a child's developing a separate sense of Self from their caregivers.[3] When adults do not feel their own sense of autonomy, their own sense of authentic Self independent from the caregivers they once relied on for survival, they will experience a diminished sense of agency.

As mentioned previously, clients with a limited sense of agency will relate to their internal world through shame. They have great difficulty being in direct relationship to their internal states, which makes it difficult for them to regulate themselves. They may feel constantly at the mercy of their emotional reactivity. Seen from this perspective, the less agency a person experiences, the more instability, dysregulation, and disorganization they will experience. Paradoxically, clients may also feel constantly at the mercy of others. Clients with a decreased sense of agency have a strong tendency to blame others and not see their own part in the relational and emotional difficulties they experience. When agency is compromised, shame and blame can become dominant ways of relating to life experience.

Agency is the opposite of blaming oneself and others. Whereas blame keeps people stuck and feeling helpless, agency helps people access their

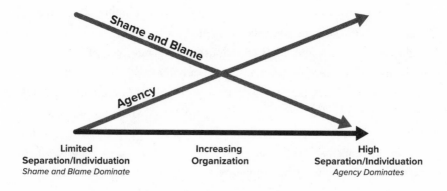

Limited	**Increasing**	**High**
Separation/Individuation	**Organization**	**Separation/Individuation**
Shame and Blame Dominate		*Agency Dominates*

own capacities to respond to real or perceived external difficulties. In fact, agency can be viewed as the source that fuels the possibility of taking action.

A good example is the difficulty so many people have in taking accountability for their actions. As imperfect humans, we all make mistakes and errors in judgment. People with a limited sense of agency might use defense mechanisms like denial and justification to not take accountability for their actions. People with a greater sense of agency will not only take accountability for their actions but also ownership for the impacts of their behaviors. Agency allows individuals to relate to others in good faith.

It is not an easy task to acknowledge the part one plays in their own life. Many people gravitate to explanations for their suffering that reinforce helplessness. They may rely on simple descriptions, labels, and reductionistic thinking, which often reinforces the feeling of being a victim of their history. For example, an adult client may say that they became an alcoholic because they were raised by parents who had alcohol issues. We know, however, that not everyone who grew up with parents with alcohol issues ends up being an alcoholic. It is very common for people to experience their personal difficulties as being caused by outside influences rather than recognizing the role they play in organizing their own reality. Reducing the complexity of one's life in this way often reinforces suffering and a sense of helplessness.

Agency introduces the perspective that we are actors in our own lives. This perspective helps adults better understand their suffering. This is tricky territory, particularly for those of us in the trauma field, as we never want to blame someone for what happened to them. That is not what agency is about. In fact, we use the word *agency* over other possibilities such as *responsibility* since responsibility is often used to blame. Agency is an internal capacity and never involves blaming Self or others. In NARM we emphasize that agency is the opposite of blame and shame. As a person starts to acknowledge their part in whatever emotional and relational difficulties they are experiencing, this leads to a decreasing sense of feeling a victim of other people and stuck in patterns from the past. This process brings with it a greater potential of feeling empowered in their life as they see increased possibilities for healing and moving forward.

When agency has not developed, individuals look outside themselves, believing that if only their partner would change, their friend would change, their boss would change, society would change, then they would finally feel OK. Without a sense of ownership related to their own emotional reactions, a person feels powerless, helpless, and hopeless. There are of course real challenges in everyone's personal and work relationships, as well as in society. We do not want to minimize the impacts of external difficulties—which regrettably psychology, without a solid trauma-informed perspective, has done by blaming and pathologizing individuals for their reactions to abnormal and traumatic situations. But when working individually with clients, our focus is on looking at how the client relates to these external challenges. As we say in our teaching: "There's what is, and there's what we do to ourselves with what is."

REFLECTIVE EXERCISE

We invite you to take a few moments to reflect on this question:

- How does it "protect" you to see the problems in a close relationship—with a partner, a loved one, a friend—as the other person's fault?

As you reflect on this question, we invite you to notice what you experience internally in your thoughts, emotions, and body.

Many people learning about agency mistakenly think of it as having to do with taking action. In NARM we differentiate between states and behaviors. Agency represents an internal state and not a behavior, although agency often initiates and shapes behaviors. For example, let's say you are feeling taken advantage of by a friend, and you've been hoping that they would recognize this and do something to remedy it. One day, you decide to talk with them about it rather than simply waiting. The action of speaking to your friend is not what we would refer to as agency. In this example, speaking up is the behavior. Agency is about relating to yourself in a way that recognizes and honors your needs and feelings—in this situation, acknowledging that you

are feeling taken advantage of and deciding that this was not working for you anymore. Agency drives behaviors. Honoring one's own needs and feelings brings the possibility of acting, or not acting, in support of those needs.

Agency sometimes gets mistaken for empowerment, and while they are related concepts, we view agency as the capacity to act, not the action itself. Empowerment occurs when individuals are able to exercise their agency into action. Empowerment is about relating to external experience and other people, while agency is about relating to internal experience and oneself.

The reality is that we are all complex human beings who organize life experience in specific ways. Humans are much more complex than simple conditioned responses. The classical conditioning model from behavioral psychology posits that an individual encounters a stimulus and responds to it. The piece we are adding to the classical conditioning model is about how humans mediate between internal and external experience. The NARM agency model demonstrates that there is always a dynamic process of how individuals organize and relate to life experience, via the "organizing Self." People encounter a stimulus, organize their internal experience, and respond to it. Therapeutically, we are holding the understanding that individuals are constantly forming and shaping their internal world by the way they view and relate to life experience.

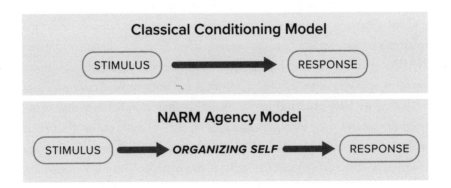

Again, it is important to acknowledge that focusing on agency does not come at the expense of validating a client's external realities. In fact, we believe a focus on agency can provide clients with more possibility in

managing external challenges. We use agency to learn about how an individual is organizing their internal experience—and what internal obstacles they may be encountering as they struggle with external difficulties.

For example, a client reported feeling targeted by their boss at work. They shared many specific examples that seemed to validate their perspective. Instead of working with this client to figure out how to address this situation with their boss, we began by exploring how they were relating to these experiences of feeling targeted. What immediately came up for this client was how familiar this pattern has been for them in their life. This opened up a much larger exploration that gave them new ways of understanding this pattern and their reactions to it. As they developed greater self-awareness, they were able to reflect on the various options for how they might respond in this work situation. When they came back the next week for their session, they proudly shared that they experienced a greater sense of confidence, which supported them to advocate for themself successfully with their boss.

A question that gets asked a lot is: How do we use agency to empower our clients and not to blame them for things that they have no control over? There are countless real things happening within a given society that impact one's sense of autonomy and self-determination. We never want to blame people for being in or responding to those situations. Although there are certainly all sorts of external challenges that rob individuals of their capacity for freedom and self-determination, we also recognize that individuals can stay connected internally to their sense of personal agency. Remember, as a therapeutic model NARM does not focus on how people act in response to external situations; we focus on how people relate to themselves and their external circumstances.

What we have observed in our careers is that as individuals start connecting more to their own personal agency, they become more effective at working in the various relationships, organizations, and systems they are involved in. The more connected individuals are to their internal experience, the more informed and effective their behaviors can be. When connecting to one's agency, there is much less likelihood of acting-in and acting-out behaviors. Instead, there is an embodied sense that we can be present to and work with our own internal experience, even when things in the external world feel distressing, painful and harmful.

In *Man's Search for Meaning*, Viktor Frankl writes about his time in a Nazi concentration camp and how he was able to stay connected to hope, love, and courage.[4] Nelson Mandela, imprisoned for twenty-seven years and facing unending isolation, forced labor, and torture, also found a way to keep connected to his dignity and spirit.[5] Oprah Winfrey has shared the incredible adversity she experienced as a child, including neglect and parental abandonment, physical and sexual violence, and racial and economic distress. As a child, she had no way of impacting her external realities. As an adult, she points to how she has learned to shift internally the patterns of early trauma as being the foundation for her success.[6]

Even when external freedoms are taken away, Frankl, Mandela, and Winfrey show us that you cannot take someone's internal freedom away. We know that not everybody can have the same resilience and fortitude as these three inspirational leaders, but their examples remind us that we can all experience an increasing sense of agency even in the face of external difficulty. When people are able to connect to how they are organizing their inner experience in the face of external challenges, including painful realities like domestic violence, incarceration, discrimination, and other forms of oppression, they gain increased capacity for agency in their lives.

REFLECTIVE EXERCISE

We invite you to take a few moments to reflect on:

- Some current life experience you are having with a friend, partner, client, or other person that feels challenging and frustrating.

- See if you are able to reflect on your role in this challenging and frustrating relational experience.

- If you are able to take accountability for your part in this relational challenge, we invite you to reflect on what impact your behaviors might have had on the other person.

As you reflect on this experience, we invite you to notice what you experience internally in your thoughts, emotions, and body.

Some clients may initially have difficulty with agency interventions. For clients who are still strongly identified with child consciousness, it can feel challenging to experience a sense of oneself as more adult in the world. But an increasing sense of agency is a key feature in resolving complex trauma for our adult clients. Even when clients are very disconnected from themselves, we are holding the possibility of ever-increasing agency and connection.

An important corrective experience for an adult who experienced developmental trauma comes when they are able to realize and embody that although they had no agency as a child, they can experience ever-increasing agency as an adult. Having a sense of their role in their current life experiences helps them deal with the ongoing challenges they face. An increased sense of agency provides individuals with new opportunities for relating to themselves and the world with greater curiosity, openness, and the possibility of increasing self-acceptance.

Agency involves self-referencing and self-reflection, and it enhances self-regulation. We've discussed the power of being able to take ownership in one's part of any given relational dynamic—not seeing oneself as just a victim to one's history. Self-referencing is learning to look inward and listen to oneself in a new way, which strengthens one's capacity for self-reflection. This ability for self-reflection brings with it an expanding capacity to be present to and regulate one's internal feelings and reactions. With increased self-regulation, people experience greater distress tolerance; they develop greater capacity to be in situations that are confusing, uncertain, challenging, and distressing with less reactivity and defensiveness. Interventions oriented toward supporting agency play an important role in structuralizing and stabilizing a client's sense of Self.

Self-activation is a term closely associated with agency. The concept of self-activation refers to awareness and expression of aspects of one's authentic Self. As an individual experiences a greater capacity for self-activation, we may observe a number of different qualities, including a more nuanced discernment of their feelings and desires, mindfulness in how to best express those feelings and desires in support of the Self, capacity to support themselves when challenged by environmental difficulties, more fluid movement and robust experience of life energy, and greater connection to

and expression of their individuation process. We believe that reinforcing agency plays a central role in strengthening these capacities.

As a client's sense of agency increases, as their sense of Self is stabilized, they have a stronger platform for processing underlying needs, emotions, and states that are tied up with their old survival style patterns. As a client experiences increasing freedom from seeing the world through a child's eyes, they deepen into embodied adult consciousness. This process of self-activation brings increasing possibilities for disidentification and internal freedom.

Internal freedom does not imply that we can do everything we want to do nor have everything we want to have. It does involve being less dependent on other people's reactions for us to feel OK within ourselves. It also involves not limiting ourselves due to how we believe others may respond to us. It is a felt sense of greater authenticity in relationship to Self and others. At the core, increasing agency and self-activation is always a movement toward increasing capacity for connection to Self and others.

Agency in Its Lived Experience

The following statements have been collected from clients about their lived, felt experience of agency in the NARM therapeutic process.

- Agency connects me to how I shape and organize my life experience.
- Developing agency has helped me feel much less like a victim and more like the co-creator of my life.
- Embracing agency gives me the experience that I am not helpless and powerless.
- Agency means that it is not set in stone about who I am—I have choice.
- Agency is the awareness of being able to choose differently than I always have.
- Agency is the feeling of sitting in the driver's seat rather than the backseat.

- Agency is an awareness that I can't control others, situations, or environments, but I am in charge of how I navigate those things and my own life.

- Agency reflects a more nuanced understanding of myself in relationship to others.

- Agency is where I connect to the truth inside me that was buried.

- Agency speaks to the ways in which I connect and disconnect from what's most authentic in me.

- Agency is owning both where I have capacity to take action on my own behalf and seeing clearly where I don't.

- When I respond to a situation with agency, the decisions that follow are authentic to the moment and not old automatic ways of reacting.

- Agency feels like an expanded sense of internal capacity.

- I experience agency as a form of self-empowerment.

- Agency supports heartful connection, inside and out.

- I experience agency as coming home to myself.

Pillar 3 in Practice

> *[Healing] can be accomplished by consistent therapeutic attention to the ways in which the patient's speech and immediate behavior fail to express, or avoid, his genuine feelings, wishes and intentions. In other words ... [enlarging] the patient's experience of agency by a consistent attention to the most immediate and general ways in which he avoids that experience.*
>
> DAVID SHAPIRO, *DYNAMICS OF CHARACTER:*
> *SELF-REGULATION IN PSYCHOPATHOLOGY*

What follows is not an exhaustive list of the ways we use agency in NARM, but we hope to provide you with guidance on how to begin applying Pillar 3 in your work with clients.

As a place to start, let's look at the therapeutic relationship itself. As we have outlined throughout this book, developmental trauma occurs for children who experienced some sort of failure in caregiver relationships. The power differential between helpless child and capable adult is enormous. When a child moves into adulthood with unresolved childhood trauma, they can be very sensitive to the power dynamics that play out in various arenas of their life, including with therapists and other helping professionals. Even with the best of intentions, therapists often meet their clients with a therapeutic agenda based on a number of complex factors including theoretical framework, organizational policies, payer requirements (e.g., health insurance), and professional expectations. When a client who was objectified and rendered powerless as a child meets a therapist or system that treats them with a level of objectification, and from a position of power, this can easily reenact the dynamics of early relational trauma.

How does a therapist engage with a client who is suffering and desperate for help without reinforcing these power imbalances? Clients can feel disempowered by the intake process and initial therapy sessions, feeling as if they must adhere to a treatment plan or therapeutic agenda that does not match their sense of and capacity for agency. An important element of not reenacting relational trauma in the therapeutic relationship is for the therapist to consistently support the client's sense of agency. This process starts with Pillar 1, clarifying what the client wants out of the therapy and collaborating with them around this intention, a foundational aspect of all the NARM interventions.

As therapists, when we do not recognize our client's agency, we may be infantilizing our clients. Infantilization happens when therapists treat their adult clients as if they are children with no capacity for agency. It occurs when therapists collude with their client's child consciousness as opposed to attuning to their adult consciousness. It can also occur due to a therapist's own challenges with agency and working from a place of child consciousness. It is not uncommon for therapists to infantilize their clients by taking over responsibility for the client's process, taking sides in the clients' internal struggles, or giving advice, to name but a few examples, thereby disrupting opportunities for clients to connect to their own sense of agency.

Supporting agency helps clients begin to relate to their symptoms and challenges from a new perspective. The pathway out of their old adaptive survival patterns is to discover that while they had no agency as a child, they do have capacities and resources as an adult that can support their intention for change. Simply choosing to begin therapy in order to change these patterns represents an expression of agency.

Using an agency orientation involves looking for "cracks" in old patterns of identity and associated survival strategies. While our clients are coming into therapy to address areas of distress in their lives, we do not just focus on their areas of difficulties. We also listen for and are curious about times when our clients experience something that is divergent from the familiar pattern; these are what we are calling *cracks*. We want to focus on and deconstruct those areas where they are feeling improved functioning, more connection, and more aliveness. When a client is talking about an area of progress or growth, we want to explore the various elements that are going into that improved functioning. Their change represents a crack in the familiar patterns, more of the authentic Self emerging. Clients' agency is strengthened by having a greater sense of awareness of what is changing that supports this emergent process.

For example, a client reports that they are finding it easier to say no and set limits with others. Rather than just accept that and acknowledge an important shift, we want to take time to support greater awareness of the process of change. In coordination with the Pillar 2 interventions of deconstruction of experience and drilling down, we would explore the elements that are going into this change in functioning. We want to understand how this individual is organizing their experience differently in relationship to boundary setting. We want to explore what has shifted that supports them to be more expressive, including saying no and setting limits with others. Out of the process of exploration, deconstructing, and drilling down into the crack in the old pattern, the client can begin to sense into the ways their personal work is supporting healing and growth.

Pillar 1 clarifies the client's intention and provides a thread for therapists to follow, which helps organize the clinical session. Holding the thread of the session also reinforces a client's sense of agency. *Threading* is

a therapeutic intervention designed to address a client's internal disorganization while supporting increased coherence in all the systems of mind and body. In the attachment field, the concept of *incoherent narrative* is used to depict a person who as a child experienced insecure and disorganized attachment and moves through adulthood feeling disorganized, disoriented, and fragmented. Threading, in service of structuralizing self-organization, acts to counteract internal disorganization by helping clients connect the dots between different beliefs, emotions, sensations, and behaviors that were previously experienced as disconnected fragments of their experience.

A basic example might be a client who was talking about his relationship with his mother, starts to experience some anger, and then says he is confused and can't remember what was just being talked about. As a threading intervention, a therapist might say: "Can we slow this down? Let's take this step by step—first you were talking about your visit with your mother, and then you noticed some anger, then you said you were confused and couldn't remember what you were talking about." As this client is supported to become more aware of the connection between his anger and the ensuing confusion, he can then begin gaining greater awareness for how he uses confusion, and other strategies, to avoid his anger.

Threading can be used as clients start telling one story and then switch to another, or during the telling just blank out. As adult clients begin to share experiences of childhood trauma, often their stories will be incomplete, fragmented, or illogical. This disorganization in the narrative does happen frequently in therapy sessions and reflects the general level of disorganization in the client's inner world. Using threading to reinforce agency helps clients connect disconnected fragments of their experience into a more unified sense of Self, part of a process of earned secure attachment.[7]

A nuanced way we apply agency in the therapeutic process is by the language of our interventions. When we mindfully hold the possibility of supporting increasing agency, we look for opportunities through wording that reflects, reframes, or even challenges the client around their own agency in a way that they can begin using for themselves.

For example, a client is describing that they are mad at their partner and says something like, "I need them to show up differently." Weaving in

agency, we might say, "What is it that you believe you need from them?" The "believe" adds space between the Self and the need. It helps create the possibility for self-inquiry about how the client themself is showing up in this adult relationship. The reality also exists that we are working individually with this client and their partner is not here, so we can only work with the person in front of us and how they are relating to their partner.

Another example of using NARM language is with a client who says, "I am helpless and powerless in this situation." We may reflect back to them, "I hear that you feel helpless and powerless in this situation." The "you feel" helps the client identify a feeling state or perception and distinguish feelings, beliefs, and perceptions from reality. It may be true that they are in a situation where they cannot effect change, but the "you feel" shifts focus from the external situation to their internal experience, which is where we may be able to help them relate to this external situation in a different way.

Or consider a client who is deeply invested in the perception that they are unlovable and that's why they can never find a partner. We might say to them, "You have this idea that you are unlovable and that's why you can't find a partner." By emphasizing "you have this idea that …" we are reflecting that they have taken something as fact that might not be a fact. We are reflecting the possibility that it might just be a perception or idea they have for themself that they are unlovable and that's why they can't find a partner, which might not reflect reality. For instance, they themself said that they are very picky when dating and acknowledged that this gets in their way of finding a relationship. So at least part of the reality here is about the way their being so picky has interfered with finding a partner.

As seen in these examples, we use agency language as a form of basic reality testing. This often occurs during the contracting process (Pillar 1). Clients will say they don't know what they want out of the therapy. When a client comes voluntarily into therapy, there is the implicit understanding that they are there for a reason. They have sought out and are sitting in front of a mental health professional, so even if the client says they do not know what they want, we will gently challenge this perceived reality. A client might say in response to the contracting question, "I don't know, I just had

to come to therapy—I had no other choice." Notice how they phrase this using non-agency language, "I had no other choice," which is not true. They are sitting in front of a therapist in a psychotherapy office; there are clearly many other choices they could have made. We might reflect back to them: "So you have this perspective that you had no choice, and yet you just said that you considered canceling and going to the bar to drink your troubles away. There are a lot of other things you could've chosen to spend your time doing, but instead you are sitting here with me, a psychotherapist." What we are doing here is highlighting agency and the way they are dismissing their own agency. We do not want to collude with their perspective that they had no other choice because it is not grounded in reality. When we collude with inaccurate beliefs, we are reinforcing child consciousness and disrupting the possibility of connecting to agency and supporting increased adult consciousness.

Here is another example of attending to agency: A client might say that they want something for themself and then act in ways that are inconsistent with this stated intention. A client has come into therapy because they want to feel better about themself and stop comparing themself negatively to others. During the course of therapy, they share with you that they are obsessively checking their social media accounts and feeling depressed to see what a good time their friends are all having. We might reflect back to them, "When you are looking at your social media accounts, is that consistent with what you said about not wanting to compare yourself with others?" A few minutes later, we might add, "And is this whole process of how you use social media helping you feel better about yourself?"

Another agency-oriented intervention is to change nouns into verbs. For example, we don't view shame as a noun, nor as an emotion. We view shame as a verb, as a process. It is a very specific process that is part of the ongoing adaptations to early trauma. Instead of an individual having a "shame-attack" (noun), we view it as an individual shaming themself (verb). If a client says, "Whenever I start to get angry at my mother, I feel shame." We might counter with, "It sounds like you shame yourself when you start to feel anger toward your mother." Turning "I feel shame" into "you shame yourself" invites agency.

We have the perspective that shame does not just appear out of the blue. We recognize that shame serves a survival function. We help clients reflect on the possibility that processes like shame serve a protective function, albeit usually outdated. This understanding of how individuals shame themselves highlights the role they play in attacking their Self, particularly around specific themes or situations. In the client example, they shame themself when they feel anger toward their mother. Although using this agency reflection as an intervention may initially be difficult for clients to accept, it begins to invite the possibility of them recognizing a self-sabotaging process that is leading to ongoing suffering.

REFLECTIVE EXERCISE

We invite you to notice how it feels to shift nouns to verbs by reading each paired sentence on the left and right. As you read each sentence pair, we invite you to reflect on a scenario in your life that may relate to the theme, first reading it through the sentence on the left (e.g., "I feel shame after I share vulnerably with my partner") and then the sentence on the right (e.g., "I shame myself after I share vulnerably with my partner"). We invite you to pause after each sentence pair and notice what you experience internally in your thoughts, emotions, body, and overall sense.

- I feel shame ➡ I shame myself
- I feel pressure ➡ I put pressure on myself
- I feel stress ➡ I stress myself out
- I feel burnout ➡ I burn myself out
- I am an idiot ➡ I tell myself I am an idiot

Using reflexive verbs helps our clients see their part in a current difficulty that they are experiencing. Nouns often reinforce helplessness ("I feel shame") whereas verbs highlight the process of what we do to ourselves ("I shame myself"). It is the difference between experiencing that things just happen versus acknowledging that I am doing something to myself.

For example, burnout is a very common challenge for many individuals. Most people view burnout as something external happening to them. They may view their burnout as caused by their job—requiring too many hours, having too many demands from employers, and feeling underappreciated. In NARM we help clients understand how they are *burning themselves out*. Whatever real external pressures there are, there is still the question of how we relate to those pressures. Many of us have stopped listening to our body and emotions. We may be driving ourselves unnecessarily hard. We may be pressuring ourselves to do things perfectly. We may not be setting realistic limits with the unrealistic expectations from our employers. Seen from this perspective, it is not about blaming the external demands; it is about paying attention to how we are relating to these demands. This gives us the increased possibility that we can start doing things differently, such as beginning to listen to our body and emotions, stop driving ourselves, and stop pressuring ourselves to do everything perfectly.

Pillar 3 interventions are all designed to invite increasing self-awareness into the way a client relates to themself. Therapists tend to focus on processing emotions with their clients, using questions such as "What are you feeling?" However, agency facilitates structuralizing of internal experience, using questions such as "How is it to notice your feeling?" When a therapist says, "Feel into your sadness," they are inviting the client into a direct experience of their emotion. When a therapist says, "What's it like to notice that there's sadness present?" they are inviting the client to reflect on how they are relating to and organizing their internal experience. These distinctions are quite subtle therapeutically, and there are times that we do want to use emotional processing questions in NARM (as you will see in Chapter 7). Our initial focus, however, tends to be on the ways a client is relating to themself that drives their feelings.

As clients gain more access to how they are organizing their life experience, they develop greater capacity to use their emotional responses in support of their adult consciousness. Moving too quickly into emotions can be overwhelming, disorganizing, and reinforcing of child consciousness. We hypothesize that agency relates to the actualization of prefrontal cortex capacities that support greater executive functioning, or what we refer to as

increasing psychobiological capacity. Included in this is the capacity to hold and process greater emotional charge from a place of more embodied adult consciousness.

The Therapeutic Process of Pillar 3

So how do you start applying Pillar 3?

Here we present an example of a young female client we'll call Destiny. This transcript captures the dialogue between her and her NARM therapist (minor editing was done for clarity and to ensure anonymity). Destiny recently moved out of an apartment with a roommate who she experienced intense conflict with. Since moving out, she has been dealing with strong reactions including obsessive thinking, hypervigilance, and avoidance of her old neighborhood for fear she might run into her roommate. When Destiny came in for this session, she said she was feeling "traumatized" and wanted to explore the reactions that are coming up for her as she tries to move on in her life.

This brief clinical example demonstrates how we use Pillar 3 to support the client's increasing sense of agency. In the following dialogue, we've added contextual elements within brackets. The dialogue picks up in the middle of the session as they are exploring Destiny's emotions in relation to her former roommate.

THERAPIST: What is it about what she said to you [about being "crazy" and needing psychological help] that makes you most angry?

CLIENT: It's just really making me feel belittled, like I'm not capable in my life.

THERAPIST: It does sound like she may be trying to make you feel that way, belittling you. But I'm curious about your response when somebody is belittling you, for example?

[I am focusing on agency here by asking about her response to the external challenge. Agency exploration focuses on how a client is relating to the challenge. Please remember, we do not want to minimize a client's

external challenges. The focus on agency is to help the client connect more to their internal experience—what might be driving their feelings, reactions, and symptoms—even when external change is difficult or impossible.]

CLIENT: I'm sort of regressing back to childhood and hiding, like I don't exist, like I'm invisible.

THERAPIST: So your roommate starts to belittle you and you regress back to childhood. And the "flame of empowerment" you mentioned a few minutes ago, what happens with that?

CLIENT: A cold tank of water was just put on it. I'm feeling shame. And the flame goes down into a pit of the earth. The shame just takes over everything.

THERAPIST: Earlier, you found the psychoeducation helpful—would it be OK if I share something like that with you again?

CLIENT: Sure!

THERAPIST: Shame is often a way of directing anger against ourselves, making ourselves feel bad about something, shaming ourselves. And when somebody belittles you, I am wondering if your reaction is to go back to a childhood strategy to make yourself as invisible as possible.

CLIENT: It seems like that.

THERAPIST: As a child that makes complete sense—what else could you do?

[I am highlighting the adaptive survival strategies we develop as a child. The comment "what else could you do?" was a communication of empathy for the child who had no other options. I am at the same time holding that implicitly, as an adult, she has many more options than she has been aware of, including the option that she mentioned—to feel anger rather than to collapse.]

CLIENT: I really appreciate that.

THERAPIST: Which part do you appreciate?

[Notice that I don't assume that I know what exactly she is feeling appreciative of. In other words, I really want to know exactly what she is finding helpful in my psychoeducation, so I ask her.]

CLIENT: I feel that I am understanding things from a different perspective, and I appreciate that. There's something that's being unlocked. Something is shifting energetically inside. [*Looking around*] Even my vision seems clearer.

THERAPIST: So as you notice what is happening in your process right now as you start to feel clearer, and as something is shifting inside, how are you relating to your inner experience?

[When I ask how she is relating to her inner experience, I am inviting her to bring awareness to the increasing embodiment that she is experiencing, reflected by her vision becoming clearer in this case. It brings increasing agency for the client to be aware of what is supporting positive shifts in their experience.]

CLIENT: I feel a greater connection.

THERAPIST: Connection to?

CLIENT: Connection to myself ... and to you.

THERAPIST: And what is it that's supporting that increasing connection right now?

[This intervention of reflecting on her relationship to her increasing sense of embodiment and connection is designed to support an increasing sense of agency.]

CLIENT: I think it's when you said, "What else could you do?" I immediately had the thought—"well, I had to make myself invisible as a child, but it doesn't have to be that way now." It's not like you're telling me what I need to do or to believe, but in a curious way you're putting out the possibility that I can relate to this in a different way, which I really appreciate.

Notice how in that last line of dialogue Destiny feels the permission and support to have her own relationship to her internal experience. As clients begin to relate to something in their own experience with an increased sense of autonomy and self-determination, this often brings with it a greater

sense of possibilities and capacities. We may view this as a client moving from child consciousness into adult consciousness. As we say in NARM: "Agency is the bridge between child and adult consciousness."

As we return to the dialogue, the therapist continues to focus on how the client has been relating to this old survival strategy of making herself "invisible" in the face of feeling belittled.

THERAPIST: So as you bring back this image of her belittling you—telling you that you're crazy, need to be in an institution, and have no business pursuing psychology—I invite you to notice what you do with that?
CLIENT: Right now I am making a choice to bring her a little closer.
THERAPIST: Why?
CLIENT: Because I feel safe enough.

[Notice how when she is experiencing an increasing sense of agency, she does not have to rely on old survival strategies. She feels more inner security to face this situation.]

THERAPIST: And what's it like for you as you choose to bring her a little closer?
CLIENT: I want to say to her: "My feelings were hurt."

[Here she is standing up for herself, channeling her aggression in a healthy way.]

THERAPIST: And what happens as you say that?
CLIENT: I'm feeling a strengthening ... and like an opening in my chest.
THERAPIST: And what happens if she doesn't get that and doesn't see that, and she keeps belittling you?

[This agency-oriented question invites the possibility that in her adult consciousness, her reaction is not dependent on the response from others. As part of the agency orientation in NARM, clients often begin experiencing themselves as increasingly independent from the environment's response in determining how authentically they can experience themselves. This is the experience of agency.]

CLIENT: I feel strong enough that I don't have to take her judgments on.

THERAPIST: OK, so what are you feeling right now as you're not going to take on what she's trying to put onto you?

CLIENT: I'm feeling a lot of relaxation. I'm breathing again. I feel settled. And I can see how I was personalizing what she was saying.

[Her ability to see how she was personalizing this experience is a great example of increasing agency.]

THERAPIST: The reality is that there are people out there that may want to belittle you. But again, the question is: what do you do with that?

[Again, reinforcing how she relates to these experiences, that she is an agent in the lived experience.]

CLIENT: I feel like I have a choice to take it on or not take it on.

THERAPIST: And how is that to have that choice?

CLIENT: I can feel the "flame of empowerment" again! [*Laughing*]

As Destiny begins to have greater awareness of and take ownership of the way she is relating to this relational conflict, her internal experience shifts. As you can see in the dialogue, this is a psychobiological process. No longer being driven by past adaptive survival strategies, which led to the symptoms that brought her into therapy, she is now feeling more organized, more settled, and a greater sense of internal security. This is an example of how clients begin to experience an embodied sense of having greater capacity in their lives through the NARM process of supporting increasing agency.

Sample Language for Pillar 3

NARM LANGUAGE EXAMPLES OF REINFORCING AGENCY

- How are you relating to that?
- What do you do with that information internally?

- What do you tell yourself when you experience that?
- What is it you believe you need?
- What's it like to be putting all that pressure on yourself?
- I notice that you really shame yourself when you start feeling _____.
- I notice that when you have these tender feelings about _____, you begin judging yourself.
- It seems like when you start to get angry, you start to guilt yourself.
- I noticed that as you mention your friend, you tighten your jaw and hold your breath.
- Is it OK for you to let the tears come?
- How is it to take that in?
- When you imagine your mother/father yelling at you, you immediately shut down; but when you imagine your mother/father yelling at your child, you get angry and feel protective. What is different for you about these two scenarios?

Therapeutic Shortcuts for Pillar 3

- Agency is about recognizing and owning one's part in internal and external dynamics.
- Any intervention that supports a client to reflect on how they are relating to their experience is an opportunity for supporting agency.
- Even when clients can't recognize, or they actively move away from, their capacity for intention and agency, we hold the possibility of increased agency.
- We use language that supports the possibility of increased agency.
- Agency emerges from the client's intention (Pillar 1).
- We then explore how what they say they want for themself is inconsistent with how they are leading their life.

- Agency interventions exist on a spectrum between invitations for self-reflection and direct confrontation.

- Agency is the *opposite* of blaming and shaming.

- Healing comes as clients recognize that while they had no agency as a child, they can experience agency as an adult.

- Agency supports exploration into the role one plays in disconnecting from one's authentic Self (child consciousness) and reconnecting to one's authentic Self (embodied adult consciousness).

- Agency is the bridge that leads clients from child consciousness to embodied adult consciousness.

Practice Exercise for Pillar 3

With a client—or with a friend or peer first if you prefer—we invite you to follow these steps:

1. Reflect with them about an area of life where they are feeling frustrated, stuck, hopeless, or ashamed.

   For example, the client may report: "I feel like I'm failing as a parent."

2. From an agency perspective, help your client identify elements of their story that do not match their feeling—do not try to convince them, just support reflection and curiosity.

   For example: "Although you have the belief that you are failing as a parent, I recall you sharing a touching moment you had last week in support of your child after they had a rough day at school. You said you were proud of how you showed up in support of your child."

3. Ask your client how it is to receive this reflection.

   For example: "How is it to notice that even though you had this belief of you failing as a parent, you shared with me something very different before?"

CHAPTER 6

Pillar 4: Reflecting Psychobiological Shifts

It is the experience of being in connection that fulfills the longing we have to feel fully alive.

LAURENCE HELLER AND ALINE LAPIERRE,
HEALING DEVELOPMENTAL TRAUMA

Pillar 4: Reflecting Psychobiological Shifts focuses on reorganization of internal states. As a neurobiologically informed, somatic-oriented model, NARM supports "the promotion of neural integration" that leads to structural and functional changes in the brain and other systems of the body.[1] While cognitive and behavioral changes are certainly important in people's lives, NARM focuses on the underlying psychobiological patterns of dysregulation and disorganization that are driving cognitive and behavioral symptoms. Reorganization occurs as clients begin to shift lifelong adaptive survival patterns into more resourced, resilient, and self-activated states. In this chapter, we introduce the ways in which we identify, reflect, and support psychobiological shifts that lead to greater organization, health, and well-being for our clients.

Real change in therapy, or any personal growth work, is difficult to effect. Many clients have shared with us that previous therapy provided

temporary relief but did not lead to long-term change. To understand why this is so, we need to look in depth at the underlying psychobiological patterns and internal conflicts left over from early trauma that are in the way of therapeutic progress. From there, we can understand ways we as therapists are able to support real change and growth for our clients.

As discussed previously, we see the possibility for change being impacted by how clients relate to their core dilemmas. We recognize that they do indeed want to grow and change, and that they are also invested in not changing. There is an unconscious loyalty to staying stuck. We know this may sound counterintuitive. Clients come into therapy desperate to change; however, growth, success, and fulfillment pose threats to the underlying shame-based identifications that shape their identity. This helps us understand why it is so hard for clients to truly own and use what they are experiencing in their therapy and personal growth. When therapists bump up against these survival patterns that do not so easily change, this is what has traditionally been called *resistance*. Clients often use elaborate strategies of self-sabotaging to "resist" real change.

Reflecting a client's psychobiological shifts is a resource-based skill to counteract the tendency to stay stuck in old trauma-based patterns. From a neuroscientific perspective, identifications can be viewed as conditioned neuropathways associated with specific brain and body responses. These neuropathways are wired in a child's brain and nervous system in response to their caregivers and environment. Shame-based identifications, emerging out of the adaptation to attachment and environmental failures, and the subsequent disruption in neuropathways, carry forward into adulthood and form the basis of child consciousness. Child consciousness involves experiencing fewer internal resources and less psychobiological capacity. In contrast, embodied adult consciousness involves experiencing greater internal resources and psychobiological capacity. We use supportive resources to elicit elements of a client's inner world that are more organized, functional, and coherent.

> ### REFLECTIVE EXERCISE
>
> We invite you to take a few moments to:
>
> - Check in with yourself and notice how you are feeling in this moment.
>
> - Recall a time in your life when you experienced fullness, richness, or abundance, even if just for a brief moment.
>
> - Reflect on the various images, thoughts, and emotional and sensory details of this experience.
>
> - Notice if you experience any psychobiological shifts in your present experience—cognitively, emotionally, or somatically.
>
> - Compared to how you felt before you started this exercise, what are you noticing now?

One of the main resources associated with embodied adult consciousness is the ability to counteract the intense shame, self-rejection, and self-hatred that have shaped one's identity with new experiences of self-acceptance, self-compassion, and heartfulness. The shift toward self-acceptance and self-compassion is generated as a client experiences increased self-awareness. Self-awareness, supported by increasing capacities for self-referencing and self-inquiry, along with a greater sense of agency, provides the fuel for the emotional completion process (which will be covered in chapter 7), which often leads to disidentification and a deeper capacity for heartfulness.

A psychobiological shift can be viewed as a "crack in the monolith" of one's survival style identifications. When we see any movements toward greater connection, regulation, and organization, these become important resources to reflect back to clients. Clients are identified with these old patterns, and it is not easy for them to notice or feel into when these internal shifts are happening. In fact, many clients will move right by them. It is our job to identify them when we observe them happening. These shifts are happening in real time and give clients an opportunity to connect and relate

to themselves through mindfulness, curiosity, and acceptance. As clients are able to experience a new way of relating to themselves—increasingly free from their old identifications and strategies—old feelings of helplessness and hopelessness can change and shift into openness and confidence.

Resourcing through Pillar 4 is about reflecting the internal capacities that our clients have or are developing in therapy. Although we are reflecting and highlighting these shifts, we are not cheerleading our clients. Of course we care about and want our clients to experience positive change in their lives, but we also understand and respect the obstacles in their way of change. We acknowledge and respect a client's core dilemma. In fact, one of the primary ways we use Pillar 4 is by tracking both connection and disconnection, a form of *dual awareness* that we cover later in this chapter. We do not promote connection over disconnection; we work with the relationship a client has with states of connection and disconnection. Choosing sides in a client's internal dilemma often leads therapists to get stuck. We do experience, however, that as the learned obstacles and fears about connection get worked through, the client experiences increasing connection, which is our natural state.

Pillar 4 is the process of observing, supporting, and reflecting the new ways clients are relating to themselves, on all levels of experience, as well as anchoring those shifts in bodily experience. When we reflect psychobiological shifts, the client may not always experience them as "positive." For example, it is common to see states of confusion, disorientation, or even dizziness accompanying significant psychobiological changes, which indicate a fundamental reorganization in the neuropathways of the brain and body. The analogy we use is that of a caterpillar metamorphizing into a butterfly. We can imagine that the caterpillar's experience of changing physical form is confusing, disorienting, and dizzying. And yet transforming into a butterfly provides the next step in its evolution.

In such moments with our clients, we want to be present to the possibility that these states, while perhaps experienced in the moment as distressing, may lead to a greater sense of expansion and growth on the other side. Like moments of more "positive" shifts, these unsettling moments can also support meaningful change. And it is these moments of embodiment—inhabiting one's body, emotions, and the full tapestry of feeling—that the subjectivity of becoming a some-"body" occurs.

Clients do often experience significant challenges in reconnection. As embodiment and organization increase, an uptick of internal distress also tends to emerge as painful emotions, negative beliefs, or other psychobiological symptoms. Dual awareness is an essential skill here. While it is not easy for most clients, we want to help them stay present with the movement toward increasing organization while simultaneously being aware of the strategies of disconnection. Clients need help to learn how to manage the distressing emotions, beliefs, and symptoms they experience from a place of embodied adult consciousness.

Many clients, as they develop their capacity to stay present to and experience greater embodiment and organization, will experience "aha" moments, as if connecting to parts of themselves for the first time. We often observe this in clients when they:

- see the world with new eyes
- feel weight lifted off them
- experience a sense of settling, ease, and quiet
- have an upsurge of energy
- feel more regulated and balanced
- experience new emotional responses
- have new insights
- have new narratives and perspectives
- connect to themselves with greater self-acceptance and self-compassion
- experience bodily tension diminishing
- describe feeling more internal space
- experience more openness and interest in social engagement
- feel a sense of "growing up," of feeling "more adult"

However, as previously mentioned, these changes do not always happen with ease and comfort. We might also observe reorganization happening when clients:

- experience confusion
- feel unsettled, disorganized, disoriented

- feel unmoored, ungrounded
- feel dizziness and nausea
- feel unclear of what they are talking about
- feel unsure of where they are going
- feel uncertain of what they're supposed to be doing
- look to the therapist for direction, guidance, answers

While we don't yet have neuroimaging studies of this phase of therapy, it is our hypothesis that this reorganization is elicited by new neural connections being formed and new neural pathways being laid down. When a child experiences attachment and environmental failures, neural networks are wired in their brain in a context of fear, helplessness, and hopelessness. We can imagine that as these deeply embedded patterns start shifting, as neuropathways are being rewired, individuals will experience various reactions to this reorganization process.

This reorganization is the healing process of complex trauma. Thus, even though it may at times feel unsettling and disorienting for clients, we support them not to run away from these internal shifts. This process of staying connected to themselves when in distress, but also when they experience expansive states, is how clients begin to build greater capacity to tolerate increasing life energy. As one client described it, "Since my session I have felt this energy freeing up and flowing outward. Like it is literally expanding my brain. Like this energy is restructuring my ego. The sense of expansion feels like coming home to myself."

A client experiencing more of their life force is a person deepening into their truest nature. Increasing psychobiological capacity is part of this larger process of post-traumatic growth and disidentification. Post-traumatic growth involves life energy no longer being used for strategies of disconnection. With life energy now increasingly available, the disidentification process promotes living life more fully and authentically. This is the experience of shifting out of child consciousness and into embodied adult consciousness.

Post-traumatic growth and disidentification involve developing greater self-awareness and mindfulness, taking our thoughts and reactions less

seriously, and leading lives with greater curiosity, openness, presence, and compassion. Individuals become less dependent on others for self-organization and self-esteem, increasingly free to follow their own autonomy and creativity, while also becoming more available for healthy connection and real intimacy. There is no longer conflict between staying connected to oneself while connecting with others. Connecting with Self and others becomes mutually supportive.

This increasing connection to Self and others rests on a deeper connection to one's life force. Intention leads to agency, which leads to activation of one's authentic Self. Over the years, psychologists have tried to explain this process by using various terms such as *integration, self-actualization, self-realization,* and *individuation.* James Hollis, a Jungian psychoanalyst, captured this process when he said, "[It is] the lifelong project of becoming more nearly the whole person we were meant to be—what the gods intended, not the parents, or the tribe, or, especially, the easily intimidated or inflated ego. While revering the mystery of others, our individuation summons each of us to stand in the presence of our own mystery, and become more fully responsible for who we are in this journey we call our life."[2]

REFLECTIVE EXERCISE

We invite you to take a few moments to reflect on:

- An area in your life that you used to feel very sensitive and self-conscious about (e.g., your intelligence, your looks, etc.) and now no longer are.

- What has helped you along the way to decrease or better manage this sensitivity?

- With curiosity, reflect on all the aspects that have led to this powerful shift in your internal world.

As you reflect on this question, we invite you to notice what you experience internally in your thoughts, emotions, body, and overall sense.

Pillar 4 in Practice

There are multiple ways to reflect on a client's psychobiological shifts throughout a session, which we are introducing in this section, but the orientation of simply watching for these shifts is where we start. While sometimes these can look or feel like minor changes, they can often be quite consequential shifts toward healing and growth.

Shifts that may disrupt old patterns and identifications happen on all levels of experience—cognitive, behavioral, emotional, physiological, relational, and even spiritual. For example, a client wanted to work on what's in his way of feeling confident and speaking up for himself, specifically in his relationship with his mother. The client reported that feeling stuck in his ability to speak up for himself is a lifelong pattern that impacts him in significant ways. The client began sharing about a recent encounter where he had felt humiliated by his mother. He'd wanted to speak up for himself but felt "frozen" in the exchange. As the client shared this experience, the therapist noticed the client relating to himself through self-shaming, self-criticism, and self-attacking. For instance, the client said about himself, "I'm so weak and pathetic. I mean, come on, I'm a thirty-three-year-old man and I still cower in front of my mother! It'll never change." The therapist noticed an overall tightening in his body, including shallow breathing and clenched shoulders and jaw. The client reported feeling sad and defeated about how small he feels when talking to his mother. Relationally, the therapist experienced the client as somewhat disconnected and distant.

The client then added that later that night, after this exchange, he was so upset that he sent his mother a text. He initially berated himself by saying that "I'm so weak that I had to send my mother a text." As the therapist inquired into the intention for sending it, the client responded that "I just had to express myself. I had to share *my* feelings for once!" Recognizing that this behavior was new for the client, the therapist reflected, first on a cognitive level, that even though this communication hadn't happened in the immediate verbal way he'd wanted it to, he had been able to speak up, which has historically been very hard for him. The client dismissed this reflection at first, but as the therapist compared this behavior to the lifelong pattern

of being unable to do what he had just done, the client recognized that he had done something different for himself. The client said he appreciated seeing it from that perspective since he had been shaming himself for being cowardly in sending her a text. "I didn't see that, I thought I was being weak, but I guess it's true—I have not been able to do that in the past."

The therapist then noticed an emotional shift. Whereas previously the client's affect had been sad and defeated, now the therapist was sensing into something different. The therapist inquired about a possible emotional shift, and the client confirmed that he was now experiencing "a little bit of pride and a little bit of confidence." The therapist then reflected that as the client named pride and confidence, he took a deeper breath and also seemed to be relaxing his shoulders and jaw. The client agreed and said, "I am feeling a bit lighter overall." Relationally, the therapist noticed that the client seemed more engaged, and the therapist reflected: "I don't know what you're experiencing, but it seems like you're more in the room now, more engaged with me?" The client nodded his head yes. Then the client added, "Even though it's just a text, this feels huge. I feel like a weight has lifted. Really, I've never done anything like this before. For thirty-three years I have been unable to share my feelings with my mother. It feels very grown up."

Sometimes it can feel like there is so much to track in terms of the client's experience. There is so much going on for humans as they work on making change for themselves. There are many things happening at once. It takes practice for the therapist to stay present, open, and curious, so as to be more receptive to the various elements that are emerging.

It is easy to get lost in a client's stories, believing that the story might effect change. Our perspective is that it is not the story that effects change, but the underlying internal states are where change happens. For many clients, though, an interesting phenomenon happens, which is that their stories start changing as the underlying internal states are shifting. Old narratives shift, and clients relate to memories differently. So while we do not want to get lost in a client's stories, we do want to pay attention to changes on the narrative level.

For example, the earlier client always called himself weak and pathetic. He recalled that even though he never acted out as a child, he was the

"stubborn and resistant kid." As he continued doing this work, he began realizing that he grew up in an atmosphere of intense shame and threat of violence. His narrative began to shift. He began to understand that it wasn't about him being weak, pathetic, stubborn, or resistant, but as a child these reflected the ways he needed to protect himself against the threats in his environment. He began to see his family, as well as himself, in new ways.

While there are many details to observe on all levels of an individual's experience, there is a larger process to supporting psychobiological shifts that involves tracking states of connection and disconnection. We are not actively trying to make connection happen. We do want to reinforce states of connection when we observe them, as these are important moments of integration and organization. This is when we reference the body, as described previously. But we do not value connection over disconnection. We understand that they go together, just like an in-breath and an out-breath. We help our clients develop the capacity for dual awareness, which allows them to be present to states of both connection and disconnection.

We want to remember that unconsciously most of our clients are stuck in states of disconnection. They are deeply invested in these adaptive survival patterns because they have served an important survival function. We need to be prepared for how the client will minimize, dismiss, distract, or outright reject our reflections of increasing connection and psychobiological capacity. Here are a few basic examples of how this might happen. A client begins touching into grief about the loss of their father at a young age when you notice that they begin to get distracted and drift away. A client begins to feel relaxed in their body and then quickly shifts into telling you how annoying it was to find a parking place outside your office. A client is feeling tender with themself and then suddenly starts judging themself. These are moments of connection moving into strategies of disconnection. Remember, these shifts can happen on all levels of experience, and Pillar 4 is about how we track these psychobiological shifts moment by moment and, when appropriate, reflect them back to the client.

It is a source of a lot of therapist frustration when our clients rely on these patterns of disconnection and resist or reject our interventions. The word *stuck* is common for so many of the therapists we provide consultation

and training for. Therapists often feel stuck with their clients, and their clients may feel stuck too. Understanding the relationship between connection and disconnection helps us better work with our reactions; it also provides a framework for how to address these patterns as they present in the therapeutic process.

When therapists feel stuck with clients, this is the time they may turn to familiar tools to effect change. Often therapists attempt to get their clients into states of connection. As mentioned earlier, we do not use Pillar 4 to make connection happen. NARM is a resource-oriented model that supports states of connection as they organically emerge in the therapeutic process. A significant resource for a client is the increasing capacity to stay present to shifts between connection and disconnection. Pillar 4 brings awareness to shifts that support a client's connection to Self and others, including increased capacity to tolerate distress and states of disconnection.

Reflecting to clients when they disconnect is an important intervention. We do this with no judgment or interpretation, simply through observation. For example, returning to the client from earlier: "You were feeling a little bit of pride and a little bit of confidence in how you showed up with your mother. But when your mother never responded to your text, you started to call yourself weak and pathetic again. How is it to be present to both sides of your experience in this moment?" This is an example of reflecting connection in the context of disconnection, both "positive" and "negative" states, which gives clients the possibility of sitting with complexity and a new way of relating to old strategies of disconnection.

We try to stay away from interpreting our clients' experience and instead rely on using observation and description. Rather than making meaning of what we see, we reflect back what we are seeing and support our clients to make their own meaning. For example, the client starts crying in response to our previous question. Instead of saying "I see that you're sad" or "I can understand your sadness," we would replace that with "I see that you are crying" or "I notice your tears." The intention of describing, and not interpreting, what we are observing is to support our client's own capacity for agency, self-awareness, and self-determination. As well as we know our clients, we will never truly know the inner world of another person. We can observe, we can

reflect, we can ask, but we want to stay away from assuming or making meaning for our clients. This allows clients to integrate their experience in the way that they need to, not according to our framework or agenda.

While we want to avoid interpretation, psychoeducation can be a very useful tool as part of supporting psychobiological shifts. Psychoeducation involves sharing information about psychological principles directly related to the client's experience, which can help promote understanding and validation. Many clients appreciate and actually enjoy learning more about trauma and how their brain and body respond to traumatic experience. This can help normalize their experiences. In fact, clients will sometimes say that before understanding what was going on they just felt "crazy," but now it all makes sense. This in itself can be organizing and healing.

There are three important aspects in using psychoeducation effectively:

1. **Keeping it relational:** This means staying in relationship with our clients and not lecturing, trying to convince, or manipulating our client's experience. The intention is to provide greater support for the reorganization that is happening. We want to reflect on how our psychoeducational comments can be most useful in support of the client's emergent process.

2. **Keeping it as embodied as possible:** This means not getting too far off into theory and intellectualization. It can be easy with some clients to get into intellectual discussions that can serve to disconnect them from the integration process. We want to keep our psychoeducational comments simple, concise, and direct, so that clients can receive this information, feel their own emotional or physical reactions to it, and use it to support integration.

3. **Checking in with how the psychoeducation lands for them:** This leads us back to the first aspect, *keeping it relational.* We want to learn about how our psychoeducational comments are being received by our client. We want to stay attuned to what impact this psychoeducational information might have on our client, including how they are able to use this information for themself moving forward (reinforcing agency) and any possible integration (psychobiological shifts).

When done with these three aspects in mind, psychoeducation can facilitate and support shifts toward increasing connection and organization. As people learn more about the mechanics of complex trauma, and how these patterns impact their lives, they often begin to see their difficulties in a new light. We have heard many examples of how NARM has been used educationally with individuals, couples, families, and groups. We have collaborated with therapists and teachers who have introduced NARM psychoeducation in residential, clinical, educational, and organizational settings. And we hope this book helps make NARM principles even more accessible to be used psychoeducationally.

Another aspect of Pillar 4 is what is referred to as *therapist self-disclosure*. When a therapist shares that they are being touched by their client, it can lead to a very meaningful moment of connection. Often therapists are moved as they experience how differently the client is relating to themself now compared to earlier in therapy. For example, a client who was very harsh and self-critical starts relating to themself through greater kindness, acceptance, and compassion. A therapist may share how it feels to be present to the client's internal shift, even something as simple as "I feel touched seeing you be kinder to yourself" or "It is nice to see you being more compassionate with yourself." Obviously it is not appropriate for a therapist to use a client's session to focus on their own life or get their own personal needs met. But when feelings are shared authentically and with attention to their impact, it enhances the possibility for deepening connection and intimacy.

An important element of Pillar 4 is providing ample space and time for the client to be present to their psychobiological shifts. We will talk more about the integration phase of NARM in chapter 8, but sometimes we refer to Pillar 4 as the savasana phase of NARM (*savasana* refers to the integration phase of yogic practices). It is easy for both client and therapist to rush by meaningful internal shifts. In fact, it can be a strategy to move quickly and not settle into any one experience. At these times, we may say something simple like, "Is it OK to just take a little time with that before moving on?"

Frequently clients want to jump quickly into another story. At these times, the therapist may need to be a bit more directive. For example, a

client begins to feel tension releasing in their shoulders and then immediately brings up another issue with their husband. The therapist might say, "I would like to hear more about your frustration with your husband, but you were just feeling into the tension releasing in your shoulders, and I wonder if it's OK if we sit with that for a little longer before moving on?"

When clients tend to disconnect quickly, therapists may need to be even more directive and challenge the pattern of connection–disconnection itself: "I notice you quickly changed the subject—how would it be for you to sit with that feeling of tension release and notice how that is?" Clients need our support as these moments can easily be missed. Again, it is OK for our clients to move into strategies of disconnection, and we do not want to try to force them into states of connection, but it is useful to invite a slowing down as we observe states of connection emerging.

As we say in our teaching, "Every new insight becomes an obstacle in the way of the next insight." We know that moments of expansion and connection are generally followed by a wave of contraction and disconnection. The threat of losing our familiar survival strategies shakes the foundation of who we take ourselves to be in the world, our identity. Who are we without our identifications? When clients get a glimpse of freeing themselves from these old personality patterns, such as in moments of inner quiet and settling, fear often arises. This is when strategies of disconnection may emerge.

For example, a client wanted to feel "more ease inside" but felt burdened by all the responsibilities in his daily life. He felt tense and agitated internally and was dealing with anxiety, insomnia, and high blood pressure. During the session, the client had just experienced a significant shift in his body, where he described feeling a sense of ease. He reported that it felt as if a burden was being lifted. He sat quietly for a few seconds and then reported that this state had passed and that he was back to thinking about the future and what he needed to do to take care of everything and everyone. He said those thoughts were creating tension and agitation in his body again. The therapist offered, "I noticed that you quickly shifted back into thinking about all you need to do, and that seemed to create tension and agitation—what would it be like

to sit with the ease just a bit longer?" The client tried several times, and each time started to feel tense and agitated. The therapist then observed: "So you experienced the ease you said you most wanted and then quickly shifted back to feeling the tension and agitation. I notice you have done this several times now. I wonder if you're OK with us exploring this further?" We can hypothesize that as the client gets closer to what he most wants, fear emerges, and he goes back into his old strategies. Without judgment, the therapist here simply invites curiosity into the relationship between both sides of the connection-disconnection process.

A powerful opportunity to use Pillar 4 is when a client is experiencing a profound shift that aligns with their original intention (from Pillar 1). A client who was experiencing social anxiety said her intention was to connect to a state of "relaxed engagement." During the session, she explored ways she felt threatened by social situations, the pressure she put on herself, and the internal discomfort that occurred for her in relationships. Even in the relationship with her therapist, she felt cautious and on edge. Near the end of the session, as she was gaining increased self-awareness of the patterns in the way of her feeling greater social engagement, she began feeling into major shifts happening in her body and rested back her in seat. After a few moments of quiet, she said, "I want to rest in my own experience. As I rest into my own experience, I feel greater connection. It feels really good." The therapist quietly observed her resting back in her seat, giving her space and time to feel into these somatic shifts. After some moments of quiet, the therapist reflected back, "I wonder if this is what you mean by 'relaxed engagement'?"

The disidentification process occurs when people are able to shift out of survival patterns and into ways of being that align with what they most want for themselves. These moments of connection with what is most authentic in themselves can be transformative. While clients may attempt to grasp and hold on to states of connection, that in itself may be a strategy of disconnection. These connected states are only happening in the present moment. As NARM therapists, we support the disidentification process by working in the present moment with the ways clients connect and disconnect. This reflects the phenomenological process of this approach. We stay

present to what our clients are experiencing. We remain curious about what is going on inside for them. And we stay mindful of the deeper dynamic of their movement toward organization, growth, resiliency, and internal freedom.

REFLECTIVE EXERCISE

For this exercise, you will need a partner.

- You can invite your partner to choose one particular theme that they would like to have more clarity about or are struggling with. For example, "I want to stop being so insecure around my friends."

- Your intention is to simply:

  1. Ask questions about this theme—how it plays out, how it impacts their life, and what are they hoping to be different.

  2. Reflect any psychobiological shifts—noticing and sharing what you become aware of as they reflect on this theme.

- Perhaps you might notice a softening in the face, a tear in their eye, a deeper breath, an expression of relief or hope, increased eye contact, or a new way of perceiving this theme. Gently reflect these shifts back without making any interpretations, just describing what you are noticing.

- You might ask them what it was like to receive your reflections.

- And for yourself, notice how it was for you to simply be curious and reflecting these (often subtle) shifts.

- Did you notice any shifts between states of connection and disconnection?

- What impact do you think even this small exercise might have on your partner in relating to this theme?

The Therapeutic Process of Pillar 4

So how do you start applying Pillar 4? We're going to provide two different examples of how NARM therapists reflect psychobiological shifts. There are considerable moments of connection for both of these clients. Please notice how the therapist uses Pillar 4 in support of the client's increasing psychobiological capacity.

The first client example is from a forty-year-old woman who is starting her life over as a single parent after leaving an abusive marriage. Her desire is to show up confidently in her life, so she can create a healthier, happier life for herself and her children. When she left her marriage, she also left a fundamentalist religious community where she felt "indoctrinated" about what it meant to be a woman and how she must serve her husband, family, and community. This exchange starts near the end of the session.

CLIENT: I've noticed that this pattern of making myself small continued up until very recently when I've started to change it.

THERAPIST: Did the work you're doing to change this pattern affect your decision in your marriage?

CLIENT: Yes.

THERAPIST: I noticed what looked to me like a little bit of a brightening when I asked you that. What's your feeling now about changing this pattern of making yourself small?

[Notice how I ask about a shift I was observing. Remember, we are tracking all levels of experience with our clients. In this moment, I noticed a brightening that showed up mostly in her face and eyes. Left on their own, many clients will move right by this, so I want to slow it down and ask about it. She just identified that she has changed an old pattern, which led her to make a significant and positive life decision for herself and her children, so checking in with the possible internal shift may support this client's sense of herself. We want to take the opportunity to support this possible integration.]

CLIENT: I'm finally able to say: "Oh wait, I actually have moved forward this far. I have chosen these steps in order to be in this place. And it wasn't just me letting all of it come and happen to me. It was actually my choice." So being able to change that perspective has been huge.

THERAPIST: Yeah. How is it for you as we talk about the progress you've been making, the choice you're making for yourself to cultivate this forward movement?

CLIENT: Well, it's actually really encouraging to me.

THERAPIST: And what do you notice internally, as you sense into that "encouraging" feeling?

CLIENT: I am able to say to myself: "This is something that I used to do—this pattern of feeling horribly about myself"—and now I'm able to not be so negative towards myself, but just: "This is where I'm at." I understand others might be nervous but I am not, because I am here. So that is awesome, being able to do that. This is a huge deal.

[Now she's reporting the experience of being able to make different choices for herself even when others might have a reaction. Despite others' reactions, she feels greater confidence in being able to stay present and connected with herself. I want to continue reflecting on her relationship to these significant shifts in the present moment.]

THERAPIST: And what do you feel right now in this moment as you're sharing this with me, this huge deal that you've made for yourself?

CLIENT: You know what? It's funny. It's funny that I can't say I feel proud. I do feel proud though. I can feel that inside. But it's hard for me to give that to myself. Which is really sad. Because I am proud! I'm proud of myself for making it through. And it was hard, I mean, it was really hard, the hardest thing I could have done, and I didn't think I would ever make it through this transition. I fought tooth and nail to get through it, and I know I was doing the right thing. So it's this beautiful experience.

THERAPIST: If it's OK, can we take a moment with it? And it's OK if something else comes up. But I'm going to invite you to just take a moment to be with that, that beautiful experience, all the work you put in, all the dedication to yourself, your kids. And notice what it's like to be present with all of that.

[Notice how I give a heads-up that disconnection might happen, and if it does, that's OK. Ultimately we want to be able to hold both connection and disconnection, and as a way to protect against loss of connection, people will disconnect. So I want to point out that this might happen, and if it does, we can still stay present with this process.]

CLIENT: Really I've noticed a lot of pattern changes to be honest, and it comes up when I have these triggers of, "Oh, I'm not good enough" or "I messed up." I'm now able to relax and say, "This is my process and this is where I'm at. It doesn't have to fit into other people's boxes. It's just where I am." And I feel like I can settle into that.

[Here she identifies an internal sense of settling, and I want to support her to stay present with it as much as possible.]

THERAPIST: Yeah, and I invite you to notice how that feels emotionally and in your body as you really sense into that.

CLIENT: That feels pretty badass! To be honest it does. I feel like … Yes!

THERAPIST: It's nice to see you connect again to that. I invite you to take your time with that feeling.

[Notice the therapist's simple self-disclosure and then an invitation for slowing down to allow time for integration.]

CLIENT: Yes, badass!

THERAPIST: And what we saw earlier, what we were learning about before, is that when you feel badass, when you feel into your strength, there's another part of you that comes up and sabotages.

[Notice again how I give a heads-up about the disconnection that has been associated with her feeling stronger and more settled within herself. This helps her increase her awareness of the old strategies, which have kept her stuck, in the context of all these new resources she's experiencing for herself.]

CLIENT: Yes.

THERAPIST: OK. So how would it be to just kind of hang here in the badass feeling and see what happens?

[Giving space and time is important to support integration. Again, clients will often want to move on to something else, and sometimes they need the invitation or direction to be with their experience in the moment. We are not trying to get them into any particular experience, but we do want to support the opportunity for them to stay present to what they are experiencing in this moment.]

CLIENT: I feel proud. I just feel so proud of myself. I feel strong in my body, and proud!

THERAPIST: I feel very touched to see you give yourself permission to feel proud. And again I notice you brighten as you are giving this to yourself.

[Notice another simple self-disclosure and then another direct observation.]

CLIENT: Yes, this is really a huge deal. I have come so far. And I know I can build on this as I move forward in my life.

We want to highlight how Pillar 4 interventions are descriptive of what we can actually observe and not interpretive. The therapist remains curious and supports the client to make meaning of her experience. The therapist tracks on all levels of experience and reflects back shifts they are observing. Notice how the therapist tracks connection and disconnection throughout this exchange. The therapist is mindful that strategies of disconnection may arise, so as he supports the client to be present with the integration of these deep resources of connection, he also reflects this within the context of old strategies of disconnection. Lastly, while the therapist discloses how he is impacted by the client's experience, he is mindful of not cheerleading or interjecting himself into the client's process. The therapist feels touched as he watches this client connect to herself in such a deeply meaningful way. Feeling into the relationship, embodying the intersubjective nature of this process, he chooses to share his response to her from his heart.

The second client example is from a twenty-seven-year-old man who desires to be more available for and connected in relationships. He has experienced challenges in relationships at work, with his family, with friends, and with romantic partners. His family immigrated to the United States, and they have all experienced cultural and intergenerational trauma. This exchange starts near the end of the session.

THERAPIST: How are you doing right now?

CLIENT: I'm able to stay connected more. I'm not disconnecting as much.

[Here he names a shift. We had been exploring these patterns of how he disconnects when in relationships, so I want to reflect back this experience of being connected right now.]

THERAPIST: And how is that, as you notice being able to connect more and not disconnecting as much?

CLIENT: It's OK.

THERAPIST: Can I share something that I observed about you physically?

[Notice how I ask permission here. It's very useful to check in to make sure clients are open to our feedback. This helps support relational connection and establish trust.]

CLIENT: Yes, sure.

THERAPIST: Your face and eyes look softer to me. I don't know what the feeling is for you, but I noticed a softening.

[I am describing my observations and being careful that he knows I am not telling him what his internal experience might be.]

CLIENT: I guess so, yeah. I guess my face feels more relaxed. After I cried.

THERAPIST: Yeah, as you said, you've been holding a lot of pain. I also heard you say that you've judged and beat yourself up for it. But as we saw, there was a really important function for you holding all this pain. You mentioned that your mom taught this to you, and how deep these patterns are in your culture.

CLIENT: And her mom taught it to her. And my dad's mom taught it to my dad. We've all received that same message.

THERAPIST: That message, yeah. And from my perspective, I think it's important not to throw away those strategies of disconnecting that helped protect you against this pain. Because there are times that people are judging you, or even more, I imagine that there may be threats sometimes? And in those moments, we need those strategies to protect ourselves against that. How is that to hear?

[This is an example of psychoeducation as well as tracking the relationship between connection and disconnection. I am normalizing the strategies of disconnection that he has judged and hated about himself and reacted to within his family. I am naming an important context here that we had previously discussed, that being a person of color and from an immigrant family living in the United States, there are real threats he faces. Previously he described feeling worried about other people's judgments, and his work will be to continue learning how to differentiate these perceived judgments from real threats. When he is under real threat, he needs strategies to protect himself. But when he is attempting to connect with another person, these strategies are getting in his way.]

CLIENT: That all makes sense.

THERAPIST: We just don't want to be controlled by these strategies, particularly in environments where we want to connect and we feel safe enough to connect.

[Further psychoeducation.]

CLIENT: You have to let them go.

THERAPIST: Yes, you are learning to modulate when you need them and when you don't need them.

CLIENT: Yes, definitely.

THERAPIST: I'm sure both your parents were doing the absolute best they could, but they might not have had the support to learn how to modulate these strategies for themselves.

[This difficulty in staying open for connection was the whole theme of the session. There are important intergenerational considerations here. I could sense how big this was for him in the moment; there seemed to be lots of connections happening.]

CLIENT: Yes, clearly they have struggled in being open to others. I can see how they guarded against letting people in. But I do want to connect with people and let people in. I didn't realize that part of me was protecting against that need for myself. I don't want my strategies to get in the way of this. I want to be open to relationships.

THERAPIST: This is what I see you creating for yourself.

CLIENT: It definitely feels freeing. There are so many layers of freedom.

In this example, the therapist threaded various pieces from throughout the session in support of the integration. Additionally, the therapist used psychoeducational comments to reinforce the integration. The respect and honoring for the adaptive survival strategies were key pieces in helping the client have a different relationship to his experience. Not only does this provide him with new possibilities of how he may relate to himself in his desire for connection, but it may also impact his relationship with his parents. Understanding the intergenerational transmission of adaptive survival strategies—and how these have impacted us and our relationships—can be truly transformative.

Sample Language for Pillar 4

NARM LANGUAGE EXAMPLES OF REFLECTING PSYCHOBIOLOGICAL SHIFTS

- What are you noticing internally?
- Would it be OK to just take a few moments to be with that?
- What's it like to take that in?
- I invite you to notice how you experience that "good" feeling.
- I notice you smile again when you say that.
- I notice how you are sitting more upright now.
- I see there are tears forming in your eyes.
- I noticed you laugh just now.
- I notice you seem to be slowing down and looking around.
- I notice you making eye contact and then looking away; what's it like as you allow yourself permission to do so?
- It sounds like you're beginning to have a sense that safety is possible.
- It sounds like you're giving yourself more permission to _____.

- It sounds like you're feeling more connected to yourself right now.

- I invite you to notice what it's like as you're able to settle a bit more here, in this moment.

- We want to give you all the time you need to allow that settling and integration to happen.

- So first you settle, and then there's a little bit of contraction.

- I think it's really helpful to see that each time you settle, then there's a little bit of tension following it. And part of the challenge is how can we allow that tension to move through us without getting caught in it.

- Last time when you felt this ease, you started getting anxious—what's happening this time as you sense into the ease?

- It feels nice to see you taking this in for yourself.

- I am feeling touched as you share this with me.

Therapeutic Shortcuts for Pillar 4

- Pillar 4 is about resourcing clients by identifying, reflecting, and reinforcing psychobiological shifts toward greater connection and organization.

- We track the physical, emotional, cognitive, behavioral, relational, and spiritual shifts that disrupt old patterns and identifications.

- We support dual awareness, which includes the capacity to track states of connection and disconnection.

- We reflect on moments of connection within the context of strategies of disconnection.

- Pillar 4 supports awareness of and importance of allowing time for *connection, reorganization, integration,* and *transformation* into new neural and physiological pathways.

- We support the possibility of increased embodiment when we reflect somatic shifts as they occur.

- When we observe psychobiological shifts, we do not interpret; we simply observe and reflect what we are noticing to the client.

- We reflect psychobiological capacities that are already established as well as those that are still developing.

- Psychoeducation, normalizing, and appropriate self-disclosure are often part of this process.

- After a significant shift that supports increased agency, psychobiological capacity, and disidentification, we may reflect on the original intention ("contract").

- Pillar 4 is about supporting and tracking our clients' capacity to tolerate increasing states of flow, connection, health, and aliveness.

Practice Exercise for Pillar 4

With a client—or with a friend or peer first if you prefer—we invite you to follow these steps:

1. Ask your client to share about a positive supportive relationship or life situation that serves as a resource for them.

2. Encourage them to elaborate on this resource: ask them to share as many details as possible about how it feels internally to reflect on this positive resource.

3. Track any observable indications of settling, relaxing, softening, smiling, or any other psychobiological shifts toward connection you may notice.

4. As appropriate, reflect back to your client your observations simply and without interpretation.

5. Invite them to pay attention to how it is to reflect on this resource, specifically any internal shift that they become aware of.

CHAPTER 7

NARM Emotional Completion Model

When I leave therapy, I feel more alive. I feel brave. By expanding the emotional spectrum, it has given me the resources to navigate my emotions and thus act differently on things. It has increased focus on my abilities. And that is what is so rewarding, the focus on my resources and capacities—not diagnoses, challenges, or limitations. Those can simply be a starting point for the exploration. The NARM process impacts all areas of my life. Where previously I only had the colors white, black, and gray on the emotional palette, now it is full of colors. And most importantly, it is me who controls the brush.

NARM CLIENT

Childhood trauma is about heartbreak. When a child reaches out to the world for support, kindness, and love and is met with the tragic reality of attachment and environmental failures, a child is left experiencing helplessness, hopelessness, and despair. A survival strategy that children use to protect against the pain of this heartbreak, and further loss, is to disconnect from their heart. As children grow up, they continue to use the strategy of disconnecting from their emotions. The disconnection from emotion creates difficulties and distress moving into adulthood and has a long-term impact on relationships, health, and well-being. Living a full life requires

humans to be moved by life experience and guided by the emotions that help them connect to themselves and others. In this chapter, we will be focusing on the clinical model for emotional completion that is a central element of the NeuroAffective Relational Model for resolving and healing complex trauma.

REFLECTIVE EXERCISE

As we start this chapter on emotions, we invite you to take a few moments to reflect on:

- A positive experience you have had in your life where you shared your heart openly with another person—an intimate partner, friend, parent, or other family member.

- As you reflect on this experience of sharing your heart openly, we invite you to notice how it affects you.

- We also invite you to reflect on how this experience may have impacted your life moving forward.

The emotional world of humans is complex. There are many psychological theories that try to capture the rich internal landscape of human emotions. Research demonstrates that emotions play a central role in how we organize our sense of Self and relate to others and the world.[1] Emotions play a role in shaping neurobiology and the internal systems that regulate attachment, behavior, motivation, perception, attention, learning, and memory. Unresolved emotions left over from early trauma create disorganization of the Self. Our intention here is to present a working understanding of how unresolved emotional responses impact child development. The NARM Emotional Completion Model supports clients to identify, connect to, and integrate unresolved emotions, a key factor in addressing complex trauma and supporting reconnection to one's authentic Self.

In the two images that follow, we are contrasting the development of secure attachment with what takes place with developmental trauma (from

chapter 2). We are expanding on how primary emotions play a central role in the development of a child's sense of Self.

In the first image, a child meets the world with core needs, starting with a need for nourishment and other basic survival needs. Emotions are a vehicle for communicating a child's basic needs. Adults might say that a baby is being "fussy" when they cry or become agitated. That fussiness is the child doing the best they can without having words yet to express that they have a need to be attended to. Often when babies communicate like this, it is because they are hungry, tired, or need changing or moving. The child's fussiness is a form of protest, an early form of anger. A child protests when they are in distress as a way to effect an environmental response. The message of the child to the environment is about needing their need to be acknowledged and attended to.

When raised in an environment with relative security and where there is continual attuned response—what we refer to as *secure attachment*—a child will have their basic needs acknowledged, attuned to, and met. When children are supported by their environment in this process of reaching out and having their needs appropriately met, the emotional response is complete. The emotion served its purpose and no longer must be activated now that the need has been met. The three-month-old child stops crying and agitating when their caregiver realizes the child is hungry and feeds them. The protest was successful in getting the appropriate environmental response. The child does not have to continue communicating to their environment once their need has been met. Instead, a child can invest their focus and energy in exploration and play. Attuned child rearing involves engaging in an attuned way with the developmental challenges a child experiences at each stage of development. This supports optimal child development.

Secure Attachment

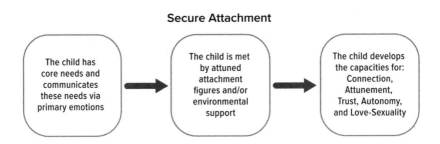

When children experience attachment and environmental failures, however, they must shut down their needs and subsequently the emotions that go with them. Imagine a child lying in their crib crying and screaming for someone to attend to them. At some point, the child faces metabolic risk if they continuously activate their precious life energy to communicate about a need that does not get met. In cases of neglect and chronic misattunement, the reality is that the child's needs most likely will not be met, at least not in a timely and appropriate manner. Additionally, in cases of abuse and violence, a child's emotional communication can invite a harmful reprisal. There are tragically too many cases of shaken baby syndrome where parents just wanted their child to stop crying. In cases of attachment and attunement failures, shutting down and disconnecting from emotional responses is a survival strategy for young children.

Psychologists have referred to *learned helplessness* to describe a giving up around the expectation of having basic needs met. *Failure to thrive* is an associated concept that is used to describe extremely neglected and traumatized children who struggle to meet basic developmental milestones and seem to have lost the will to live. When there is nothing a child can do to impact an environmental response—here are the origins of disrupted agency—the child gives up, collapses, and disconnects from feeling as a way to manage the unbearable pain and hopelessness—here are the origins of emotional repression.

In the second image, the strategies a child uses to disconnect lead to disrupted developmental capacities and impact childhood development. This is clearly outlined in the research around adverse childhood experiences (ACEs). Here we are focusing on the role emotions play in this developmental process. The expression of emotions is a way children communicate their needs to others. When faced with environmental failure, and with the prospect of not having these core needs met, children start to associate emotions themselves with threat. They learn to disconnect from their authentic feelings as a survival strategy. Children rely on patterns of disconnection as survival mechanisms in place of authentic connection and communication. Just in the same way that a bird in a cage might stop trying

to fly, a child shutting down needs and emotions makes survival sense. Yet for humans, there is a high cost to this survival mechanism. As outlined in the ACEs pyramid, early trauma is linked to psychological, social, and physiological illness later in life. The adaptive survival styles stunt a person's life and lead to ongoing distress and suffering that brings individuals into therapeutic treatment.

Attachment, Relational, and Developmental Trauma

| The child has core needs and communicates these needs via primary emotions | ➡ | The child experiences attachment failure and/or environmental failure | ➡ | In order to survive attachment and/or environmental failure, a child must rely on strategies of disconnection | ➡ | Childhood trauma leads to compromised core capacities and default emotions | ➡ | The child develops adaptive survival styles |

REFLECTIVE EXERCISE

We invite you to take a few moments to reflect on your relationship to your emotions— the ways you both connect to and disconnect from your emotions.

- *Connection to emotions:* Whether "positive" emotions like joy, gratitude, and love or "negative" emotions like fear, anger, and grief, we invite you to reflect on the ways that your emotions might contribute to and possibly enrich your adult life. As you reflect on the role emotions play in supporting your adult life, we invite you to notice what you experience physically and emotionally.

- *Disconnection from emotions:* We invite you to take a few moments to reflect on the ways you have learned to avoid and push away your emotions. As you reflect on the ways you have learned to disconnect from your emotions, we invite you to notice how it feels internally.

While humans experience a wide spectrum of emotions, we focus on two main emotions that are directly associated with environmental failure: *anger* and *grief.* For a child, anger and grief feel too threatening to experience, so these emotions become disavowed from conscious awareness. Authentic emotions of anger and grief become split off, repressed, denied, dissociated, displaced, somaticized, and distorted in other harmful ways. When it no longer feels safe for a child to connect to their authentic emotions, they can no longer use emotions as means to communicate their basic needs for survival, growth, and well-being to their environment. Authentic emotional responses become embedded in a child's brain and body as incomplete, unresolved emotional communications. This comes at a great cost.

Working through the unresolved emotional responses of anger and grief plays a central role in healing patterns of developmental trauma. Although other emotional responses certainly play a role in how individuals heal from trauma, we will be mainly focusing on how NARM supports the resolution of unresolved anger and grief. Before we move further into discussing anger and grief, however, it is important to recognize the roles *fear* and *anxiety* play in developmental trauma as well.

Fear and Anxiety

In NARM we differentiate between fear and anxiety. *Fear* relates to our response to potential mortal (life-and-death) threat. Fear is closely associated with responses to shock trauma, which reflects those life-and-death experiences that require immediate reactions. The function of fear is to trigger neurophysiological systems designed to respond to an immediate life threat. If you are in the forest and a bear jumps out at you, fear is triggered to activate a threat response system that optimizes your chances for survival. Fear activates subcortical brain processes that mobilize the basic survival responses of fight, flight, and freeze.

For children, environmental failure triggers fear. The threat of attachment loss is the single greatest fear for a young child. For a child who is 100 percent dependent on their caregivers for survival, relational loss

is experienced as a mortal threat. As adults, we become less dependent on others for our survival. Loss of relationship can be profoundly devastating, but in most cases it does not pose a mortal threat. In fact, adults are designed to survive relational loss, even the loss of their parents. Despite how painful relational loss is for adults, in most cases they are responding not with fear but with anxiety. Although there are many forms of shock trauma that do pose a mortal threat for adults and trigger a fear response, much of what drives complex trauma symptoms involves anxiety and relates to incomplete emotional responses.

The process of *anxiety* relates to an internally driven source of threat, which is not an immediate mortal threat but a threat to the security of one's sense of Self. This tends to appear as an anticipated threat of something that could happen to us. We refer to this as *futuristic memory*, a process of projecting into the future something that has already happened to us. Futuristic memory correlates with the "internal working model" theory, which helps explain that early development shapes how people view themselves and their expectations of others.[2] For example, if a child experienced rejection from their caregivers, they may move into adulthood believing they are unworthy of being loved and worrying about being rejected in relationships. As an adult, they may be in a relationship with a partner who is very committed to them and has no intention of leaving the relationship. Yet no matter the evidence to the contrary and how many times their partner reassures them, the individual still believes that their partner will reject them and has strong reactions to this possibility of relational loss. Real or imagined abandonment can provoke intense emotional and behavioral reactions.

We use the term *anxiety* similarly to the psychoanalytic term *signal anxiety*, meaning that the psychobiological reaction of anxiety communicates to us about something internal that is unresolved and needs attending to.[3] What is generally unresolved for adults has to do with a child's basic needs and emotions that were not adequately met in their early life. In the previous example, the child's need to be accepted and securely attached was not adequately met during childhood, which led to unresolved emotions of grief and anger. As an adult striving to securely connect in an intimate relationship, they experience anxiety. Seen from this perspective, anxiety is

not the problem—it is the communication that there is already a problem. We support our clients to listen more deeply to the anxiety and what it is trying to communicate. This is similar to the pain response, which alerts us to a specific part of our body that needs attention.

As we describe in the following sections, anxiety is often signaling that anger or grief is arising. Returning to the previous example, we can imagine the deep pain of rejection this person felt as a child. We can imagine the strong emotional responses that the child did not feel safe to communicate. And we can imagine how getting closer in an intimate relationship triggers these incomplete emotions. By working with the primary emotions that anxiety is signaling, we can begin to unravel the unresolved emotional patterns that keep our clients stuck and in distress.

Another example of how anxiety may be signaling unresolved emotions can be seen in a client who has a lifetime of intense social anxiety. The client met a potential new friend and had the idea to invite this person out to dinner. As she prepared to ask, she began feeling anxious about asking. The futuristic memory is strong, as she has the belief that if she asks, she will be rejected. This anxiety is not based on present experience, as the client is under no immediate threat. In reality this new friend would probably very much like to connect and would be happy to go out to dinner. But the client is perceiving reality in a distorted way, for example by telling herself that her friend would just say yes to be nice but doesn't really want to go. Based on this distorted perception, she has a physiological reaction, experiencing a racing heart or sweaty palms. She may also berate herself that this is really not such a big deal and shame herself about being so dramatic. In these moments of anxiety reflecting a futuristic memory, people meet the present through the filters of their child consciousness. This also shapes behaviors, because in this circumstance, the client felt so anxious that she decided not to ask this person out to dinner after all, and she potentially missed out on a meaningful friendship.

In one's present life, the anxiety often has nothing to do with reality. Even if this client did get rejected upon asking this person to dinner, this is not the same as a child being rejected by a caregiver that they are fully dependent on. The reality is that adults are going to be rejected at various

times in their life. Adults have the capacity to manage rejection much differently than they did as dependent and helpless children. But anxiety is not realistic because it does not relate to actual threat. When anxiety is triggered, it points to underlying, unresolved patterns of identity distortion, disconnection, self-rejection, and disorganization that need to be addressed.

While we do not want to take clients further into their anxiety, we do want to understand the underlying internal dynamics that are seeking resolution. As a way of helping clients learn what their anxiety may be signaling, we invite curiosity about their anxiety. We reflect on these questions: *What are they afraid of? What are the underlying dynamics that are eliciting anxiety?*

Anxiety is often an indication that the client is getting closer to a core dilemma. For example, if a client opens their heart in a new relationship, they dread they will be rejected or abandoned. The anxiety experienced in the present moment signals unresolved emotions associated with past experiences. By inquiring into our clients' anxieties, we can support our clients to connect to unresolved primary emotions.

We can view anxiety as an embedded desire. The hidden desire is the resolution of childhood trauma. The irony of not running from anxiety is that the more we listen to it and understand what it is communicating, the quieter it gets.

REFLECTIVE EXERCISE

We invite you to take a few moments to reflect on:

- Your relationship to your own anxiety. Perhaps pick something specific you may feel anxious about—for example, something in your relationship, at work, or making a life decision.

- What deeper need or emotion might your anxiety be signaling?

- If you're able to identify this, what do you notice as you reflect on this deeper need or emotion underlying your anxiety?

- What do you notice internally as you reflect on your relationship to anxiety?

Anger

If we understand that anxiety is often a signal for an unmet need, then we can begin to understand how anxiety often signals an unresolved protest. Children whose core needs are consistently not being met will foreclose anger and protest. The emotion of anger, mediated by the sympathetic nervous system, feels too threatening for a young child. So they turn the anger inward. As they get older, protest and anger are replaced by resignation and collapse. When they begin to feel anger as an adult, they disconnect from it and are left experiencing anxiety. While many clients will be able to recognize the anxiety, they struggle to connect to the unresolved protest that is driving the anxiety. As we will describe, reconnecting to and integrating unresolved protest and anger are important elements in helping clients fundamentally change their relationship to Self.

When a child is faced with the threat of attachment loss and environmental failure, they will activate a protest response. While it is never the child's first choice to be angry at their caregivers, the original intent of protest is to impact and change their environment in order to get their needs attended to and met. Protest, as an expression of anger, is therefore a communication to their environment that whatever is happening is not OK. Seen in this way, activating the emotional response of anger in response to the failure of needs not being met is an expression of a child's needs, an attempt to get these needs met.

A young child who feels they deserve to be fed, held, or soothed will start screaming until someone attends to their basic need. There is an intention to that protest. If the caregivers are able to attune and attend to the need, the emotional response is complete—the protest was successful. If the need is not attended to, the protest was unsuccessful and the core needs are left unfulfilled. This feels threatening to a child. The protest may increase and turn into aggression and rage. But more often, children give up the hope that someone will attend to them, and they learn to disconnect from their core needs and the emotions that express them.

As mentioned earlier, protest and anger toward caregivers are frightening for a young child. For many children, expressing anger or aggression

at their caregivers is a real threat as it might provoke reprisal, which for a young child threatens their survival. Additionally the felt sense of anger can be very intense and potentially overwhelming for a young child with little capacity to hold high sympathetic nervous system arousal.

When protest isn't responded to by caregivers, this creates an impossible bind for a child. Children cannot hold love and intense anger toward their caregiver at the same time. Anger at the caregiver represents a profound threat to the child. One of the ways children manage this dilemma is through splitting. As described in chapter 2, from a child's perspective it is better to be an unlovable child of loving parents than to be a lovable child of unloving parents. If the child experiences caregivers as not having the capacity to love them, there is no hope left.

Splitting and identifying with the "bad self" provides hope. If they can get rid of the parts that are seemingly not liked by the caregivers, then they imagine they will be loved. Or if they work really hard to be what their caregivers expect of them, then they will be loved. Internalizing the environmental failure as their failure leads to shame-based identifications that feel protective and maintain hope. It protects the attachment relationship. It preserves the possibility that there is still love in the universe. As painful as it is to feel defective, faulty, and unlovable, it gives a child hope that they maybe can fix themself, and that maybe then they will be loved.

This shame-based process involves splitting off elements of experience and banning them from consciousness. Shaming oneself is a parasympathetically dominant shutting-down process that protects a child. As mentioned previously, protest and anger that cannot be directly experienced or expressed often lead to anxiety. They also lead to various acting-in and acting-out behaviors for children, and later as adults. For children, we see acting in through disengaging, withdrawing, regressing, and self-harming behaviors, and acting out through hitting, screaming, lying, bullying, and other oppositional and defiant behaviors. For adults, we see acting in through self-shaming, self-hating, codependence, maladaptive eating, substance use, and self-harming behaviors, and acting out through blaming, controlling, manipulative, abusive, and violent behaviors.

For example, a client who grew up with chronic misattunement and abuse did not learn how to deal with underlying anger and learned instead to disconnect from it. As an adult, she reports that she struggles with constantly judging herself (acting in), as well as judging others (acting out). She is unaware of how she is transferring and projecting her unresolved anger onto herself and others, and how these acting-in and acting-out patterns are related to unresolved anger. When the therapist reflects back the intensity of her attacks toward herself and others, she may use that information to further attack herself for being an angry person (acting in), as well as blame others for making her angry (acting out). This ongoing cycle of activation of anger in response to needs not being met, and the acting in and acting out of anger toward oneself and others, leads to a multitude of psychobiological symptoms. Without working with the underlying unresolved emotional state of anger, it will be very difficult to address the symptoms.

Many symptoms and disorders can be understood through the lens of anger that has been split off and foreclosed from awareness. For example, we can view forms of projection and paranoia through this lens. Let's take a child who is afraid of what lives in their closet. The split-off anger that the child is unable to connect to in response to whatever is going on in their life may be transferred and projected as a monster in the closet. We see this with adults as well in all sorts of projections, paranoia, and conspiracy theories. When an individual doesn't know how to deal with their anger, they will disconnect from the anger and direct a distorted version of it toward themself or others. Therapists can be on the receiving end of this from their clients. Quite a number of people are suspicious of psychotherapy and believe that "shrinks" are practicing some sort of mind control, just doing it for the money, or harboring ulterior motives. This can create difficulties in establishing therapeutic alliance.

When children cannot express their anger directly in their environment, when they have disconnected from their capacity to act assertively in order to get needs met in their environment, they are left feeling helpless, vulnerable, and lacking a sense of agency. This carries forward into adulthood in the way that adults experience their life. While clients may appear resistant or adversarial, underneath is often an experience of hopelessness.

For a child, protest initially brings hope. A child who is able to protest against environmental failure is still connected to their sense of hope—the belief that something external might change and they will be OK. When a child shuts down their protest and gives up, hopelessness arises and leads to expectations that nothing in the external world will change and they will not be OK. Years later, depressed clients will say to us, "What's the point?" or "It'll always be like this." These are expressions of hopelessness.

As we will discuss later, helping clients reconnect to the primary emotion of anger can reawaken hope. It is the hopefulness of an adult who feels confident in meeting their life with agency, self-determination, and self-activation.

REFLECTIVE EXERCISE

We invite you to take a few moments to reflect on your relationship to your own anger:

- Do you feel angry easily?

- Does it take a lot to make you feel angry?

- Do you never feel angry?

- What are some ways you might turn anger in against yourself?

- What are some ways you might turn anger out against others?

- What do you notice internally as you reflect on your relationship to anger?

Grief

Childhood trauma does not just make a child angry—it breaks a child's heart. A child comes into the world with the expectation to be welcomed into and supported by their environment. A child's brain is wired to interact with others in a way that supports their healthy development. When this does not happen, when the early environment fails a child, there is profound loss.

As we've discussed, initially there will be a protest as a way of communicating needs and initiating the possibility of connection. If the protest isn't responded to, or not responded to in a supportive manner, the child learns that connection and support are not possible. As a child loses the hope that their caregivers can attune to and support their developing needs, the child will experience profound grief.

Grieving is a way humans come to terms with irrevocable loss. Grieving is the experience of processing relational loss. It is an important survival mechanism that humans can experience loss and still continue their lives. Grief helps us move on. Because most Western cultures tend to ignore grief, we view sadness as a negative emotion, something to avoid. From a NARM perspective, when given the appropriate support to stay connected with one's sadness, grief can be heart-opening and life-affirming. We see from other cultures and cultural traditions that grieving can help us heal our broken hearts.

In NARM we view grief as an emotion that reconnects us to our heart. When we discussed Pillar 1, we used the phrase *heart's desire*. We see the therapy process as being fueled by a largely unconscious desire to be in one's heart again, what we call *the heart in search of itself*. A child who experienced early trauma had to disconnect, reject, and repress their core emotion of sadness in order to survive, thereby maintaining disconnection from their heart. Whereas a child needed a caregiver to attend to their loss, as adults, grieving allows people to attend to their own losses. As such, grief acts as a reconnection to one's heart. When a client is able to truly grieve what they have lost, grief can be deeply heart-opening and enlivening.

As essential as it is for the client to complete and integrate their anger, the underlying grief of not having their basic needs met must also be addressed. There is deep grief for a child in not having their core needs met. Additionally there is deep grief for a child in not having the relationship they wanted and needed with their caregivers. Acceptance of this reality is part of the movement from child consciousness into adult consciousness. Adults have the ability to grieve deep losses and use this emotional experience to enrich their lives.

A clinical challenge we face is that many clients are used to running away from their grief; they fear that if they stay present with their grief, they will fall into a bottomless pit of despair. Some clients fear that if they begin

crying, they will never be able to stop. We differentiate between *depression* and *grief*. We view depression as a collapsed energetic state associated with feeling stuck, despair, and hopeless. We view grief as an energetically alive state associated with feeling new possibilities for growth, transformation, and rebirth. Grief is a completion of and a way to come to terms with permanent loss. It allows people to reconnect with the pain associated with the loss, to process it, and to move forward in their lives.

When people avoid the experience of loss, they shut down their heart. When they spend their lives disconnected from their heart and avoiding feeling loss, the pain is unrelenting. While it is true that reconnecting with one's grief can be difficult and painful at times, it is nothing compared to the never-ending pain of denying this core feeling.

This was wonderfully demonstrated in the 2015 Pixar movie *Inside Out*, which used a neuroscientific understanding of emotions to depict what happens when loss goes unprocessed for a child.[4] Riley, the main character, is having a difficult time accepting the impact of her family moving to a new city. Doing whatever she can to avoid her grief, she experiences herself moving toward despair and depression. Everything changes when Riley is finally able to connect to her grief and begin accepting her loss. This story demonstrates the centrality of grief in the service of personal healing and relational connection.

As individuals stop running from themselves, grief serves as a reconnection to and expression of their life energy. As they develop the capacity to stay present to grief, they also develop the increased capacity to experience other heart feelings such as tenderness, gratitude, compassion, and love.

REFLECTIVE EXERCISE

We invite you to take a few moments to reflect on your relationship to your own grief:

- Do you allow yourself to feel the grief of significant loss?
- Does it take a lot to make you feel grief?
- How do you differentiate between grief and depression?

(continued)

- Can you remember a time that you allowed yourself to fully grieve?

- What do you notice internally as you reflect on your relationship to grief?

Primary vs. Default Emotions

NARM differentiates between two aspects of human emotions, what we refer to as *primary emotions* and *default emotions*. We ask these questions: *Does feeling this emotion support increasing psychobiological capacity (adult consciousness) or stronger identification with old adaptive patterns (child consciousness)? Does this emotion serve connection or disconnection?*

Primary emotions serve to support deeper connection with ourselves and the movement toward disidentification. Default emotions serve to reinforce disconnection, keeping us bound to old survival style identifications and patterns. Any emotion can be either primary or default. There are many varying factors and it's quite a complex process, but the focus therapeutically should be on whether the emotion is reinforcing strategies of disconnection (child consciousness) or supporting movement toward increasing connection and disidentification (adult consciousness).

REFLECTIVE EXERCISE

We invite you to reflect on:

- Emotions that are more familiar to you and that you more commonly experience—noticing your relationship to these emotions, including how it feels internally to reflect on them.

- We then invite you to reflect on emotions that are less familiar to you and that you less commonly experience—noticing your relationship to these emotions, including how it feels internally to reflect on them.

Default emotions are habitual and automatic emotional reactions that take an individual into familiar territory within themself. These emotions have a regressive quality, in the sense that they reinforce a child's helpless perspective on themself, their relationships, and the world. No matter how many times a client feels into this emotion, it does not fundamentally shift their internal experience. Individuals may experience default emotions internally as physical contraction, overwhelm, stuckness, low energy, and little or no sense of agency. These emotional reactions drive dysregulation and disorganization. Functionally, default emotions feel familiar as they are part of the adaptive survival strategies that serve to protect against primary emotions that felt threatening to us as children.

For example, a client who experienced a series of disappointments would always respond with anger. Recently this client felt they were being treated unfairly in several situations, such as when they had a conflict with a family member, when they were not invited to participate in a community event, and when a friend did not return their call. Each time this client responded with blame and anger. They felt victim to these experiences and said, "This sort of thing always happens to me. It's always my fault. But what about them? They're the ones not treating me fairly!" And yet, no matter how many times the client would feel into and express their anger, nothing seemed to change. In fact, the client felt increasingly resentful and reactive.

No matter how much this client attempts to process disappointments in this familiar way, by using blame and anger, they will most likely get the same result—more disappointment and more anger. Generally, we inquire if there are primary emotions being avoided by the client's default emotions. A NARM therapist may start by asking a simple question: "Is anger a familiar emotion for you?" Or if the therapist has worked with this client for some time, the therapist may be even more direct: "I notice that in all of these situations where you experienced a disappointment, you responded with anger. Might there be any other emotions that you are aware of?" This question leads to an inquiry about other emotions that might be underneath their anger.

Perhaps as a young child, this client felt profound grief in the face of the losses they experienced, and the helplessness became too much to bear.

In order to move away from this helplessness and pain, this person may have adapted to situations of potential or perceived loss by responding with anger and blame. Resolution of the experience of helplessness and pain likely won't come through processing the familiar emotion of anger (default emotion). For this client, resolution will more likely come through processing the unfamiliar emotion of grief (primary emotion).

Primary emotions bring increasing connection and support emotional depth because they are the authentic, spontaneous feelings of our inner experience. Primary emotions lead to increasing separation-individuation, a sense of agency, and self-activation. Internally, they tend to be experienced as more settling and grounding, supporting a sense of expansion and flow. They are energetically alive states. Functionally, primary emotions support internal regulation, coherence, and increasing psychobiological capacity. Therapeutically, primary emotions also support a client's disidentification process and engagement with their authentic Self.

The following chart provides a simple summary of these emotions' differences.

DEFAULT EMOTIONS	PRIMARY EMOTIONS
Familiar, habitual, automatic	Unfamiliar, authentic, spontaneous
Reinforce regression	Support separation-individuation
Reinforce superficial emotionality	Increase emotional depth
Reinforce helplessness and powerlessness	Support agency and self-activation
Somatically tense or collapsed	Somatically grounded, relaxed, or expansive
Generally acted out and acted in	Generally felt in an embodied way
Often experienced as uncontained and overwhelming	Often experienced as contained and organizing
Often lead to feeling drained and exhausted	Often lead to feeling refreshed and energized

DEFAULT EMOTIONS	PRIMARY EMOTIONS
Reinforce disconnection, dysregulation, and disorganization	Support connection, regulation, and organization
Disrupt psychobiological capacity	Increase psychobiological capacity
Reinforce survival style identifications and child consciousness	Support disidentification and embodied adult consciousness

REFLECTIVE EXERCISE

We invite you to:

- Make a list of your *default emotions*—the emotions that are familiar and easy for you to access.

- Make a list of your *primary emotions*—the emotions that may be unfamiliar and more difficult for you to access.

As you reflect on your lists, what do you notice in your internal experience as you reflect first on your default emotions and next on your primary emotions?

We often see sadness as a default emotion for clients who have lost connection to the primary anger that once drove their protest. For example, we see many clients who feel sad and begin crying in reaction to all emotional triggers in their life, even at times when it seems that anger would be the appropriate response. As mentioned previously, anger feels threatening to children, and many adults have learned to distance themselves from their anger. Additionally some psychological and spiritual approaches reinforce methods for bypassing anger. If we bypass anger, we run the risk of reinforcing disconnection, anxiety, and depression.

Many clients avoid their anger because they equate emotions with behaviors. It is useful to help clients differentiate between *emotions* and *behaviors*. For children who experience early trauma, this differentiation is

difficult. Many children learned to fear their emotions because emotions became associated with frightening impulses. Many people still experience this association in adulthood. They may fear that if they feel their emotions, they will be compelled to act out their impulses. In some cases, clients feel that they have no control over their actions, so they repress emotions to avoid triggering any impulses to act out.

For example, many clients fear feeling their anger because they are afraid of acting out violently. Many individuals have fantasies of acting out aggressively toward others or themselves. We want to help differentiate violence from the primary emotion of anger. Violence is generally aimed at hurting, punishing, or destroying another person, people, or objects. Anger, as it becomes contained and integrated, is an energetically alive state that communicates a protest. Whereas violence keeps us stuck in old self-defeating patterns, the primary emotion of anger mobilizes us to actively get our needs met. As adults, primary anger manifests as assertiveness, confidence, and healthy aggression.

As essential as it is for the client to complete and integrate their anger, the underlying grief of not having their basic needs met also must be addressed. There is deep grief around not having the relationship we wanted and needed with our caregivers. Grief helps us complete the loss. Clinically, as a client connects to their primary anger, they often begin to experience primary grief for the caregivers they never had, for the childhood they never had, and for other significant losses from their life. When grief is not used as a default strategy in order to run away from protest and anger, there can be deep healing in the grieving process.

Just as default grief can be used to avoid primary anger, default anger can be used to avoid primary grief. For example, we see many clients who rage no matter what is happening in their life. They may act out their rage toward others, objects, or systems, or act in their rage toward themselves. For many of these clients, grief feels threatening. Anger might feel like it fuels them to do something, anything, whereas grief feels like a giving up. Feeling the arousal associated with anger may give them the sense that they can defeat the pain of loss. Many clients have tremendous anxiety about connecting with their grief for fear that they'll fall into a bottomless pit of despair and never get out.

Many people equate grief with depression. In NARM we view depression as a default emotion. It is often experienced as a collapsed state; it feels like deadness. We view grief, however, as a primary emotion. Despite it being painful, grief can also be experienced as an energetically expansive state. We want to support clients to differentiate between the default emotion of depression that leads to collapsed and stuck states, and the primary emotion of grief that brings us back into balance and reconnects us with our wholeness. The primary emotion of grief supports us to come to terms with irrevocable loss. It allows us to reconnect with the hurt we experienced and to truly let go and move on.

As a NARM therapist shared with us after the sudden and tragic loss of her child, "When I allowed myself to feel the love that I had for that child, dead or alive, and I felt the sharp prongs of intense grief and loss and pain, when I felt all that—and it hurt—I felt connected to him. And in this, I felt connected to myself."[5]

One of the biggest sources of pain for humans is disconnecting from their heart. When people avoid their relationship to loss, they shut down their heart. Grieving connects people back to their heart. When they're no longer running from themselves and the losses they have experienced, emotional completion becomes possible.

Learning to tolerate emotions without reacting is an essential ingredient for developing embodied adult consciousness and increased self-organization. NARM is a therapeutic approach that works directly with internal states, and not behaviors, and therefore focuses on emotional containment, and not expression. Whereas many therapeutic models support more expressive ways of processing emotions, NARM uses a containment approach to strengthen a client's capacity to be in connection to their primary emotions. We help clients experience deep, difficult feelings from an increasingly embodied, adult perspective, where they learn to be present to internal states without acting them in or acting them out. This is the containment process—not to run from our emotions but rather to acknowledge, feel, and tolerate them, as well as understand what they are communicating. In this way, focusing on the structuralizing of self-organization becomes a platform for the processing of emotions (we will introduce this therapeutic process in the next section).

The intention of the NARM Emotional Completion Model is to support an individual in learning to stay present with their primary emotions, be informed by them, and be enlivened by them. Embodying and integrating one's primary emotions, after years of disconnection, change one's relationship with the Self. As clients increase their capacity for tolerating affect, they are more able to stay present with all their feelings without feeling overwhelmed and needing to disconnect. As we support our clients in building greater capacity for being present with the "positive" feelings of connection, expansion, aliveness, and pleasure, they are also developing greater capacity for being present with the "negative" feelings of disconnection, contraction, distress, and pain. This capacity to be connected to one's full range of authentic emotional states leads to increasing emotional and relational capacity.

REFLECTIVE EXERCISE

We invite you to reflect on:

- The ways you have learned to stay connected to yourself emotionally.

- What has helped you learn to stay present with your emotions?

- How has this impacted your personal and professional life?

The Therapeutic Process of the NARM Emotional Completion Model

When we are in touch with all of our emotions ... we are more verb than noun, more a movement than a thing.
FRANCIS WELLER, *THE WILD EDGE OF SORROW*

The NARM Emotional Completion Model describes pathways for connection to primary emotions en route to resolving developmental trauma.

However, in NARM we don't encourage emotional expression before the client has clarified what they want for themself out of the therapy session (Pillar 1) and before agency has been established (Pillar 3). When moving prematurely into processing emotions before the contract and agency are established, clinicians run the risk of reinforcing default emotions and, by extension, child consciousness.

Clients may want their therapist to begin processing emotions right away, believing that they will feel better when they can express feelings and "get them off my chest." Since we focus primarily on containment, not on expression or catharsis, we do not want to move into processing emotions prematurely. Otherwise, we run the risk of working directly with default emotions. We recognize that working with default emotions will not lead the client into new territory and generally fortifies old maladaptive patterns, including disconnection, fragmentation, and disorganization.

From our perspective, one of the mistakes that some therapeutic approaches make is to try and get clients into their emotions. Remember, clients have spent their entire lives running from their emotions for a reason—emotions have felt overwhelming and terrifying. We take a different approach. We understand the function of disconnecting from one's emotions. If we try to get clients into their emotions, we may be overriding their protective strategies against feeling their emotions and missing the opportunity to truly understand the important survival function of disconnection.

We start where the client is, which usually means exploring the client's aversion to their primary emotions. We "go with the resistance," meaning that we work with the fear of the feeling as opposed to trying to get them into their feelings directly. Once clients form a different relationship to these protective strategies, they often feel less compelled to protect against emotions, which gives them more direct access to their primary emotional states.

We are looking for and working with the primary emotions as they emerge in the therapeutic process. As we say in NARM, *primary emotions ride the back of agency.* That is to say, access to primary emotions increases in a virtuous cycle as agency develops. Therapists do not have to go searching

for primary emotions in clients. As clients connect to a greater sense of agency, their inner world structuralizes in a way that allows for the stability needed to process once-threatening primary emotions. Again, it is important to highlight here that moving too quickly into processing emotions without structuralizing through contracting and agency can lead to regressive states of child consciousness, which can further destabilize clients. We focus on creating the conditions for clients to reconnect to their emotions in a way that supports the possibility of greater connection, integration, organization, and transformation.

The NARM Emotional Completion Model relies on three clinical steps for using affect to resolve complex trauma and support disidentification:

1. **Identify the Primary Emotion**

   This step begins as a client acknowledges and takes ownership of the primary emotion that has been split off and defended against.

2. **Reflect on the Emotion's Communication**

   This step is about inviting a reflection on the implicit communication in the client's emotion—what is the emotion about? What is it trying to effect?

3. **Support a New Relationship to Unresolved Emotional Conflicts**

   This step supports a client to be present to and help contain the energy inherent in the emotion—not focusing on expression, discharge, or catharsis but on integration, organization, and transformation.

Step 1: Identify the Primary Emotion

The first step in the emotional completion process is about psychological ownership—in other words, supporting a client to be present with, and not run from, their primary emotions. People can spend their entire lives running away from themselves, using numerous strategies to avoid feeling their authentic feelings. In this first step, we help clients recognize their avoidance behaviors. We use various interventions to challenge their survival mechanisms designed to avoid feeling. The question we are always asking: *Is this thread of emotion leading to the possibility of emotional completion?*

Using the framework of the adaptive survival styles, we can begin to understand some of the adaptive strategies for avoiding feelings:

- **Connection:** A client may use avoidant strategies such as dissociating, splitting, intellectualizing, and spiritualizing. They may generally narrow their lives by limiting emotional awareness and social engagement.

- **Attunement:** A client may avoid attuning to their own emotions or may feel that they do not deserve to have their own needs and feelings. They may focus on being there to meet others' needs and feelings at the expense of connecting to their own needs and feelings.

- **Trust:** A client may work to limit situations where they are not in control, including any situation where they are asked to be vulnerable with their needs and feelings. They may set up situations where they can avoid sharing their emotions.

- **Autonomy:** A client may avoid self-referencing and direct expressions of their authentic Self. They may avoid situations where speaking directly about their authentic feelings would be appropriate and useful.

- **Love-Sexuality:** A client may avoid authentic emotions by focusing on achievement and performance. They may avoid intimacy and other relationships where they might be invited to share their heart.

As introduced earlier, a familiar strategy people use to disconnect from and protect against primary emotions is only engaging with default emotions. We want to explore the possibility that there may be other emotions available besides those that feel most familiar and automatic. For example, when working with a client who we know goes easily into "depression," we may want to explore other possibilities as they navigate an experience of feeling mistreated by a coworker. The client says to us, "I just feel so hopeless and depressed. Why would they do this to me?" We may respond by inquiring if there are any other emotions they are aware of. We might say something like, "So your coworker has spoken negatively about you to your staff, lied about something you did, and refuses to admit there's any

problem. When I asked you how this was for you, you said you felt hopeless and depressed. I wonder if there might be any other emotions that you feel as you think about this situation with your coworker?" Without leading them into any specific emotion, we simply inquire as to any other emotion that may be less obvious to this client.

Sometimes just a little time and space are needed for a client to reflect internally, and they will begin experiencing a primary emotion. In this case, the client may say: "I just feel hopeless. Nothing changes. I suppose it's also a bit frustrating that they keep doing this to me." Now that the client has introduced the word "frustrating," we would want to drill down further into how they relate to the frustration. It is possible that this could be the first step for them to connect to the primary emotion of anger. There may be an energy of protest beneath the depression. In this case, hopelessness and depression would be considered default emotions, and the frustration (anger) emerging toward the coworker would be considered a primary emotion.

Another example is a client who frequently comes into sessions wanting to process rage about their relationship. You know from previous sessions that anger is very easy for them to access and that acting out in aggression is a familiar strategy they use in relationships. No matter how many times they express their anger about their partner, nothing seems to change for them or in their relationship. In this situation, we might want to bring inquiry into what function this acting-out strategy serves, including inquiring into the possibility that there may be other emotions besides anger. For example, we might say, "We've explored your anger toward your partner in depth together, and yet as you just told me, nothing seems to change. Might it be possible that there are other feelings besides anger you are experiencing in your relationship?"

At times, we will directly challenge our client's survival strategies designed to avoid feeling. This is an invitation for the client to increase ownership of how they are relating to their internal emotional world. For example, a client has recently been left by a romantic partner and, instead of experiencing the primary emotions associated with this loss, cycles between intense blame and shame, actively blaming their ex-partner or themself. We

might reflect something like, "I notice that every time you begin talking about your ex-partner you either blame them or blame yourself. If you weren't blaming yourself or your partner, what feeling do you think you might feel?"

Often it feels challenging for clients to reflect on their primary emotions. We don't expect that our clients will so easily answer such direct questions. We use other approaches to support them in identifying their primary emotions. One example is inviting them to empathize with others. Let's say this client who was left by their partner keeps going back into blame and shame; we might follow up with a question like, "What if this was your best friend who just got left by their partner? What do you imagine they might feel in response to this rejection?" Sometimes redirecting the focus off the client's direct experience and using a loved one can open up other emotional possibilities. In this case, the client responds, "I guess they'd be feeling pretty angry." We might just let them reflect on that. Or perhaps, if we choose to be more direct, we could say, "So they'd be feeling angry—and how about you?"

Although we are not pushing for emotional feeling and expression, we also don't want to collude with our clients in moving away from their emotions, even if these emotions seem distressing or scary. We support our clients' increasing capacity to relate to their emotions from adult consciousness, where they experience greater agency and stability.

An example from one of our clinical trainings may help illuminate the power of this process. In a small group practice, we had two students practicing the basic NARM skills as therapist and client. The client was reflecting on her relational difficulties with her mother and began feeling "activated." She reported feeling tension and agitation in her shoulders. The therapist began to suggest ways to resource these distressing sensations as a way to manage the activation. At one point, the therapist shared that she had previous somatic training and asked if it'd be OK to provide gentle touch on the client's shoulders as a way to help settle the activation. The client agreed. After a few minutes of gentle touch on the client's shoulders, the client reported that the activation felt more settled. The therapist went back to her chair and the session proceeded. After the session ended,

we moved into debrief of this practice session. During the debrief, one of the observers asked the client how it was to receive direct touch from the therapist as a way to resource the activation. The client answered that even though it did settle the agitation and tension, she did not like it. She said: "I think the activation I was feeling was part of me tapping into the anger I have long buried toward my mother. It felt very scary for me to get closer to that, but I felt that by settling this activation, it actually reinforced a bypass I've used for so many years in avoiding my anger. I have avoided it for too long and I want to feel it. So I felt a missed opportunity in learning to feel it and tolerate it. I think the anger is trying to express something important. It may carry answers that I have not been able to figure out yet in relating to my mother." (quote minimally paraphrased)

People get stuck when they fight against their primary emotions. Many people are unconsciously using significant life energy fighting hard not to feel their authentic emotions. We support clients' connection to their inner emotional world with openness, interest, and curiosity. The first big step toward integrating once-threatening primary emotions is for our clients themselves to connect to their internal experience through openness, interest, and curiosity, as opposed to a goal-driven process of making something happen, changing it, or fixing it. By simply acknowledging their relationship to primary emotions, clients begin to get the sense that their deepest emotions do not have to feel so scary and overwhelming but can in fact be experienced as liberating, enlivening, and empowering.

Step 2: Reflect on the Emotion's Communication

The second step in the NARM emotional completion process is about understanding the implicit intention in one's primary emotion. We reflect on these questions: *What message is the emotion attempting to convey? What is the emotion trying to accomplish?*

As discussed previously, we view emotions as messages to both the Self and the environment. When a person is able to identify a primary emotion, we would then inquire into what it is that the primary emotion is trying to communicate. It is essential to know what our client's emotions are actually about.

We can never assume we know exactly what our clients are feeling or what may be driving their emotions. We stay open and curious in order to learn.

As we introduced earlier, primary emotions are the vehicles for children's basic needs. When a child experiences environmental failure, they learn to adapt to this failure by disconnecting from and rejecting their core needs and feelings. In adulthood, the developmental window for those needs to be met has long passed. The emotional process of attempting to communicate those needs, however, has not yet completed and remains unresolved. So while attempting to get the need fulfilled reinforces child consciousness, helping the client reconnect to the emotion that attempted to communicate the original need can support resolution of child consciousness.

Understanding the intention in primary emotions is a critical step toward completing the process of unresolved emotions. But this step does not in itself lead to emotional completion. For example, some therapeutic approaches may guide a client to get in touch with their unmet needs so they can express the emotions associated with them. Often this is done in the name of "empowerment." Feeling empowered activates one's needs, provides energy to express them, and often feels good temporarily, but without moving toward the third step—be present to and contain the energetics of the emotions—it does not necessarily shift emotional patterns and support increased psychobiological capacity. In fact, focusing on just feeling empowered by "getting our emotions out" can lead to increased acting-out and acting-in behaviors.

For example, an adult client was getting in touch with their childhood anger toward a parent and expressed: "Screw you! You don't own me!" This felt empowering to the client. They have long feared their aggression and have never been able to feel and express it before. Some therapists may cheerlead this accomplishment and coach them on how to bring this new-found empowerment into their current relationships, for instance, as a way of helping them stand up for themself.

However, this client came back the next session and shared that while they are standing up for themself in relationships, they still feel very reactive, like there is something left unresolved. "Once I opened the floodgates to my anger about not getting my needs met, it's like I am just angry at

everyone and everything." Although initially this anger felt empowering, the client began to realize that these needs and emotions were associated with creating separation and individuation from their primary attachment figures and did not necessarily relate to their adult relationships. This client's "reactivity" started getting in their way of showing up openly and vulnerably in their intimate relationships, something they wanted for themself. In fact, they noticed they were now pushing people away.

As part of drilling down into step 2, the client was asked, "What do you think the 'You don't own me!' is trying to communicate?" Upon self-reflection, the client answered, "I am my own person." This statement is an embodiment of separation-individuation. The client became more aware of their lack of sense of independence and autonomy as a child, which has contributed to their reactivity as an adult. Continuing the drilling down, the therapist asked what it meant for the client to be their "own person." The client expressed an even deeper acknowledgment: "I can have my own thoughts and feelings and still be OK." As the client began exploring how they related to this acknowledgment, a process which will be described in step 3, the client described feeling themself "landing," and after a few moments of quite reflection, "inner quiet, no longer feeling angry and reactive ... coming home."

Reconnecting to the Self through emotional completion provides increasing psychobiological energy available for self-activation in one's adult life. This second step in the emotional completion process leads to and supports the third step, which focuses on supporting embodied adult consciousness. As clients move forward with completing unresolved emotional responses, they begin to relate to themselves in new ways that support the possibility for an increasing sense of internal freedom.

Step 3: Support a New Relationship to Unresolved Emotional Conflicts

The third step of the NARM Emotional Completion Model supports clients in learning to integrate the powerful life energy inherent in primary emotions. NARM is containment based, meaning we support our clients to stay present to their primary emotions in an embodied way. This approach

focuses on providing new ways of relating to one's internal states that generate increased psychobiological capacity and disidentification.

In NARM we differentiate between emotional expression and emotional completion. We do not use interventions that encourage emotional expression, discharge, or catharsis. Although it may feel rewarding for clients to express intense emotional responses, this can be done in a way that bypasses staying present with and integrating emotional energy. Instead, clients learn to tolerate and contain the life-affirming energy of these deep and powerful affects. We trust that as clients integrate the energy inherent in their primary emotions, this shifts their relationship with Self and others, giving them more possibilities for how to relate to their present needs and express their authentic emotions.

Unresolved emotions serve as a glue that keeps the shame-based identifications and survival strategies in place. Completion of these primary emotions occurs as clients are able to own, feel, and integrate the emotional energy, thereby dissolving the glue and shifting old identifications and survival strategies. Self-organization increases as a person finds a new way of structuralizing their internal experience away from self-shaming and self-rejection toward greater self-acceptance and self-compassion.

For example, a client recently learned that his partner had cheated on him again, which was the third time (he knew of) during their five-year relationship. In dealing with past experiences of hurt and betrayal, he had used all sorts of strategies to stay away from his anger, mainly blaming himself and going quickly into hopelessness and resignation. As he was supported through the NARM process to reflect on his reaction to this recent experience, he was able find a new way to relate to this experience. Although self-blame initially emerged, the therapist was able to help the client identify that he really felt angry (step 1). As he was invited to reflect on the intention of his anger (step 2), he stated, "I don't deserve this." As he was invited to notice what it was like for him to say this (step 3), he immediately said, "Confident!" The therapist asked him what else he noticed about feeling confident, and he said, "I feel more settled, balanced, and stronger. Like I can do this!" Whereas in the past he would blame himself and ignore these transgressions—his mantra was "forgive, forget, and move on"—he now felt that he had the capacity to approach this situation with new possibilities.

This client's statement "I don't deserve this" and his embodied sense of confidence reflect a shift out of shame-based identifications, a shift from child consciousness into adult consciousness. Instead of relating to himself through shame and self-hatred, feeling that he deserves the bad things that happen to him, he was able to stay present to and own his personal truth. Even though he still felt unsure about what to do in regards to his partner, he no longer felt compelled to run away from his authentic feelings. He said that it felt "life-changing" to feel confident in knowing that he would do his best and that, no matter what happens, he'd be OK.

Step 3 of the Emotional Completion Model overlaps with Pillar 4, where we are supporting clients to be present with psychobiological shifts. We use somatic mindfulness, slowing down, and inviting self-reflection in helping clients learn to tolerate the expansion that comes with feeling their authentic emotions. It may be as simple as asking, "Is it OK for you to sit with the grief in this moment?" At other times, we may be more specific in our questions—for example, "What are you noticing in your internal experience as you give yourself this time to feel into your grief?" And sometimes we may be very specific—for example, "You mentioned that it actually feels good to feel your grief—where exactly in your body are you noticing these good feelings?"

The energetics of emotional responses, particularly anger and grief, are very powerful. When a client begins experiencing this expansion of energy, it may quickly turn and feel distressing. As a way to manage this emotional charge, clients will often begin using acting-in or acting-out behaviors. Therapeutically, we can anticipate this movement from primary emotions into old strategies as part of the Pillar 4 focus on tracking connection and disconnection. As clients begin to connect to their primary emotions, they will often begin using old strategies to disconnect. In these situations, we might say something like, "So as you're being present with your anger, you begin telling yourself that anger is a waste of time and you just need to focus on being positive. What's it like for you to notice both—your anger and the impulse to move away from your anger?" Even if a client is only able to stay with the emotional energy for a brief moment, we view these moments as opportunities for building increasing capacity to be present with their life energy.

When an individual is able to stay present longer with their primary emotions in an embodied way, it leads to increased affect tolerance. This supports a deeper capacity for tolerating a wide range of affects, including being with complex and even conflicting emotional states. For example, an adult client who as a child was harmed by their caregivers may experience deep healing as they are able to stay present with their complex and conflicting feelings toward their caregivers. As the client learns to stay present to their love, anger, and grief toward their caregivers, without having to split, avoid, or use any other strategy to move away from their primary emotions, resolution and healing are possible.

In NARM our focus is on supporting clients to tolerate increasing charge and aliveness, which we track over the course of sessions by using the NARM Personality Spectrum for assessing psychobiological capacity (coming in chapter 9). Profound healing occurs in re-owning disowned, rejected, and split-off aspects of oneself. The emotional completion process provides clients with an inner knowing that they can stay present to their emotional responses—even intense and powerful ones. Instead of life energy being channeled into long-standing strategies and symptoms, there is more energy available for expansive, heart-centered human states like connection, joy, pleasure, love, intimacy, creativity, confidence, compassion, humor, play, gratitude, and a sense of aliveness.

REFLECTIVE EXERCISE

We invite you to take your time in reflecting on your relationship to the following emotional states:

- Connection
- Compassion
- Confidence
- Hopefulness

- Play/humor
- Pleasure
- Aliveness
- Gratitude

As you reflect on these internal states, we invite you to notice what you experience internally in your thoughts, emotions, and body.

Therapeutic Shortcuts for the NARM Emotional Completion Model

The NARM Emotional Completion Model supports clients to:

- own their primary emotions
- understand the implicit intention in their emotions
- be present to and help contain the energy inherent in the emotion, not focusing on expression, discharge, or catharsis

Practice Exercise for the NARM Emotional Completion Model

With a client—or with a friend or peer first if you prefer—we invite you to follow these steps:

1. Ask your client to reflect on a challenging relational experience that they've recently had and if they are able to *identify* any emotion related to this challenging relational dynamic.

2. If they are able to identify an emotion, ask them what that emotion might be *communicating* about this experience.

3. As they reflect on the message of this emotion, invite them to notice how they are *feeling internally*—how is it for them to be present to their internal state?

CHAPTER 8

NARM Relational Model

Learn to differentiate between the sound of your intuition guiding you and your traumas misleading you.

UNKNOWN SOURCE

Although this chapter focuses on the client-therapist relationship, this model also applies to all sorts of relationships. We invite you, while you're reading this chapter, to reflect on how the NARM Relational Model could support your other professional and personal relationships as well.

Where Therapists Get Stuck

The *R* in *NARM*—the relationship between therapist and client—is central to the effectiveness of this work, as we describe throughout this chapter. We are working with multiple levels of unresolved relational trauma, and the therapeutic relationship is a key element to the restoration of relational health. This certainly adds to the complexity of the work, but it also adds to the dynamic engagement of the therapeutic process. We can learn to more effectively use the therapeutic relationship to shift deeply entrenched psychobiological patterns. Focusing on the relational elements makes the change process come alive.

The NARM Relational Model provides therapists with an approach to support their own well-being too. Many therapists at our professional

trainings are there because they feel stuck with clients. They might not know what to do or what to say with clients. They may feel that their interventions aren't working. They might blame themselves for not being a good enough therapist. They might blame their client for not being a good enough client. Their difficulties with clients might lead them to experience ongoing confusion, doubt, and distress. Traditionally referred to as *countertransference*, a therapist's internal experience holds a lot of information for what is happening within the therapeutic relationship.

The reality is that when working in the field of complex trauma, the work with clients will often be complicated and challenging. Our clients come in with complex histories. Many of us, as therapists, have our own complex histories. Then we are establishing a relationship between two complex human beings. The mix of our client's unresolved trauma and our own unresolved trauma leads to potentially a very challenging relational dynamic. Managing the complexity can lead therapists to feel stuck, frustrated, and helpless. But from our perspective, these feelings are not the problem; the problem is when therapists attempt to minimize, deny, or avoid these feelings. We see the stuckness, frustration, and helplessness as messages that we can listen to and learn from. When therapists are able to stay connected to their internal experience with openness and curiosity, we see countertransference as a very useful aspect of healing complex trauma.

No matter in which country or setting we teach, there is one common thread running through so many of the helping professionals that attend our trainings—they are all working so hard. We refer to *efforting* as the experience of therapists working extremely hard, pushing and pressuring themselves in various ways, and at times also pushing and pressuring their clients. Many therapists feel driven to attune, understand, figure out, solve, and fix issues for clients. For many therapists, this drive to solve and fix is precisely what brought them into this profession in the first place. Therapists tend to be good at that. Many therapists grew up being the one other people would turn to in times of difficulty. They found value in being there for others. But this being there for others is, at least in part, a compensation and a strategy to avoid their own needs and a way of "earning love." When faced with the complexity, and at times helplessness and hopelessness, that

arises within therapy, what do therapists do with it? Oftentimes they double down on their efforting. They try even harder.

In the United States, a high percentage of therapists report experiencing burnout in any given year. Compassion fatigue, which includes burnout as well as secondary exposure to traumatic stress, is a real occupational risk in our field. We have created the NARM Relational Model for enhancing therapeutic engagement while minimizing the risk of compassion fatigue. Without understanding the complexities of working relationally with clients dealing with unresolved developmental and relational trauma, we run the risk of burning ourselves out, and even harming our clients in the process.

REFLECTIVE EXERCISE

We invite you to take a few minutes to reflect on why you chose to become a therapist or helping professional:

- Were there any early life experiences that might have impacted or inspired you to choose this profession?

- What did you learn from your early life experiences that supports you to be effective in this job?

- What did you learn from your early life experiences that might make it difficult for you in this job?

As you reflect on these questions, we invite you to notice what you experience internally in your thoughts, emotions, and body.

Many therapists experienced helplessness as children. At an early age, we may have learned to become proficient at attuning to and reading our environment. These abilities provide a child with a way of feeling in control. Underneath these abilities, however, is often a profound sense of feeling out of control and helpless. For most children, no matter what they did, they were unable to change their environments.

Our early experience with helplessness may have inspired us as adults to help others. As therapists, when we attune to our clients, most of whom have also experienced early helplessness, it may trigger our own sense of helplessness. We might question if we can truly help this person. Many clients deeply believe that they are fundamentally flawed and cannot be fixed. They may not believe that you, or anyone, can help them. Our own sense of helplessness can become mixed with our clients' sense of helplessness and can lead to a situation where therapy feels stuck.

It is essential that we, as therapists, acknowledge our helplessness in order to face the real limitations we experience with clients. The basic reality is that we cannot help everybody, as hard as this might be to accept. Additionally, we may not be the right therapist for every client we meet. Therapists may put immense pressure on themselves to be there for and to meet all their clients' needs. Therapists may struggle to accept the real limitations that they are faced with. Therapists may stay in relationships with clients at all costs. When therapists are unable to acknowledge their helplessness, they resort to old survival strategies that have significant impact on their health and well-being.

As the old joke goes, "How do you regulate a therapist? Put a client in front of them." Taking care of others as a way of taking care of ourselves is an old survival strategy that helped us at one point in our lives. It also motivated many of us to become therapists. Those very skills that as children we were so proficient at can have consequences for us as helping professionals.

Therapeutic skills that support us in being open and attuned to another person's suffering are what can eventually contribute to burnout and compassion fatigue. It puts therapists in a bind, because the exact thing they are so good at—being empathic and responsive with their clients—can be part of what leads to therapists feeling stuck, frustrated, helpless, and overwhelmed. While we know that these therapeutic skills are being offered to clients with the best of intentions, it is our perspective that if we do not understand what is driving them, they can disrupt effective relational therapy.

Because we're helping professionals, it is important for us to be clear about our impulses to help. Knowing the intention underneath an intervention is important. When sitting with a client, we might ask ourselves: *Where*

is my helping impulse coming from? How exactly do I know in this moment what kind of help this client needs from me? Am I trying to avoid or dismiss feelings in my attempt to help? What is the intention underneath this intervention? What impact might this intervention have?

The empathic impulse to help relieve another of their suffering is strong in humans. Empathy gets activated by social brain circuitry to provide us with the resonant, felt experience of what another is experiencing. The benefits of empathy are that it allows us to meet others where they are, deepens awareness and understanding of what another person is experiencing, allows us to be affected by others, and provides opportunities for enhancing states of safety, connection, and shared pleasure.

REFLECTIVE EXERCISE

This exercise requires you having a partner. This exercise has several names: sometimes we call it the Mirror Neuron Dance, the Attunement Dance, or the Resonance Dance.

- With your partner, choose who will be the leader and who will be the "mirror."
- Once you've set up the roles, the leader will take five minutes, and during this time they can move as freely as they wish within their environment.
  - The mirror's job is simply to follow and mimic the behaviors and expressions of the leader.
  - During this time, it is best for both of you to be silent, so as to direct focus on your internal experience.
- Once complete, check in first with the leader and ask how it felt to be mirrored.
  - What did you (the leader) notice about the mirroring?
  - What did you notice especially when your partner (the mirror) was in tune versus when they were not in tune?
  - How did this impact your internal experience?

(continued)

- Then check in with the mirror and ask how it felt to be the mirror.

  - What did the mirror notice about attuning and following you?

  - What was going on internally for the mirror—were they trying really hard to do it right, were they judging or criticizing themself when they felt they did it wrong, were they able to be present within and engaged with their partner at the same time?

- After you've completed the check-in, switch roles, and follow the same process in your new roles.

While empathy is generally regarded as an essential ingredient in any effective support, therapists must be mindful of the pull of *unmanaged empathy*. Unmanaged empathy can look and feel like caring but may be driven from impulses that relate to the ways we avoid deep feelings, particularly the feelings of helplessness. We are vulnerable to our sense of helplessness when we empathize with but are not able to impact another's suffering. For many of us who experienced early trauma, this leads us directly back to our own fear of helplessness. We might ask ourselves: *How can I be with another person's suffering? Am I able to stay present? Or do I try to compulsively effect change?*

The main risk of unmanaged empathy involves overidentifying with our clients and their suffering. We may experience a blurring of boundaries, having difficulty differentiating our feelings from our client's feelings. We may start to feel overly responsible for our clients, perseverating or even obsessing about their well-being (this is different than professional responsibility for our clients). This over-responsibility can lead to infantilizing our clients and fostering for our clients an unhealthy dependence on us as therapists. Reflecting on unmanaged empathy is important to assure we are not acting out on our clients, and it is equally important to assure we are not acting in on ourselves.

We want to share two examples of helping professionals who both came to see us due to burnout, which illustrates the risks of unmanaged empathy.

The first was a therapist in private practice who started running overtime in sessions with clients. He felt guilty about ending and wanted to give them more time. It led to the therapist responding to calls, emails, and texts in the evening and over the weekend. Initially he felt that he was helping his clients by being there for them, but he began to feel burdened by the expectation that he had to be there for his clients no matter what. This culminated in a client who said they needed even more time with him and began coming to the therapist's home and stalking him in public places. He sought out his own therapy because this inability to set boundaries was impacting his personal life. He confessed that he was seriously considering closing his practice and going into a new profession.

The other example was a client who worked in social services and was required to go to therapy as part of her being out on stress leave. She was extremely dedicated to the work she did in serving the most vulnerable people in her community. During her initial session, she proudly stated how many vacation and sick days she had accrued and never used. And yet here she was out on stress leave. She herself had been involved with social services as a child and said that she couldn't rest knowing that one child was unsafe. Although she clearly had a generous, caring heart, her inability to take care of herself had led to serious emotional and physical health issues. This led to further distress being on leave because she was unable to do the work she was called to do. She said it herself, "Empathy might just be the death of me."

Many therapists identify with being the caring, attuned therapist who will work tirelessly to help their clients. This identification leads to therapists having difficulty recognizing when their therapeutic engagement might be driven by unmanaged empathy. We are certainly not suggesting that therapists become distant, aloof, and disengaged. We believe it is essential for therapists to relate to their clients with warmth, care, and active engagement. However, therapists have to find a balance where they can meet their clients from a place of authentic care and compassion while at the same time respecting the client's agency and their own practice of self-care. And when a client needs more services or time than a therapist can provide, it is essential that unmanaged empathy does not cloud a therapist's

professional duty in assuring optimal client care, which may include the therapist seeking consultation, therapy, and further training, recommending additional resources for the client, or creating a transition plan for an appropriate referral.

REFLECTIVE EXERCISE

Helplessness

We invite you to take a few moments to reflect on:

- Helplessness and your relationship to your own helplessness.

- Consider ways your unconscious sense of helplessness may affect your therapeutic engagement with your clients.

- We invite you to take a few moments to notice how you are feeling overall—specifically noticing how you are feeling about yourself.

Empathy

We invite you to take a few moments to reflect on:

- Empathy and the various ways you experience and demonstrate empathy in your life.

- Consider ways your sense of empathy may affect your therapeutic engagement with your clients.

- We invite you to take a few moments to notice how you are feeling overall—specifically noticing how you are feeling about yourself.

Helplessness + Empathy

We invite you to take a few moments to:

- Differentiate your sense of empathy from your need to do something with it.

- Consider ways these might play out for you as a therapist.

- We invite you to take a few moments to notice how you are feeling overall—specifically noticing how you are feeling about yourself.

For some therapists, doing anything other than leading with unmanaged empathy feels too distant, too neutral, not caring enough, and the pull to become a caretaker or cheerleader takes over. We want to remind therapists who feel the need to demonstrate their empathy that a caring presence is cultivated not from what we do but from who we are. Being a helping professional should not be performative. It is the quality of connection with ourselves and others that creates meaningful engagement and therapeutic effectiveness. In other words, our therapeutic presence is cultivated not from *doing* but out of *being*. Out of *being* emerges presence, curiosity, receptivity, attunement, and the capacity for openhearted connection with our clients.

Using the NARM Relational Model

To simply be present, available, and congruent—to be a real human being—is what [our clients] need most ... Presence must be the basic orientation to the treatment. There may be continued temptation to retreat from the demands of a real relationship to the security of technique of whatever kind. But to come home to the reality of the human relationship, as difficult as that may be at times, will be a relief to both client and therapist and will be the real cement which holds all the rest of the treatment together.

STEPHEN JOHNSON, *CHARACTEROLOGICAL TRANSFORMATION*

It is clear that our current field of psychotherapy is populated by highly empathic individuals. It really shouldn't be any other way. However, as explained earlier, unmanaged empathy can get therapists off track and leave clients feeling fundamentally missed, and even mistreated. For example, imagine that a client dealing with symptoms of distress and pain comes in to see a therapist who is practiced at being highly attuned. The therapist attunes to the deep levels of distress and pain, and from there they immediately jump to implementing therapeutic skills in order to effect change in

the client's symptoms. That might not sound so bad. The therapist is trying to help their client relieve their suffering. But clients are not objects to be fixed. It's not like dropping your car off at a mechanic. The relationship is central to the healing process. If a therapist jumps too quickly into attempting to fix, there may be important steps they are missing along the way. And without these steps, a therapist may very well be acting out their own countertransference onto clients.

The NARM Relational Model supports therapeutic presence by cultivating states of *being* within two human beings—the therapist and client. It promotes a process of intersubjectivity. Although we are presenting it in an outlined model, we encourage you not to pressure yourself to try and get it right. It is not a manualized approach. It is an embodied, dynamic process that is intended to support you in showing up with your clients more in your 50-50 balance.

For sake of clarity and ease of learning, we have deconstructed a holistic interpersonal process down into distinct internal states that shape and inform relational skills (see following image). The three internal states are curiosity, presence, and self-inquiry. The five relational skills are attunement, acceptance, reflection and exploration, mindful interventions, and integration.

Application of the NARM Relational Model

INTERNAL STATES   RELATIONAL SKILLS

Internal States:
- Curiosity
- Presence
- Self-Inquiry

Relational Skills:
- Attunement
- Acceptance
- Reflection and Exploration
- Mindful Interventions
- Integration

Although we are presenting these therapeutic skills in a sequence, their implementation will be interwoven throughout a session. Just like in learning to play an instrument, there are many things to remember initially, but with more practice, eventually the steps recede into the background and the process flows more organically.

Given the right kind of relational support, clients will become experts of their own internal world, and the change process will be driven from within them. The NARM Relational Model, and particularly the internal states the therapist embodies, supports the Four Pillars and Emotional Completion Model presented in earlier chapters, as well as the relational skills presented in this chapter. The three important internal states we start with are *curiosity*, *presence*, and *self-inquiry*.

Internal States: Curiosity, Presence, and Self-Inquiry

NARM is the first training I have done in which the therapist mattered. Other trainings talked about countertransference, but NARM really took the time to unpack countertransference, and bring it into an embodied, lived experience. This made all the difference in my work with complex trauma.

NARM STUDENT

Cultivating a state of curiosity supports our ability to be open, receptive, flexible, and in a perpetual mode of learning. Curiosity allows us to remain present with complexity. Instead of pressuring ourselves to know it all, or allowing others to put pressure on us, we can simply remain present and receptive to learning.

A good starting place is the simple acknowledgment that we truly do not know what our client's inner experience is, and that we will never fully know it. Instead of striving to be the all-knowing expert therapist and seeing the client as a passive recipient of our interventions, we hold the perspective that therapy is a collaborative, exploratory process. It is an opening to the complexity of another person's experience, as opposed to reducing the

complexity of another person's experience by using labels or theory to define their inner reality.

By meeting a client with curiosity, we are able to learn about their present experience and how old adaptive patterns are impacting their ability to live more fully, freely, and healthfully in their present life. We set the intention to be there to learn from and about our clients, and to support them in the process of learning more about themselves.

Developing stronger therapeutic presence emerges out of curiosity. To be able to attend to the here-and-now experience of the client, therapists also need to be able to be present themselves. While there are many internal capacities that shape one's ability to be present, here are just a few competencies that are directly relevant to the NARM relational model:

- To be open to new, emergent experience and not always pressuring ourselves to know

- To acknowledge and respect that the client is the final expert of their inner state

- To be open to truly learning, even from mistakes

- To be nonjudgmental with Self and others

- To meet our clients from a state of receiving, not doing

- To meet our clients with an open heart, from a place of heartfulness

As therapists are able to be more firmly rooted in the present moment with clients, new information becomes available. We rely on a phenomenological approach, which focuses on experience in the here and now. As our clients are telling stories from their past or detailing symptoms they're experiencing, we are curious about how they are relating to these stories and symptoms in the here and now, and what the symptoms are trying to communicate. This is an ongoing, moment-to-moment process of attending to complex dynamics as they appear in the present moment.

In order to track the intersubjective dynamics, therapists must develop the capacity to be in a receptive state. When in an active "doing" state, mediated by the sympathetic nervous system, therapists may miss important elements emerging within the therapeutic process. For example, there are often somatic

and emotional shifts for both client and therapist that can be easily missed as therapists become overfocused with thinking, analyzing, strategizing, and implementing. All of this *doing* leads to a lot of internal noise within the therapist. This noise can become distressing and overwhelming; it can create confusion for therapists, leading them to overcompensate by compulsively doing whatever they can to be helpful and see themselves as a helpful therapist. This internal noise, and the strategies that emerge from it, can become a habitual pattern for therapists and interfere in the intersubjective process.

In NARM we try to make it simpler for therapists. Instead of pressuring ourselves to "fix," we aim simply to be open to the client in the present moment. When in a receptive *being* state, mediated by the parasympathetic nervous system, therapists may notice important elements emerging, including the somatic and emotional shifts that are central to the therapeutic process. Remember, all details matter in the relational process of therapy. Instead of seeing these details from a place of feeling compelled to do something about them, we can shift internally to a place of being open, curious, present, and receptive. Developing these relational capacities supports an internal quietness for therapists that allows them to be more receptive to what is happening for their clients and ultimately be more efficient in supporting the resolution of old trauma patterns.

REFLECTIVE EXERCISE

We invite you to take a few moments to reflect on your internal strategies of doing and efforting when working with clients:

- It might help to choose a specific client and reflect on the internal volume of your strategies—you can imagine a volume control that goes from 10 (most internal noise) to 0 (least internal noise).

- Where is your internal noise volume as you sit with this client?

- How does your internal noise volume impact your capacity for presence and curiosity?

- What else do you know about the impact of your internal noise?

As therapists are able to move into deeper states of curiosity and presence, internal quietness becomes a gift to both client and therapist alike. Working from a place of internal quietness with clients, even when there is a lot going on during therapy, requires therapists to cultivate an ongoing relationship to their own internal experience as they sit with clients, being mindful of their 50-50 balance. This self-inquiry process is central in strengthening all relationships.

Self-inquiry as a relational capacity creates an opportunity for earned secure attachment in our adult clients. One of the essential ingredients for secure attachment, often missing for many children, is active self-inquiry by their caregivers. What children need to feel seen and valued is for their caregivers to reflect on their own inner experience in relationship to their children. Specifically, a child needs the feeling that their caregivers are able to reflect on how they are impacting their child. Much developmental damage would be averted if caregivers, and our society in general, would be more mindful about children's inner worlds and how caregivers' behaviors are impacting their children.

Understanding these attachment dynamics provides the basis for understanding the importance of a therapist's self-inquiry process. Especially when working with the impact of attachment and relational trauma, it is essential that therapists have the capacity to reflect on how they are impacting their clients. Failure to self-reflect often leads to therapeutic misattunement and a poor prognosis for treatment. One major obstacle in the way of self-inquiry and self-reflection is therapeutic countertransference.

Our understanding of countertransference dates back to Dr. Sigmund Freud, creator of psychoanalysis, who warned against letting a therapist's feelings get entangled with their client's feelings. Since then, there have been many different interpretations of the processes of transference and countertransference. Mostly, countertransference has been viewed as a negative aspect of the therapeutic process. As we outlined previously, unmanaged empathy and efforting are two good examples. Without having much awareness, therapists can act out on their clients even with the best of intentions. While we agree that countertransference can be a major obstacle in therapy, we also see that it can be used mindfully to deepen the therapeutic relationship.

In NARM we refer to *Big C countertransference* and *little c countertransference*. This is in line with the more current psychological perspective on countertransference that differentiates between "personal countertransference" and "diagnostic countertransference." While personal countertransference has to do with what is being evoked within the therapist (Big C), diagnostic countertransference informs us about what is happening within the client (little c).

Big C countertransference refers to the idea that if we are not able to become aware of the unconscious, emotional reactions we are having with clients, it interferes with the therapeutic process. When therapists are not able to be present and see their clients clearly and directly for who they are and the capacities they have, they may relate to their clients through the lens of their own acting-out and acting-in strategies. For example, a therapist may identify as the savior or as the inadequate helper, seeing their clients as either needing to be saved or unable to be saved.

Little c countertransference—also referred to as *diagnostic countertransference, somatic countertransference,* or more simply *resonance*—refers to the generally unconscious process of picking up information from our client through nonverbal means. As we discussed earlier, therapists may be attuning to many levels of information in their clients. Resonance allows for learning on the level of nonverbal communication. For example, therapists may feel different body sensations, like pain in a specific area of their body that they had not noticed before. They may have a somatic reaction, like suddenly being overcome with exhaustion or nausea. They may feel impulses, like a sudden urge to flee or attack. They may feel a strong emotion, like a sense of sadness wash over them. They may have a sudden image come to them, like a person's face or a situation. These dynamics, which come up in countless ways, can all contain useful information for helping us develop greater understanding of how our clients are organizing their internal worlds.

While Big C countertransference has historically been viewed as pathological, meaning that these internal reactions interfere with the therapist's ability to connect with a real person sitting in front of them, little c countertransference can be extremely beneficial. Little c countertransference can

be seen as an extension of meeting clients with openness, curiosity, receptivity, and empathy. When we are impacted by our clients, it allows us to better understand our clients and the relational process of therapy. Similarly, noticing the relational impact also helps therapists better understand themselves as they engage with their clients.

What becomes difficult, however, is how to discern if we are experiencing Big C or little c countertransference. For example, how do we know if the sudden urge to flee is coming from our clients or may be our own internal reaction? To make it easy, in NARM we teach that the only thing therapists need to *do* with their countertransference is to simply *be present and curious about it*. This is the practice of self-inquiry.

As we are able to stay present and curious to our internal experience—whether it might be coming from Big C or little c countertransference—we reflect on this information, where it may be coming from, and how it might support us in relating to ourselves and our clients. As we become more grounded in our connection to our internal feelings and reactions, our interventions can be more aligned to the client sitting in front of us in this very moment. Self-inquiry is an ongoing process that enhances internal states of curiosity and presence for the therapist and supports greater attunement with our clients.

While we need to be mindful of discerning Big C countertransference and acting-out strategies, the willingness to be affected by our clients is central to the relational process. This discernment process helps differentiate between authentic empathy and unmanaged empathy. When we have discerned that we are being moved by authentic empathy, personal disclosure can be a powerful relational intervention. For example, we may share something like "It's painful for me to watch you hurting yourself" or "It's touching for me to see you being kinder to yourself." When done judiciously, these self-disclosing comments can reinforce agency. For example, a client might respond, "Thank you—it's painful for me to hurt myself too, and I want to continue learning why I'm doing this to myself" or "I really want to continue being kinder to myself, that is what I want moving forward." When a therapist's sharing comes from authentic empathy, clients feel seen and supported, and they may be able to use the therapist's communication

for further internal shifts toward adult consciousness and disidentification. This may also enhance the relational connection.

Without active self-inquiry, therapists have a greater likelihood of acting out on their clients and fostering dependency. The identification around caretaking and empathy-providing is often very strong in individuals who end up as therapists. This can be confusing because it often feels good to both therapist and client to set up this caretaking relationship: the client wants to be helped and the therapist wants to be the helper. But without establishing a space of self-inquiry, there is the potential of this leading to a reenactment, where the therapist acts as the "good parent" for the help-less client. While clients may feel rewarded in receiving the nurturing they never received, this therapeutic framework does not support increasing capacity for the client. In NARM we do not work in child consciousness, which reinforces infantilizing and dependency. To the degree possible we work in adult consciousness, always oriented toward increasing psychobio-logical capacity.

REFLECTIVE EXERCISE
Difficulty in Relationship

We invite you to choose a current client or relationship you are strug-gling with.

- Bring their image into your mind.

- If possible, recall your last meeting, or a particularly challenging meeting.

- We invite you to reflect on the following questions:

    - What feelings, sensations, or impulses are you noticing?

    - How are you showing up with this client/person?

    - What is your relational impact on this client/person?

    - Are there relational patterns here that you are familiar with from past relationships?

(continued)

Transforming through Relationship

We invite you to choose a current client or relationship you feel happy or confident about.

- Bring their image into your mind.

- If possible, recount your last meeting, or a particularly fulfilling meeting.

- We invite you to reflect on the following questions:

  - What feelings, sensations, or impulses are you noticing?

  - How are you showing up with this client/person?

  - What is your relational impact on this client/person?

  - Are there relational patterns here that you are familiar with from past relationships?

The internal states of curiosity, presence, and self-inquiry create the foundation for the relational process that supports the resolution of complex trauma patterns. We now introduce the five relational skills that inform and guide the interventions we use in NARM.

Relational Skill 1: Attunement

The intention of attunement is to be present to both the client's distress and their intention for change. The attunement we are describing includes inviting inquiry into layers of internal experience that the client is often not in touch with and may be actively guarding against. It also includes inviting inquiry into our own sense of receiving this client, including any countertransference reactions, and the relational dynamic between therapist and client. In this first phase of the NARM Relational Model, we are simply wanting to experience how it is for us to sit with this client.

Attunement is built upon authentic empathy and describes the relational capacity to be present with and sense into another person's experience. It is the capacity for "feeling with the heart of another" that allows us to be accurately responsive in relationships.[1] The most obvious example is a

parent with their infant. An infant is not able to express themself in words, and yet the parent and child share a communication that is beyond words. The attuned caregiver is deeply engaged with the child's experience and progressively develops a felt sense knowing of the inner world of the child. Another example will be obvious to most anyone who has an animal in their life. Humans and animals can often create a similar nonverbal understanding that is demonstrated in various ways. This empathic attunement is one of the main reasons that animal-assisted programs have been so successful for mental health treatment.

Therapists do demonstrate high levels of attunement. It comes easy for many therapists to feel into the depths of pain and suffering within their clients. Because of this, it also makes them susceptible to unmanaged empathy, burnout, and all the other acting-in and acting-out strategies we named earlier. From the very beginning of working with a new client, it is essential that therapists are aware of their boundaries around attunement, so as to protect against Big C countertransference.

Little c countertransference, however, uses authentic empathy and resonance to help us attune to what is emerging from all levels of the client's experience. This is an ongoing, moment-by-moment process of paying attention to our clients' inner experience and observable behaviors, all the implicit and explicit ways clients express their inner reality. We rely on the client's self-reporting and our own observational tracking, as well as our capacity for resonance.

An important point to reinforce is that, in NARM, we are not primarily focused on behaviors but are attuning to our client's inner states. Some therapists believe that attunement means to meet their client's needs. Clients may say that their therapist was "misattuned" to them when the therapist didn't give them what they wanted. For example, a client might say, "Can't you just tell me what to do?" Or "Can you simply agree with me here?" Generally we want to be mindful about not colluding with clients' requests just because they expect us to "attune" to them in specific ways.

While we respect what the client says they need, we do our best to differentiate when these needs might be driven from child consciousness versus adult consciousness. Attuning to child consciousness in our adult

clients means we are attuning to strategies of disconnection, which reinforces disorganization and lack of capacity. We focus on attuning to adult consciousness, where there are untapped internal resources that allow the client to move toward greater organization and increased psychobiological capacity.

It is important not to foster the belief that a client will receive perfect attunement in therapy. This belief interferes with agency and reinforces child consciousness. It supports the fantasy of an idealized parent who will always be there for them no matter what, which places the client in a role of helpless child. Instead, we recognize that in adult relationships there will always be some level of misattunement, as we never truly know another person's inner world. Attachment research demonstrates that securely attached caregivers are only in attuned states with their children for roughly 30 percent of their interactions.[2] This means that even for those of us who are very attuned with our clients, approximately 70 percent of the time we may be in some level of misattunement. In support of adult consciousness, we reinforce a client's capacity to stay connected while tolerating the perceived misattunement they experience. We remain attentive to the client's distress and bring curiosity into what may be driving their distress, including if there are real ruptures in the therapeutic relationship in which we may need to take accountability for and work toward relational repair.

Donald Winnicott used the term "holding environment" by a "good-enough mother"[3] and later applied this understanding to effective therapists as well, which highlighted that attunement was not about perfection but about responsiveness. Therapists can take pressure off themselves by not striving to be perfectly attuned and instead focusing on staying open, receptive, and responsive. This includes practicing self-inquiry of the various levels of our internal experience while we're sitting with our clients and noticing any impulses, thoughts, judgments, emotional responses, or somatic reactions that might get in our way of being present.

We want to always keep in mind that we may be the first, and only, person who has ever provided this level of attunement, seeing our adult clients not as helpless but as agents in their own growth. We are holding

space for deeper capacities and possibilities than even clients may hold for themselves. Often the gift of attunement alone can go a long way in helping our clients stop running from themselves, become curious about their inner worlds, and begin to reconnect to their own healing capacities.

THE APPLICATION OF RELATIONAL SKILL 1: ATTUNEMENT

Before your client comes into your office, we invite you to practice quieting your mind. Give yourself a little time to attune to your own experience. When the client sits down in front of you, see if you're able to stay in a quieter mind. Notice what happens inside you as you begin to connect with your client. Notice any thoughts, pressure, judgments, or strong impulses to act that may be creating more noise in your mind. Reflect on your 50-50 balance in this moment.

You may feel tempted to move quickly into *doing something*, especially if the client is asking something from you directly. We invite you to give yourself permission to not immediately act on your impulses or their request to have you do something. We invite you to practice simply *being with* your client—connect to your curiosity, presence, and self-inquiry.

From this place, begin observing and feeling into the different levels of the client's experience—somatic, emotional, behavioral, cognitive, and spiritual. Notice also the relational field and how it feels to be in contact with this client and how it is to receive your client. It can be difficult to stay present to all these levels of our clients' experience if they are talking and you are trying to track their story. We invite you to give yourself permission to not track the story as well as you might normally do and instead create space for noticing other levels of their experience. We want to invite you to particularly notice what you are picking up from your client's internal states and not let yourself get lost in their stories, behaviors, and symptoms.

Throughout the session, as you reflect on your capacity to stay open, present, and curious with your client, we invite you to notice your internal noise (remember the exercise on our internal noise volume from 10 to 0). We invite you to practice slowing down, using fewer words, and taking a pause to reflect before you respond. We also invite you to practice being patient with yourself as you try on a new way of attuning to your clients.

Relational Skill 2: Acceptance

The intention of acceptance is to allow for complexity. As humans, we are faced with managing an extremely complex world. Preconceived knowledge, beliefs, and agendas are often used to manage the complexity of the therapeutic process, but they can also get in our way of being present and open to the direct experience with our clients. To truly understand another's internal world, we have to free ourselves from what we believe we know, to the best of our abilities, so as to be able to make real contact. Once we can say "I don't know," we can be open to new learning and greater complexity. As philosopher Jiddu Krishnamurti taught, "You can learn only if you do not know."[4] The reality is that we will never fully know our client's internal experience, but we can continue to learn as we deepen into relationship with them.

One of the ways we try to manage complexity is by reducing it and making things simple. For example, how many of you have heard a colleague refer to a client as "borderline" or "resistant"? While diagnostic labels and psychological concepts can be useful in helping us understand common themes across different clients, they can also conceal more than they reveal. Additionally these labels can be reductionistic in a way that can lead to objectification.

Once a person has been objectified, it creates a disconnect in the human-to-human relationship. And often these labels are used pejoratively. This could be driven by Big C countertransference. A therapist may be having a reaction to their client, and simplifying the complexity by labeling them helps the therapist manage their own reaction. Most clients can feel when this happens. How would it feel for you if you were sitting with someone who was supposed to be listening and understanding you and instead they reduced your experience to being "borderline" or "resistant"? Even with the best of intentions, when therapists simplify their clients' experience, the therapeutic process suffers.

We train NARM therapists to do something that is very hard for humans to do—recognize and respect the complexity of who our clients are and not reduce their complexity. This challenges us to be in a place of not-knowing, relying on curiosity and interest. Attempting to be with

the not-knowing evokes helplessness in many therapists. A therapist may respond desperately to this challenge with: "*I have to know or I can't help!*"

It is important for therapists to identify and monitor their agendas for clients. Pillar 1 helps us by focusing on the client's agenda for themself, not our therapeutic agenda for them. We recognize and respect the client's own process, even if we don't fully understand or know exactly how to help. As a NARM therapist wrote, "We are [not] responsible for [figuring it all out]. The client, the contract, and our willingness to stay curious holds that for us. The client holds the content, and we hold the process. Taking our agendas out of the therapeutic process of what health is supposed to look like respects the client's autonomy and keeps our own pride as 'knowers' in check."[5]

Another way therapists reduce complexity is by taking sides in a client's internal conflicts or becoming goal-oriented. Many therapists attune to a nascent impulse toward agency within their clients and want to guide and promote this for them. At these times we want to remember that the movement toward agency is only one side of a complex internal conflict. Therapists need to be able to hold both sides of the dilemma—both the movement toward agency and what may be blocking agency.

For example, a client has been dissatisfied in her marriage. She believes she may be finally done with her husband and is considering leaving him. Her therapist agrees that leaving him is the right thing to do and encourages next steps. The therapist is behaviorally taking sides with the part of the client who wants to leave, which ignores the part of the client who is invested in staying with her husband. She has been considering leaving for several years but has not done it yet. It may feel empowering for her in this moment to consider leaving, but NARM therapists are focused on internal states, not behaviors. We would want to explore the internal shifts that have led her to be considering this decision. Of course, we ultimately respect whatever decisions a client makes for themself, but it can be a trap for therapists to get caught into advice giving or taking sides in an internal conflict around such complex topics. Not taking sides in our client's stories helps reinforce agency. Ultimately, the client is the one who must live with the consequences of their choices, and that must be acknowledged and respected.

Much of our difficulty in staying open to the complexity of our clients relates back to our difficulty in accepting our own helplessness. While we attempt to meet our clients with acceptance, we also attempt to be accepting of ourselves. If we start noticing our own impatience, sensing we're not doing it right, or feeling we should be somewhere else in the process, those are good reminders to practice self-inquiry by reflecting on what is going on inside us. What we do not want to do is to simply start throwing out exercises or interventions in order to make something happen because we don't know what else to do. Allowing our lack of knowing, and whatever feelings might come with this, to lead the way can actually be an important step in connecting deeper with ourselves and our clients. We are in this learning process together with our clients.

THE APPLICATION OF RELATIONAL SKILL 2: ACCEPTANCE

As you are present with your client, we invite you to practice holding acceptance for both your client and yourself. Starting with your client, allow yourself to truly hold a place of not-knowing. Even if you have worked with this client for a long time or have an extensive history on them, see if you are able to be with them in the present moment without having to understand or make it all fit. As much as possible, just hold an open space to listen, take in, and let wash over you all that the client is sharing on all levels of their experience. Notice the different aspects of what you're taking in around the client's story, beliefs, emotions, body, and the way they are in relationship with you. We invite you to practice "beginner's mind" with a lack of preconceptions and set beliefs.

We also invite you to practice holding acceptance for yourself. As you're sitting with your client, notice any pressure to figure out, do something, fix, or get someplace other than where you are in this very moment. You might even try out the feeling of "I don't know" and see what this brings up for you and if you are able to lean into it a bit more. It might feel unfamiliar and uncomfortable to hold this larger space for yourself and your client. We invite you to give yourself time to explore this and how it reverberates within you, your client, and the therapeutic process.

Relational Skill 3: Reflection and Exploration

The intention of reflection and exploration is to begin understanding how a client organizes their inner world. As we engage deeper with our client's way of organizing their experience, we begin to reflect on their core dilemma and how it may be influencing them in this moment and in their life. We hold the understanding that our clients are still being impacted by this internal conflict between their authentic Self and the adaptations they had to make as children in order to survive. We are curious about the core dilemma as it is being expressed in the client's present life.

The therapeutic contract (Pillar 1) helps us begin reflecting on the core dilemma. We inquire about the client's intention and what is getting in their way of actualizing this intention. For example, a client comes in because they want to develop more social relationships and yet they've been feeling lonely and isolated. While their intention is to establish more social relationships, the behaviors they describe involve spending all their time alone playing video games. We can begin seeing both sides of the dilemma—what they desire for themself (relationships) and the obstacles in the way of getting what they most desire (isolating behaviors and what is driving these behaviors). In NARM we reflect on and explore both sides of this dilemma as well as the apparent contradiction.

It is difficult to adequately address the problem if we do not understand what is at the root of the problem. If a therapist decided to work behaviorally with the client and gave them a homework assignment to cut down their solo video game playing to three hours a day so as to create more time for engaging in social relationships, they would be working to change one side of the dilemma while ignoring the function that this behavior has in relationship to what the client says they most want. The organizing theme emerging from the contracting process is focused on the internal conflict between the desire for connection and the difficulty with connection. If the client consents, this internal conflict—not the behavior—becomes the organizing thread of further exploration.

This process depicts the development of a working hypothesis. The working hypothesis informs and guides our exploratory questions (Pillar 2),

the ways we reinforce agency (Pillar 3), and our reflection of psychobiological shifts (Pillar 4). It also allows us to sense into what authentic emotions may be missing from the client's awareness and how to support them in the emotional completion process.

As part of the inquiry process (Pillar 2), we use the answers and feedback to our questions to refine, adjust, or shift our working hypothesis. Becoming too attached to one's hypothesis could reflect a Big C countertransference acting out—needing to understand it all right now in order to feel secure in what we are doing. It is better to "hold lightly" our developing understanding. This requires ongoing practice of self-inquiry.

For example, in working with the previous client, they originally named that their isolation was due to feeling scared of people. As the therapist continues exploring, the client then clarifies that they isolate themself not because they are scared of others, but because when they are in relationships, they feel burdened by other people's expectations. Whereas the behaviors around isolation have not changed, what the client identifies as driving these behaviors has shifted. This gives us important information to use in further exploration. Our working hypothesis is always subject to continual revision as we continue the therapeutic process with clients.

THE APPLICATION OF RELATIONAL SKILL 3: REFLECTION AND EXPLORATION

As you are present with your client, we invite you to give yourself space and time to reflect on how your client is organizing their internal world. Without straining to figure anything out or connect any dots, notice the various levels of the client's experience and what draws your attention.

What are you noticing about your working hypothesis? Perhaps you notice specific ways the client is relating to themself—for example, particular moments they begin shaming themself, avoiding certain topics, or relating to old familiar (default) emotions. What are you noticing about their engagement with you? What are you aware of in your own internal experience, particularly around any countertransference?

As you begin to reflect on your understanding of how the client is organizing their internal experience, how they are relating to you, and how you

are relating to them, are you able to hold all this information lightly? From this place, what do you become curious about? What seems important here? What might be a priority to explore now, and what might be bookmarked for later exploration? How might your working hypothesis inform the questions you ask and the interventions you use? As you move forward, we invite you to see if you are able to adjust your understanding as new information presents itself.

Relational Skill 4: Mindful Interventions

The intention of mindful interventions is to hold the possibility that our clients can begin to relate to themselves in a new way with increased capacity for connection to Self and others. Instead of relating to themselves through the filters of old survival style patterns—based on shame, self-rejection, and self-hatred—clients can begin to relate to themselves with greater capacity for openness, curiosity, and eventually self-acceptance and compassion. Ultimately, as a client receives support to address what is in the way of connection to their authentic Self, they begin to build greater psychobiological capacity for healing and growth.

How do we, as therapists, most effectively support this process? It begins with a therapist staying in connection with themselves. Psychiatrist James Masterson taught that when therapists get in the way of the client's growth process, it often comes because therapists become so focused on fixing or helping the client that they lose connection to themselves. Masterson believed that many of the interventions a therapist uses are being driven by a therapist's Big C countertransference. He cautioned, "You have no right to intervene unless you have a theoretical reason and hypothesis as to the result. If you have no hypothesis, you are probably intervening because of your own feelings. If that happens, forget about the patient. Let the patient struggle on her own while you figure out your own feelings, because your feelings interfere with treatment at this point."[6]

Mindfully applying interventions relates to an intersubjective process that supports us, in connection with our inner world, to stay in relation with our client's intention and inner world. We practice self-inquiry around

our intention for interventions, including any countertransference reactions that may be driving our engagement. We give ourselves permission to slow down, to pause, to make mistakes, and to learn. We give ourselves permission to be human within our therapeutic role. Centering our humanness helps create a platform of mindfulness in which the NARM skills and techniques can be effectively used to deal with the complexity of our clients' internal worlds.

The therapeutic skills and techniques we use emerge from the Four Pillars. While we have already presented how we apply the Four Pillars to address unresolved complex trauma, we want to emphasize that the "mindful" part of using interventions is evaluating why you are using a specific tool and how this fits with your working hypothesis. We do not use interventions to push for outcomes, to caretake, or to protect clients from their reactions. We use interventions in supporting our client's capacity for increasing depth of experience.

Remember, it is not only applying these skills that matters. It's also being open to and receiving the feedback in response to the interventions. We must always be willing to reevaluate based on new information we are receiving from the client, from our own internal process, and through the therapeutic relationship. We can learn so much by observing how the clients use for themselves the interventions we provide.

THE APPLICATION OF RELATIONAL SKILL 4: MINDFUL INTERVENTIONS

As you are present with your client, we invite you to reflect on how you are engaging with your client using interventions. This begins by being mindful of how the working hypothesis is informing your interventions. As you are working directly with your client, we invite you to bring self-inquiry as to the intention around each specific intervention you choose to use. Questions that might help you in this process: *What am I hoping to elicit or effect by using this specific intervention? What am I noticing about how the client responds to this intervention? What is the impact of my interventions? How does this impact relate to my working hypothesis, particularly around their intention (Pillar 1) for what they wanted for themself out of this session?*

We invite you to notice if the interventions you are using seem to be supporting connection and disidentification or seem to be reinforcing disconnection and old identifications. If you feel as if the interventions are reinforcing old strategies or not having the intended impact, see if you are able to stay open to the learning, rather than pressuring yourself to figure out what to do next. If you need to adjust your way of engaging or check in with the client about their experience, this in itself is a mindful intervention of engaging with openness, curiosity, and humility.

Relational Skill 5: Integration

The intention of integration is to support increasing psychobiological capacity. In yoga there is a pose called *savasana*, otherwise known as resting or corpse pose, which is generally introduced at the end of a yoga class to support integration of the practice. Some yoga teachers prioritize the active poses, which leads them to cut into the time they allow students for savasana. But the integration phase is essential in supporting the long-term health benefits of yoga practice. Similarly, many of the most widely used therapeutic models emphasize the activity of therapy—what we do in therapy—minimizing the integration that supports long-term change and growth. This brings us back to the theme of this chapter about meeting our clients from a place of *being*, and not primarily focused on *doing*.

Clients may have difficulty with integration. Many of our clients will want to jump very quickly to something new after feeling more settled or having a new realization. Many people do not give themselves time to settle, catch their breath, and allow states of relaxation and ease. People tend to be invested in keeping themselves busy and making things happen. Allowing time for integration is difficult not only for most of our clients but also for many therapists. Therapists also may feel discomfort with the "resting" phases and will jump quickly to something new, which usually comes in the form of another intervention.

After a successful intervention has been employed, it is common that a client experiences some sort of psychobiological shift toward increased organization. For example, clients may report feeling relieved, less burdened, more

settled, more relaxed, more balanced, more expansive, more spacious, more clear, or more engaged with you. Clients may attempt to minimize these shifts by moving quickly past these moments. Remember, there is deep investment in staying stuck in disconnection, identifications, and survival strategies, even when they no longer serve us. Yet integrating these internal shifts can reinforce movement toward greater psychobiological capacity, allowing the client to meet the world with increased presence, engagement, agency, and self-activation.

By using Pillar 4, we want to support, and at times guide, our clients to be present with their internal experience. Cultivating somatic mindfulness is one way we encourage integration of these shifts. This involves supporting *interoception*, which is a person's awareness into the present experience in their body. From our perspective, the sensations associated with these psychobiological shifts are an expression of significant inner change. By inviting clients to take time to notice and sense into these internal shifts, we are encouraging embodiment and perhaps the rewiring of neuropathways.

It is important that we provide clients with an opportunity for integration. Slowing down, even when our clients want to jump to the next thing, is a critical step of supporting this process. Often this means accepting and dropping into silence, which for many therapists and clients can be uncomfortable and even excruciating. It is important not to push the process and make something happen just because it's uncomfortable for the therapist or client. Change can be uncomfortable at times.

While it can be new, and at times intimidating, to trust in the flow of this organic process, slowing down and silence can become major resources for someone who is so used to running from their internal experience. This supports the organismic impulse moving toward connection, health, and aliveness and possibilities for reorganization, healing, and transformation.

THE APPLICATION OF RELATIONAL SKILL 5: INTEGRATION

As you are present with your client, we invite you to notice how much might be going on for the client, even beneath their conscious awareness. If you notice yourself missing what is going on for the client, we invite you to take your time, slow down, shift your active *doing* mindset to a receptive *being* mindset, and practice your 50-50 balance.

If your client moves quickly away from states of connection and expansion into disconnection and contraction, notice how you relate to this and what you do in relation to their shifts. If you are putting pressure on yourself to make something different happen, expedite the process, explain something, or neatly wrap up the session, see if you are able to bring more presence to what is happening without the need to control or direct it.

We invite you to take time to sense into the relational field. Questions that might help you in this process: *Am I being impacted by the client's experience in any way? If so, how am I being impacted? Does how I am feeling right now give me any information about my client's experience? How is it for me to be present as the client is having new experiences? How is it for me to be present in this relationship?*

Practice Exercise for NARM Relational Model

We invite you to take a few moments to reflect on a client you are struggling with. It may be helpful to reflect on a specific recent session you had with this client.

1. Reflect on your capacity to attune to your client. As you imagine yourself sitting with this client right now, what aspects of their experience are you attuning to?

2. What is your sense of your client as you attune to their experience? Are you able to stay present and open to their experience without feeling compelled to say or do anything?

3. What do you know about your own reactions to your client and what they share with you? How does being with this client impact you?

4. What is your working hypothesis? In other words, how might you understand how your client organizes their internal world?

5. As you begin to understand the way your client is organizing their internal experience, how might you proceed in supporting your client while maintaining connection with them?

Overall, on a scale from 10 to 1 (10 being high, 1 being low), what would you say your capacity is to stay open to this client with curiosity and presence?

Heartfulness

The object of your practice should first of all be yourself. Your love for the other, your ability to love another person, depends on your ability to love yourself.

THICH NHAT HANH,
TRUE LOVE: A PRACTICE FOR AWAKENING THE HEART

Although it is difficult to capture in words, we might define *heartfulness* as a felt sense in one's heart of being connected—both with oneself and with another person. It is an experience of depth in connection with Self and others. The capacity of our depth of connection with another is dependent on the depth of connection we are capable of within ourselves. As individuals deepen into the authentic and intimate relationships within themselves, a sense of shared heartfulness with others becomes possible.

REFLECTIVE EXERCISE

We invite you to take a few moments to reflect on a time that you were able to stay present and connected in yourself while staying connected and openhearted with another person.

- What do you notice about your capacity to connect with heartfulness and love?

- We invite you to take a few moments to notice how it feels to reflect on this—specifically noticing how you are feeling in your heart.

Heartfulness in the therapeutic process starts with the therapist. NARM therapists direct attention within themselves before they focus attention on clients. When connecting to themselves through curiosity, presence, and self-inquiry, therapists have more capacity to show up in presence and create the conditions for intersubjectivity. A therapist who has greater access to

their heartfulness can support their clients in building greater capacity for heartfulness within themselves and with others in their lives.

The more therapists are in their countertransference strategies, the more they are in some degree disconnected from their hearts. Unmanaged empathy, running from helplessness, and other familiar strategies like compulsive efforting and caretaking can be a function of shutting down our hearts from being in true, intimate relationship with ourselves and our clients. Being present in one's heart is the counterpoint to these old familiar strategies and leads to meeting oneself, and therefore one's clients, with greater understanding, acceptance, and compassion.

Developmental trauma is about heartbreak. The resolution of developmental trauma is about heartfulness. We strongly encourage all therapists to engage in their own healing process. As individuals reconnect to their hearts, they often have a feeling of opening a door to a place within themselves that has long been shut. It is very difficult to guide someone else to internal places we have not been ourselves.

Emotional completion, and the larger disidentification process, is about reconnecting to our hearts. As we begin to dissolve our old identifications and strategies, we feel more connected to our heart feelings and let those guide us. An intention that once started as a whisper, a longing of the heart's desire, can be actualized. This can lead to significant personal changes as well as enhance our capacity for relational connection.

REFLECTIVE EXERCISE

We invite you to take a few moments to:

- Set an intention from your heart for yourself moving forward in your life.

- What might be the optimal outcome if you are able to actualize your heart's desire moving forward?

- As you reflect on your heart's desire, we invite you to notice what you experience internally in your thoughts, emotions, and body.

- *We especially invite you to take a few moments before moving on to feel into your heart.*

CHAPTER 9

NARM Personality Spectrum Model

There's no such thing as immaculate perception—we see things through the filter of our experience.
DANIEL SIEGEL, *THE DEVELOPING MIND: HOW RELATIONSHIPS AND THE BRAIN INTERACT TO SHAPE WHO WE ARE*

When working with clients who have experienced complex trauma, it is very helpful to have a framework that allows therapists to understand the psychobiological capacities of their clients. These capacities are foundational elements of the Self. When a child experiences and adapts to adverse childhood experiences, their developing psychobiological capacities are impacted, which leads to disorganization of the Self. In psychology, this has been described through the classification of *personality disorders,* also referred to as *disorders of the self.*

We do not rely on the more widely accepted framework for understanding personality disorders—for example, within the *DSM-5.* Instead, in order to help therapists provide more effective treatment, we have created a spectrum model that uses a psychobiological perspective for assessing levels of Self-organization.

Throughout the history of Western philosophy and psychology, defining the concept of the Self has been elusive. *Personality* tends to be the most commonly used concept in modern psychology; *character* and *identity* are

related concepts that are often used interchangeably. We view Self as much more than character, identity, and personality. A very basic definition of Self describes one's own subjective experience and sense of being; it attempts to capture the lived experience of "being human." Although we use "personality" in the NARM Personality Spectrum to stay consistent with current psychological understanding, it is really a framework for understanding the nature of a client's unique organization of Self. The NARM Personality Spectrum recognizes the link between unresolved developmental trauma and levels of disruption to self-organization. As Fritjof Capra says, "The ideas of self-organization are very important to understand the autonomy, the authenticity and basic humanity of people."[1]

Any therapist who works with trauma will be working with personality disorganization every day. It is estimated that 15 percent of the United States' population—over thirty million people—meet diagnostic criteria for at least one personality disorder.[2] But as therapists and other helping professionals, do we have adequate training to assess for and work with such complex psychobiological patterns? For most of us, that answer is no.

A general clinical understanding of personality, and specifically personality-disorder dynamics, has been lost because of the current trends in modern psychology with less emphasis on depth-oriented models. Many therapists have not done specialized training, nor are they receiving clinical supervision, for working with personality disorders.

To make it even more challenging, many therapists overestimate the organization of their clients. This largely has to do with therapists seeing the best in people, not wanting to view their clients pathologically, and mistaking life functioning with personality organization. Clients can be functioning quite well in their lives—for example, as doctors, nurses, teachers, business owners, and politicians—and still have profound disorganization of the Self. In fact, sometimes overfunctioning can be a strategy used by clients with significant internal disorganization.

This leads us to a very important point. The NARM Personality Spectrum focuses on the organization of the Self, and not specifically on functioning. When focused on functioning, therapists can get pretty far down the road of therapy until they realize how disorganized the client actually

is. They missed truly seeing the client because they were focused on how well the client was able to function in some areas of their life. Once they recognize the client's level of disorganization, it can be hard to shift gears therapeutically. Clients on the more disorganized end of the personality spectrum will require a different approach to treatment than clients on the more organized end of the spectrum. So the earlier a therapist is able to assess the client's level of internal organization, the more responsive they can be to the client's capacities, and therefore the more effective they can be in treatment.

Additionally, overestimating our clients can be a countertransference reaction for some therapists. As young children, we needed to view our caregivers and other adults in our lives as more organized than they often were; recognizing that they were failing us would've been unbearable. The fantasy of having highly organized adults in our early environment becomes a projection we carry into adulthood. This projection can lead a therapist to have an inaccurate assessment on the level of disorganization within a client. Additionally, if the therapist runs into challenges with this client, they may unconsciously blame themself, just as they did as a child. As mentioned in the previous chapter, when therapists begin to feel they are failing with their clients, they then begin relying on various strategies including pressuring themselves, working harder, compulsive caretaking, or giving up. If therapists have not been able to adequately resolve their own developmental trauma patterns, they tend to view their clients through a distorted lens and thus be less effective in their clinical work.

Another challenge in our field is the common belief that personality disorders are rare. While it may be true that clients meeting the full *DSM-5* criteria for a personality disorder diagnosis might be uncommon, most clinicians are unaware of how many of their clients are impacted by often undiagnosed personality disorder traits. Because personality disorders are viewed as more extreme diagnoses, and because of the emphasis on cognitive and behavioral symptoms in our clients, mental health professionals might not capture the depth of their client's psychobiological distress. Additionally, many psychotherapists are wary of taking on clients who have a personality disorder diagnosis due to various factors, including

feeling underprepared to work with such severity, not wanting to be overwhelmed, and being cautious around the risks associated with these clients. No matter how we might feel about working with clients dealing with personality-disordered dynamics, when we work with complex trauma, we cannot escape the reality that many of our clients will have high levels of disorganization of the Self.

An additional challenge for therapists is that the relationship between complex trauma and personality disorders is not very well defined. Symptoms of complex trauma have quite significant overlap with symptoms of personality disorders. Differential diagnosis helps us create an accurate assessment that informs therapeutic scope, interventions, and prognosis. It is beyond the scope of this book to compare and contrast the NARM Personality Spectrum with the various diagnostic systems in use. The main emphasis for us is that prevailing diagnostic systems focus on classifying symptoms and behaviors, whereas we focus on the common underlying psychobiological dynamics—driven by unresolved complex trauma—that fuel the various personality disordered manifestations.

By using ten specific psychobiological traits that we will be defining, the NARM Personality Spectrum provides a roadmap for identifying where our clients are on the spectrum from Organized Self to Disorganized Self, and the various positions in between. We are using the term *Disorganized Self* to differentiate from *Personality Disordered*, the latter of which implies the specific framework as outlined in the *DSM* and *ICD* systems, including such personality disorders as borderline, narcissistic, schizoid, dependent, and antisocial.

We do not use the NARM Personality Spectrum as a categorization for different manifestations of psychopathology. As NARM therapists, we use it as a framework for assessing our client's psychobiological capacity. The NARM Personality Spectrum provides a clearer understanding of a client's inner world, including the disorganization of psychobiological states that are driving their distressing symptoms and maladaptive behaviors. As such, this model is designed to help shape and individualize our therapeutic interventions depending on where our clients are on the personality spectrum.

The NARM Personality Spectrum is intended to create a roadmap that provides a clearer sense of where the client is in the moment regarding their ability to engage with and benefit from the therapeutic process. This is important because it answers this question: *Does this client have the capacity to benefit from the intervention that I think might be a good one for them right now?*

The NARM Personality Spectrum is designed as a spectrum of psychobiological capacity as outlined here:

Organized Self   **Adaptive Self**   **Disorganized Self**

The full breakdown of this spectrum starts on p. 270. We also provide a worksheet for using this framework in therapeutic practice in Appendix B. The key takeaway is that unresolved early trauma disorganizes the Self to lesser or greater levels depending on multiple factors, including both nurture and nature. When we're assessing new clients, this framework helps us organize:

- our workng hypothesis of where our clients are on a wide range of personality dynamics (their psychobiological capacity)
- how the client's level of internal organization relates to their symptoms
- our own countertransference reactions
- an accurate and realistic prognosis
- how to most effectively treat clients based on where they are on the Personality Spectrum

In order to accurately assess a client's level of internal organization, we define three different ranges on this spectrum: *Organized Self, Adaptive Self,* and *Disorganized Self.*

Organized Self: Children who have experienced more secure attachment and less developmental trauma will move into adulthood with a more organized, coherent sense of Self. They meet life more firmly grounded in

embodied adult consciousness. They experience greater internal security, sense of agency, and authenticity. They have the capacity to stay in balanced relationship between Self and others, experiencing greater depth within themselves while experiencing greater intimacy with others. They generally have more developed capacity for traits like self-awareness, insight, openness to learning, and a desire for change and growth.

Adaptive Self: As children experience more insecure attachment and more developmental trauma, they will move into adulthood with a more disorganized sense of Self. The more these individuals are identified with their survival styles, the more they get stuck in seeing the world through a child's eyes (child consciousness). As adults, their psychobiological capacity will be compromised, which shows up in their limited capacity for self-awareness, insight, and openness to learning. They are more identified with limiting and self-defeating narratives, stories, and perspectives. Opportunities for growth and change can feel threatening, leading them to relate to new experiences with avoidance, rigidity, resistance, and other acting-in and acting-out strategies. As clients, they may question their progress in therapy, and at times both client and therapist may feel frustrated with the therapeutic process.

Disorganized Self: Children who suffer significant early trauma will experience even more disruption to their developing Self. They will move into adulthood with an even more disorganized and disordered sense of Self. As adults, they will relate to the world through child consciousness, meaning they often view the world as happening to them and will feel that they are helpless victims in an unfair and punishing world. They cannot tolerate depth. They struggle with complexity and nuance, and tend to keep things superficial and simplistic. They may have developed minimal capacity for self-awareness or insight and can be defensive, resistant, suspicious, and even paranoid. Therefore, these clients have less room for learning, confronting dysfunctional patterns, and engaging in change and growth. When they do begin to experience change or growth, they may start acting in and acting out, often in extreme ways. They may act out on multiple people in their life—including their therapist. Both client and therapist may perceive that there is a significant lack of progress in therapy, and both may feel dissatisfied with the therapeutic process.

Many therapists experience difficulty in working with clients on the Disorganized Self range of the spectrum. For example, Pillar 1: Clarifying the Therapeutic Contract can be much more challenging with these clients than with those in the Organized Self or Adaptive Self range of the spectrum. Clients in the Disorganized Self range will often come in with vague, unclear, or conflicting intentions, often focused on wanting the environment or other people to change so that they can be OK. Other times they might place expectations, demands, or even threats on the therapist to "fix them."

Similarly, Pillar 3: Reinforcing Agency can also be very challenging for clients in the Disorganized Self range. They often make the therapeutic process about others; they may blame people in their life and have great difficulty accepting any ownership of the distress they are experiencing. They may unconsciously project negative traits onto others, which validates their use of distrust, resistance, and rage. This can get particularly challenging when these dynamics are directed at their therapists. These clients may begin by appreciating or idealizing the therapist but soon switch over to blaming and attacking. They may even become threatening or cross boundaries in ways that leave the therapist feeling uncomfortable or unsafe. These situations may leave the therapist with the sense that they are not on the same team as their clients, feeling trapped in adversarial therapeutic relationships.

For example, a client at the end of a first session said to her new therapist, "I have been to over twenty therapists and healers and knew right away that you are exactly what I've been looking for." This began several sessions of this client praising the therapist. She would say things to the therapist like "you so get me," "you are a lifesaver," and "where have you been all my life?" But as soon as the therapist began to ask her more depth-oriented questions, she began lashing out. For example, in one session she shared that her intention was to feel more grounded, more balanced, and less reactive in herself in her relationship. During that session, she began recounting a recent experience where she was lashing out violently against her partner for a perceived slight that she interpreted as her partner distancing herself. As the therapist began asking agency-oriented questions

about this incident—for example, "What was it about her behaviors that you took as distancing?" and "What was it that she said that led you to feeling unbalanced and reactive?"—she began glaring at the therapist suspiciously and said, "You're going to take her side, aren't you?" It quickly escalated, and she began raising her voice, saying things like "you always take her side," "why don't you just go and work with her then," and "you just don't ever get me."

These clients have often been through countless therapists and other helping professionals and frequently get labeled as "treatment resistant." They may have the feeling that despite all their efforts to receive treatment, they are not feeling met or satisfied, or not making the kind of progress they expect. The therapist also may feel stuck and that therapy isn't progressing in the way they'd like it to be. Or they feel like they take one step forward and then five steps back.

The therapist may be unaware that their client is in the Disorganized Self range, but they generally are aware of the strong reactions these clients elicit within them. We use the psychoanalytic term *countertransference strain* to describe a therapist's strong internal reactions to clients in this range. An example is a therapist who looks at their schedule for the day and sees their 2 p.m. client and feels a knot in their gut. Another example is a therapist who stays up at night worried or scared about a client. One last example is a therapist who fantasizes about a client quitting or even themself moving away to get rid of the client. We've seen therapists who have had very strong reactions to such clients, understandably so. These clients can be extremely difficult to work with and can leave therapists feeling stuck, hopeless, and frustrated.

At the same time, these are often the clients who send therapists back into supervision, further learning, and even postgraduate trainings. Many therapists coming into NARM trainings report feeling desperate to find better ways to support the clients they find most challenging. They do not feel fully equipped to effectively work with these clients. From this perspective, the personal experience of countertransference strain can be the catalyst for important professional development.

Therapists can get hooked by these clients and burn themselves out if they are assuming client buy-in or attempting to reach unattainable goals and their clients do not have such capacity. Therapists may have a compassionate but ultimately misguided desire to do whatever they can to help their client. A therapist may believe that if only they could get their client to open up, trust them, recognize that they are truly there for them, and let them help them, then maybe their client would make progress. Unmanaged empathy can lead to an inaccurate read on the psychobiological capacity for such clients, and it leads to ongoing countertransference strain and struggle in providing effective treatment.

REFLECTIVE EXERCISE

We invite you to take a few moments to reflect on three different clients:

- An "easier" client: one who is engaged, collaborative, thoughtful, hard-working, and enjoyable to work with.

- A "more challenging" client: one who has made some progress, and can at times be enjoyable to work with, but has also been difficult.

- A "more problematic" client: one who feels stuck, resistant, or adversarial and has created problems for you in terms of boundaries, stress, or other countertransference strain reactions.

As you reflect on each client, we invite you to notice your internal experience.

The NARM Personality Spectrum provides a map for identifying areas of both strength and challenge for clients. Areas of strength can be used for reflecting on various resources and progress in developing increasing capacity. Areas of challenge can be used for normalizing and providing psychoeducation as a means for developing understanding, agency, and self-compassion. No matter where a client is on the spectrum

of their personality organization, this framework can support therapists in meeting their clients where they are and providing more attuned and refined interventions, tailored to where the client is in terms of their psychobiological capacity.

The NARM Personality Spectrum: Ten Traits of Psychobiological Capacity

What are the core psychobiological traits shaped through childhood that we are using to better understand the organization of Self? While this isn't an exhaustive list, it does does help us capture essential traits that represent the characteristics of an individual's personality. By identifying and assessing capacity with each of these ten characterological traits, we gain greater awareness of the internal dynamics leading to a client's symptoms and distress.

One note before going further into this assessment tool. We want to acknowledge that this is a theoretically designed tool that has not yet been put through research trials, and therefore we are not promoting it as an evidence-based evaluation model. We offer this framework in support of a therapist's ability to be more effective in assessing and treating their clients. Additionally, we have found that clients themselves enjoy learning about the NARM Personality Spectrum. We hope that it can be used to also support personal growth for those who are interested in using it in this way.

The NARM Personality Spectrum helps us gauge progress as we are supporting our clients with the possibility for increased psychobiological capacity. A concept similar to "window of tolerance" or "range of resiliency," psychobiological capacity represents movement toward greater organization within the Self. When there is coherence internally, these ten traits are working in cooperation and support the capacity for health, growth, and aliveness. When there is disorganization internally, these ten traits are

disrupted and lead to various psychobiological symptoms. Many of our clients who are dealing with unresolved trauma have disruption of some or all these psychobiological traits.

The ten psychobiological traits we use are (full descriptions on following pages):

1. Connection

2. Separation-Individuation

3. Self-Regulation

4. Agency

5. Intimacy and Therapeutic Alliance

6. Empathy

7. Self-Awareness and Insight

8. Consensus Reality

9. Self-Activation

10. Presence

REFLECTIVE EXERCISE

What we invite you to do over the next pages is to choose a client, preferably a client you find challenging—perhaps someone you have already been thinking about as you've been reading this chapter—and as you go through each of these ten psychobiological traits, score your client on each category. As you'll see, the scoring scale is between 10 and 1; 10 represents the highest capacity with this psychobiological trait, and 1 represents the lowest capacity with this psychobiological trait. Once you go through all ten categories, you will have a score somewhere between 100 and 10. On page 292 you can calculate the final score of your client and answer the reflective questions provided there.

Connection

ORGANIZED SELF	ADAPTIVE SELF	DISORGANIZED SELF
More Connection	**Disrupted Connection**	**Profound Disconnection**
• Internalized subjectification; experiencing oneself as a subject	• Limited experience of internalized subjectification; experiencing oneself less as a subject	• Internalized objectification; experiencing oneself as an object
• Increasing connection to one's physical, emotional, psychological, and spiritual Self	• Disrupted connection to one's physical, emotional, psychological, and spiritual Self	• Very little connection to one's physical, emotional, psychological, and spiritual Self
• More coherent and stable sense of Self	• Less coherent and stable sense of Self	• Lack of coherent and stable sense of Self
• More embodied, less symptomatic, more resilient	• Less embodied, more symptomatic, less resilient	• Highly disembodied and symptomatic, not resilient
• More socially engaged and greater ease in connection with others	• Less socially engaged and less ease in connection with others	• Socially disengaged and difficulty in connection with others
• More fulfilled in one's relationships with others and life experience	• Less fulfilled in one's relationships with others and life experience	• Unfulfilled in one's relationships with others and life experience
• Greater capacity for heartfulness and love	• Compromised capacity for heartfulness and love	• Minimal capacity for heartfulness and love
Organized Self	**Adaptive Self**	**Disorganized Self**
10–7	**6–4**	**3–1**

REFLECTIVE EXERCISE

- Think of a client in terms of:
    - Capacity to experience themself as a subject
    - Capacity for connection to themself (physical, emotional, psychological, and spiritual self)
    - Capacity for stability in themself
    - Capacity for resilience
    - Capacity for social engagement
    - Capacity to feel fulfilled by relationships and life experience
    - Capacity for heartfulness and love
- Provide them with a score between 10 and 1: _____

Separation-Individuation

ORGANIZED SELF	ADAPTIVE SELF	DISORGANIZED SELF
More Separation-Individuation	**Disrupted Separation-Individuation**	**Minimal Separation-Individuation**
• Capacity for differentiation and psychological independence from attachment figures and others in one's life, leading to a stronger sense of Self	• Compromised capacity for differentiation and psychological independence from attachment figures and others in one's life, leading to a more unstable sense of Self	• Very little capacity for differentiation and psychological independence from attachment figures and others in one's life, leading to a fragmented or minimal sense of Self
• Less identified with old identifications and object relations, adaptive strategies, and coping mechanisms	• More identified with old identifications and object relations, adaptive strategies, and coping mechanisms	• Strongly identified with old identifications and object relations, adaptive strategies, and coping mechanisms
• Increasing awareness of unconscious protection against attachment and relational loss	• Strong unconscious protection against attachment and relational loss	• Extreme unconscious protection against attachment and relational loss; fusion with parents and significant others
• More identified with adult consciousness	• More identified with child consciousness	• Strongly identified with child consciousness
Organized Self	**Adaptive Self**	**Disorganized Self**
10–7	**6–4**	**3–1**

REFLECTIVE EXERCISE

- Think of a client in terms of:
    - Capacity for differentiation and independence from others
    - Capacity for freedom from identifications and adaptive strategies
    - Capacity for awareness of unconscious protection against attachment and relational loss
    - Capacity to live in adult consciousness
- Provide them with a score between 10 and 1: _____

Self-Regulation

ORGANIZED SELF	ADAPTIVE SELF	DISORGANIZED SELF
More Self-Regulation	Disrupted Self-Regulation	Dysregulation
• Increasing capacity to regulate one's internal states (i.e., physiology, emotions, behaviors)	• Compromised capacity to regulate one's internal states	• Minimal capacity to regulate one's internal states
• Increasing capacity for object constancy, affect tolerance, and distress tolerance	• Compromised capacity for object constancy, affect tolerance, and distress tolerance	• Minimal capacity for object constancy, affect tolerance, and distress tolerance
• Less reliance on others and one's environment to regulate and soothe	• Increasing reliance on others and one's environment to regulate and soothe	• Demanding while at the same time resisting and rejecting others and one's environment to regulate and soothe
• Greater ability to relax and feel balanced	• Less ability to relax and feel balanced	• Very little ability to relax and feel balanced
• Increasing states of physiological fluidity and flow	• Increasing tendency toward states of physiological tension and collapse	• Experience chronic states of physiological tension and collapse
• Increasing overall state of health and well-being	• Increasing tendency toward anxiety, depression, and other mental and physical disorders	• Experience chronic anxiety, depression, and other severe mental and physical disorders
Organized Self	**Adaptive Self**	**Disorganized Self**
10–7	**6–4**	**3–1**

REFLECTIVE EXERCISE

- Think of a client in terms of:

    - Capacity to regulate their internal states (i.e., physiology, emotions, behaviors)

    - Capacity for object constancy, affect tolerance, and distress tolerance

    - Capacity for less reliance on others and their environment to regulate and soothe

    - Capacity to relax and feel balanced

    - Capacity for states of physiological fluidity and flow

    - Capacity for overall state of health and well-being

- Provide them with a score between 10 and 1: _____

Agency

ORGANIZED SELF	ADAPTIVE SELF	DISORGANIZED SELF
More Agency	**Disrupted Agency**	**Minimal Agency**
• Increasing capacity to take ownership for one's life	• Compromised capacity to take ownership for one's life	• Very little capacity to take ownership for one's life
• Taking ownership for one's emotions, reactions, and behaviors	• Difficulty taking ownership for one's emotions, reactions, and behaviors	• Inability to take ownership for one's emotions, reaction and behaviors
• Less tendency to reactivity, blame, and feeling the victim of others and external circumstances	• Increasing tendency to reactivity, blame, and feeling the victim of others and external circumstances	• Strong sense of reactivity, blame, and feeling the victim of others and external circumstances
• Less dependent upon environmental response for one's well-being	• More dependent upon environmental response for one's well-being	• Strongly dependent upon environmental response for one's well-being
• Feel more firmly grounded in one's adult self; more connected with adult consciousness	• Less grounded in one's adult self; more identified with child consciousness states	• Very little access to adult self; highly identified with child consciousness states
Organized Self	**Adaptive Self**	**Disorganized Self**
10–7	**6–4**	**3–1**

REFLECTIVE EXERCISE

- Think of a client in terms of:
    - Capacity to take ownership for their life
    - Capacity to take ownership for their emotions, reactions, and behaviors
    - Capacity for less reliance on reactivity, blame, and feeling victim
    - Capacity for less dependency upon environmental response for their well-being
    - Capacity to be grounded in their adult Self
- Provide them with a score between 10 and 1: _____

Intimacy and Therapeutic Alliance

ORGANIZED SELF	ADAPTIVE SELF	DISORGANIZED SELF
More Therapeutic Alliance & Capacity for Intimacy	**Disrupted Therapeutic Alliance & Capacity for Intimacy**	**Weak Therapeutic Alliance & Capacity for Intimacy**
• Increasing capacity for intersubjectivity and intimacy	• Compromised capacity for intersubjectivity and intimacy	• Minimal capacity for intersubjectivity and intimacy
• Experience therapist and others in one's life as being resource for support	• Compromised ability to experience therapist and others in one's life as being resource for support	• Minimal sense of therapist and others in one's life as being resource for support
• Acting in collaboration with therapist and others	• Experience increasing ambivalence about support from therapist and others	• Act adversarial or outright rejection of support from therapist and others
• Able to experience therapist or other people as real human beings	• Increasingly experience the therapist or other people through the filter of transference and projections	• Do not experience the therapist or other people as real human beings but through the filter of transference and projections
• Ability to develop trust, goodwill, and warmth with therapist and others in one's life	• Increasingly challenged in developing trust, goodwill, and warmth with therapist and others in one's life	• Do not trust therapist and others in one's life, viewing them as objects that intend to exploit, deceive, or harm
• Acknowledge therapeutic and relational boundaries and respect boundaries of therapist and others in one's life	• Acknowledge therapeutic and relational boundaries but are increasingly less clear or comfortable with boundaries of therapist and others in one's life	• Deny, reject, or directly challenge therapeutic and relational boundaries with therapist and others in one's life
Organized Self	**Adaptive Self**	**Disorganized Self**
10–7	**6–4**	**3–1**

REFLECTIVE EXERCISE

- Think of a client in terms of:

    - Capacity for intersubjectivity and intimacy

    - Capacity to experience therapist and others in one's life as resources for support

    - Capacity to act in collaboration with therapist and others in one's life

    - Capacity to experience therapist and other people as real human beings

    - Capacity to develop trust, goodwill, and warmth with therapist and others in one's life

    - Capacity to acknowledge and respect the therapeutic and relational boundaries

- Provide them with a score between 10 and 1: _____

Empathy

ORGANIZED SELF	ADAPTIVE SELF	DISORGANIZED SELF
More Empathy	**Disrupted Empathy**	**Minimal Empathy**
• Capacity to relate to what another person is experiencing from within the other person's frame of reference ("put yourself in their shoes")	• Difficulty relating to what another person is experiencing from within the other person's frame of reference	• Inability to relate to what another person is experiencing from within the other person's frame of reference
• Ability to sense into what another person may be feeling	• Difficulty sensing into what another person may be feeling (increasing failure of empathy)	• Failure to sense into what another person may be feeling (failure of empathy)
• Capacity to have greater accuracy in differentiating one's own feelings from another's feelings	• Difficulty in differentiating one's own feelings from another's feelings (increasing unmanaged empathy)	• Inability to separate one's own feelings from another's feelings (unmanaged empathy)
• Comprehension and appreciation of another's experiences and motivations	• Increasingly challenged in comprehension or appreciation of another's experiences and motivations	• Do not comprehend or appreciate another's experiences and motivations
• Curiosity and tolerance of differing perspectives	• Compromised capacity to have curiosity and tolerance of differing perspectives	• Disregard and intolerance of differing perspectives
• Recognizing, understanding, and caring about the effects of one's behaviors on others	• Difficulty in recognizing, understanding, and caring about the effects of one's behaviors on others	• Inability to recognize, understand, and care about the effects of one's behaviors on others
Organized Self	**Adaptive Self**	**Disorganized Self**
10–7	**6–4**	**3–1**

REFLECTIVE EXERCISE

- Think of a client in terms of:

  - Capacity to relate to what another person is experiencing from within the other person's frame of reference

  - Capacity to sense into what another person may be feeling

  - Capacity to differentiate their own feelings from another person's feelings

  - Capacity for comprehension and appreciation of another's experiences and motivations

  - Capacity for curiosity and tolerance of differing perspectives

  - Capacity to recognize, understand, and care about the effects of their behaviors on others

- Provide them with a score between 10 and 1: _____

Self-Awareness and Insight

ORGANIZED SELF	ADAPTIVE SELF	DISORGANIZED SELF
More Self-Awareness & Insight	**Disrupted Self-Awareness & Insight**	**Minimal Self-Awareness & Insight**
• Capacity to inquire and explore inward, to question beliefs and assumptions	• Compromised capacity to inquire and explore inward, to question beliefs and assumptions	• Very little capacity to inquire and explore inward, to question beliefs and assumptions
• Ability to tolerate uncertainty and complexity; accepting not-knowing	• Difficulty tolerating uncertainty and complexity; reducing complexity to simple answers	• Inability to tolerate uncertainty and complexity; relying on polarized, all-or-nothing thinking
• Capacity for self-discovery	• Less capacity for self-discovery	• Minimal capacity for self-discovery
• Less need of mirroring from others and environment for their sense of Self	• More dependent on mirroring from others and environment for defining their sense of Self	• Strongly dependent on mirroring from others and environment for defining their sense of Self
• Interested in developing increasing understanding and depth	• Interested primarily in cognitive/behavioral change and symptom reduction	• Disinterested in new learning about Self
Organized Self	**Adaptive Self**	**Disorganized Self**
10–7	**6–4**	**3–1**

REFLECTIVE EXERCISE

- Think of a client in terms of:

    - Capacity to inquire and explore inward, to question beliefs and assumptions

    - Capacity to tolerate uncertainty and complexity

    - Capacity for self-discovery

    - Capacity for less reliance on mirroring from others and environment for their own sense of Self

    - Capacity for interest in developing increasing understanding and depth

- Provide them with a score between 10 and 1: _____

Consensus Reality

ORGANIZED SELF Clearer Consensus Reality	ADAPTIVE SELF Disrupted Consensus Reality	DISORGANIZED SELF Distorted Consensus Reality
• Ability to differentiate between what is real and what is not	• Difficulty differentiating between what is real and what is not	• Inability to differentiate between what is real and what is not
• Capacity for reality testing	• Challenges with reality testing	• Extreme distortions in reality testing (i.e., delusional thinking)
• Capacity to relate to commonly accepted worldview	• Adherence to inaccurate beliefs about oneself, others, and the world	• Adherence to false and distorted beliefs and perceptions (i.e., delusions and hallucinations)
• Increasingly less identified with and living free from the filters of identifications, projections, transference, thoughts, beliefs, guilt, shame, and anxiety	• Increasingly identified with and living through the filters of identifications, projections, transference, thoughts, beliefs, guilt, shame, and anxiety	• Significantly identified with and living through the filters of identifications, projections, transference, thoughts, beliefs, guilt, shame, and anxiety
Note: "reality" is culturally dependent and must be assessed in a culturally-respectful manner.		
Organized Self	**Adaptive Self**	**Disorganized Self**
10–7	**6–4**	**3–1**

REFLECTIVE EXERCISE

- Think of a client in terms of:
    - Capacity to differentiate between what is real and what is not
    - Capacity for reality testing
    - Capacity for relating to (culturally dependent) commonly accepted worldview
    - Capacity to live free from the filters of old identifications, projections, transference, thoughts, beliefs, guilt, shame, and anxiety
- Provide them with a score between 10 and 1: _____

Self-Activation

ORGANIZED SELF	ADAPTIVE SELF	DISORGANIZED SELF
More Self-Activation	**Disrupted Self-Activation**	**Minimal Self-Activation**
• Increasing connection to one's life force and sense of aliveness	• Compromised connection to one's life force and sense of aliveness	• Very little connection to one's life force and sense of aliveness
• Ability to channel impulses in constructive and creative direction	• Compromised ability to channel impulses in constructive and creative direction	• Channeling impulses in unhealthy direction, including acting-in and acting-out strategies
• Capacity for self-acceptance and self-compassion	• Compromised capacity for self-acceptance and self-compassion; frequently relate to oneself through self-rejection, self-criticism, and self-hatred	• Minimal capacity for self-acceptance and self-compassion; regularly relate to oneself through self-rejection, self-criticism, and self-hatred
• Capacity for healthy aggression	• Increasingly unhealthy aggression, toward oneself and others	• Unhealthy aggression, directing violence toward oneself and others
• Ability to initiate, carry through, and set the course of one's own life	• Less ability to initiate, carry through, and set the course of one's own life	• Inability to initiate, carry through, and set the course of one's own life; active self-sabotage
Organized Self	**Adaptive Self**	**Disorganized Self**
10–7	**6–4**	**3–1**

REFLECTIVE EXERCISE

- Think of a client in terms of:
  - Capacity for connection to their life force and sense of aliveness
  - Capacity to channel impulses in constructive and creative direction
  - Capacity for self-acceptance and self-compassion
  - Capacity for healthy aggression
  - Capacity to initiate, carry through, and set the course for their life
- Provide them with a score between 10 and 1: _____

Presence

ORGANIZED SELF	ADAPTIVE SELF	DISORGANIZED SELF
More Presence	**Disrupted Presence**	**Lack of Presence**
• Increasing capacity to be in the here & now and live in the present moment	• Compromised capacity to be in the here & now and live in the present moment	• Inability to be in the here & now and live in the present moment
• Sense of future and relationship to past are coherent and integrated with the present	• Foreshortened sense of future and repression of past memories; internal conflict with past and future disrupt the present	• Inability to perceive a future different from the past; profound internal conflict leads to fragmentation of past and future and dissociation from the present
• Increasing capacity to experience expansion, aliveness, flow, creativity	• Compromised capacity to experience expansion, aliveness, flow, creativity	• Inability and often resistance to experience expansion, aliveness, flow, creativity
• Increasing capacity for pleasure and enjoying life	• Less capacity for pleasure and enjoying life	• Minimal capacity for pleasure and dissatisfied with life
• Increasing sense of psychological, emotional, and spiritual freedom	• Less sense of psychological, emotional, and spiritual freedom	• Very little sense of psychological, emotional, and spiritual freedom
Organized Self	**Adaptive Self**	**Disorganized Self**
10–7	**6–4**	**3–1**

REFLECTIVE EXERCISE

- Think of a client in terms of:
    - Capacity to be in the here and now and live in the present moment
    - Capacity to have an organized, integrated present, past, and future
    - Capacity to experience expansion, aliveness, flow, and creativity
    - Capacity for pleasure and enjoying life
    - Capacity for sense of psychological, emotional, and spiritual freedom
- Provide them with a score between 10 and 1: _____

Final Scoring for Your Client

ORGANIZED SELF	ADAPTIVE SELF	DISORGANIZED SELF
Total Score	Total Score	Total Score
100–70	69–40	39–10

REFLECTIVE EXERCISE

- Provide them with a final score between 100 and 10: _____

- Questions to reflect on (based on client's final score):

  - What's your overall sense looking at your client through this lens?

  - What might this suggest about treatment?

  - What might this suggest about prognosis?

  - What other support may be indicated?

  - How might this relate to your work with this client?

  - How might this relate to your feeling about your client?

  - How might this relate to how you view yourself as a therapist?

The Therapeutic Application of the NARM Personality Spectrum Model

Clients will show up with a wide range of psychobiological capacity, and we must be able to align our therapeutic approach to the human who is sitting in front of us. It is important to remember that humans are complex, and one way of working does not work for every client. Even across multiple sessions, a client may experience different levels of internal capacity. The NARM Personality Spectrum model helps therapists assess the client in the present moment in order to tailor and guide treatment in response to the client's psychobiological capacity.

Our understanding of psychobiological capacity helps us reflect on a client's *distress tolerance*, which refers to how much challenge a person can tolerate without disconnecting. Having an accurate read on our client's present capacity helps us to reflect on the use of specific interventions—for example, "Does my client have the capacity to use the intervention that I think might be useful?" Depending on the answer, we may need to adjust our interventions accordingly. While we are working to facilitate the possibility of increased psychobiological capacity, we want to do so within the client's capacity for being receptive to our support.

The NARM Personality Spectrum can be used as part of an intake process. We can use this assessment over time and evaluate a client's score over the course of multiple sessions. This can help us have a more informed perspective on how therapy is progressing. It can also be used collaboratively with a client for encouraging and reinforcing self-reflection.

What we don't use it for is to pathologize our clients. Levels of organization do not define who someone is, and we do not make judgments based on the scores. Unfortunately, there are psychological diagnoses—specifically the various personality disorders—that carry a heavy weight of stigma. We want to make sure that readers understand that the NARM Personality Spectrum is not intended to judge someone. It is used to understand the impact of complex trauma on the Self. From this understanding, therapists ask themselves how they can create the most humane treatment possible in supporting the resolution of their client's complex trauma patterns.

The reality is that, like most therapeutic approaches, NARM will generally be more effective and progress faster when working with clients in the Organized Self end of the spectrum, and be more challenging and progress slower when working with clients in the Disorganized Self end of the spectrum. While the NARM organizing principles remain consistent no matter who we are working with, the clinical process does need to be adjusted based on the client's present level of disorganization.

For example, a client that scores in the Disorganized Self range may not respond well to therapeutic skills like attunement and empathy. They may distrust "touchy-feely" therapists who want to talk about feelings and show care and affection. They may feel that their therapist is out to get them in

some way. They might act in a resistant, hostile, or threatening manner. This can be very hard for therapists who rely on relational skills like attunement and empathy for building a strong therapeutic alliance. However, knowing that a client is compromised in psychobiological traits such as intimacy and empathy helps us understand how to adjust our therapeutic approach.

Again, the more a client falls in the Disorganized Self range, the more a therapist may feel like they are not on the same team as their client or begin experiencing countertransference strain in other ways, such as doubting, shaming, or pressuring themself. Therapists may feel like they're not doing well enough. Remember, this is not a personal indictment against you, the therapist. Often, the reality is that therapists are doing very good work; it's just that some clients are more limited in their ability to respond positively. If you are struggling this way with a client and you score them in the Disorganized Self range, this might be a good time to reach out for clinical supervision or perhaps further clinical training. And if your countertransference strain is impacting your personal life, it is important to receive personal support. We'd recommend you consider bringing these reactions into your own therapy. The gift of our most challenging clients is that we can use these challenges for our own professional and personal growth.

The reality is that clients in the Disorganized Self range often need more support than therapists may be able to provide alone, particularly those who work in private practice. It is important to reach out to their other healthcare providers and work collaboratively to support this client. Consider referring clients out if you feel you are working beyond your scope of competence or scope of practice. Often other clinicians or facilities are better suited to work with a client, which does not mean you have failed. Making wise professional decisions includes taking your client's unique situation into consideration and making the most supportive treatment choice you have available. In fact, if you are noticing resistance to considering referring a client out to another provider or facility, that may be a sign of a countertransference reaction and something for you to reflect on. There are generally other options available, and we encourage therapists to be open to all possibilities for optimal support for our clients.

Our hope is that this NARM Personality Spectrum model will help you with the wide variety of clients you are working with. The intention is that it can help you better understand your clients' internal worlds. By seeing our clients more clearly, we can establish an even stronger process of intersubjectivity in supporting our clients in healing from complex trauma.

REFLECTIVE EXERCISE

We invite you to take a few moments for a personal reflection using the NARM Personality Spectrum:

- In your life now, we invite you to reflect on your present capacity on each of these ten psychobiological traits, and use those to reflect on your overall psychobiological capacity in your present life. We invite you to go back through the ten psychobiological traits and score yourself if that feels useful. If you scored yourself, please write this present score down.

- Then think back to an earlier time in your life, perhaps as a teenager or young adult; we invite you to reflect on your capacity on each of these ten psychobiological traits at that point, and use those to reflect on your overall psychobiological capacity at that time. We invite you to go back through the ten psychobiological traits and score yourself if that feels useful. If you scored yourself, please write this past score down.

- Now we invite you to compare where you are now (present score) to where you were then (past score).

  - If your present score has increased from your past score, what has helped you shift in terms of increasing your psychobiological capacity?

We invite you to notice your internal experience as you reflect on this exercise.

PART III

Applying NARM
with Clients

CHAPTER 10

Clinical Transcript Demonstrating the NARM Organizing Principles

Aiyana is a fifty-year-old, divorced mother of two adult children, living in the small-town community where she was born and raised. She identifies as Native American and was raised within a Native American family and community. She left home at seventeen with a college scholarship and became a professor, author, and expert in her professional field. After many years away working at a major university, she returned to her hometown to take care of her elderly parents. Since returning, she has also moved into a caretaking role for several of her siblings who have been dealing with significant substance abuse and mental health issues. She commutes over an hour each way so that she can still teach at the university, though recently her family responsibilities have her considering teaching online, cutting back her teaching schedule, or even taking early retirement.

Aiyana reports that she has a history of anxiety and depression and has managed her symptoms by being a "workaholic." She has been treated by a psychiatrist off and on since college. She had tried hypnotherapy, meditation, and yoga previously but had never been in psychotherapy before. She had a series of panic attacks upon returning home, which led her to seek out psychotherapy. Since being back home and living among her family of origin, she began to recognize the extent of her adverse childhood

experiences and wondered if her depression, anxiety, and panic might be related to her unresolved trauma. She heard about me (Brad), and my work in trauma, from a friend who had been a client. This is from our second session together.

In the transcript of the therapy session, running commentary in the form of clinical annotations has been added to help readers identify the NARM principles and skills we have presented throughout this book. We also include our own personal reflections—including our working hypothesis, counter-transference reactions, and self-disclosure. These clinical annotations are designed to demonstrate transparency in how we organize NARM therapy sessions and promote greater ease in applying NARM interventions.

Please note: This transcript is of a real client session. The client's name and other revealing information have been changed to protect confidentiality, and the text was minimally edited for clarification and to avoid repetition. Otherwise, this captures the full NARM session with this client.

SPEAKER	TRANSCRIPT	ANNOTATION
Brad	What would you like to get out of our time together today?	Pillar 1: Clarifying the Therapeutic Contract [chapter 3]. There are different ways to state this contracting question, but I prefer to keep it simple.
Aiyana	Something keeps coming up for me. It's anger. But it's really about my inability of accepting myself. I'd like to be real. So I guess it will be self-appreciation, caring for myself.	Often clients will have difficulty with this initial contracting question. I notice right away that Aiyana has answers, but she gives me several answers, and none were said very confidently. I am interested in this statement "caring for myself," because I see what she's doing right now, being in therapy, as an act of caring about herself. Highlighting how she is caring for herself right now might be an avenue to explore with her around agency [chapter 5], but at this point, I am

SPEAKER	TRANSCRIPT	ANNOTATION
Aiyana *(continued)*		going to reflect on this statement in service of continued clarification into her intention for our session (Pillar 1).
Brad	What's it like to say that—that you'd like self-appreciation and caring for yourself?	As I continue to ask clarifying questions around her intention, my intention here is to see if this "self-appreciation" and "caring for herself" feels right for her in terms of what she'd like to get out of our time together. We do the best we can to use our client's exact words. Also, notice the agency language that I use in asking about how she relates to her internal experience—"what's it like to say that?" as opposed to something more open like "how does that feel?" This is an example of the structuralizing (versus processing) process described in chapter 5.
Aiyana	It's hard. I'm telling myself, "Oh, that's fake."	I notice how quickly she self-attacks. This may reflect a process of connection-disconnection. It was my impression that her stating that she wants to care for herself is a movement toward greater connection, and as we have discussed throughout this book, self-attack is a strategy of disconnection.
Brad	So there's part of you that brings up that you want to care for yourself, that you'd like self-appreciation. And then really quickly, it sounds like that there's another part that says that that's a fake concept to want for yourself.	I am just reflecting back the two sides, connection and disconnection, without choosing sides or asking her to choose sides. I want to see how she might relate to this.

SPEAKER	TRANSCRIPT	ANNOTATION
Aiyana	Right. Like phony, selfish.	She's giving me an understanding of how she relates to her intention to care for herself, calling it "fake," "phony," and "selfish." I am also aware that there may be cultural and intergenerational binds here as well. Aiyana is a Native American woman who left her home community and created a life for herself different than the expectations of the family and cultural systems she was raised with and is now back interacting closely with. My early working hypothesis [chapter 4] is that there could be a bind here where caring for herself, seen from a certain perspective, is labeled fake, phony, and selfish. She may have also internalized this.
Brad	Selfish? Phony?	I am reflecting back these words to see if they still feel resonant for her and if she has any more she wants to add.
Aiyana	Yeah, those are the words that come up.	The wording she uses here, "the words that come up," is not from an agency perspective. The way she says it makes it sound like it just happened. But from an agency perspective, a more accurate description is that when she wants something for herself, she tells herself she is being selfish.
Brad	OK. Are those words familiar? Like when you've tried to care for yourself in the past— *[she jumps in to answer before I finish my sentence]*	This clarifying question emerges from my early working hypothesis. The words may not be at all familiar to her, or they may be very familiar to her, and either way it will give

SPEAKER	TRANSCRIPT	ANNOTATION
Brad (continued)		me information that I will use to continue understanding how Aiyana is organizing her experience, specifically in relationship to her intention of self-appreciation and caring for herself.
Aiyana	Yes. Because it doesn't feel like I'm worthwhile to do that. I'll go through the motions of self-care …	Not feeling worthwhile is what we refer to as a *shame-based identification*. This could also be an example of splitting—the way as children we protect our caregivers by making us bad, or using her words, not feeling "worthwhile."
		As she was saying this, I also started feeling sad, and she reports this same feeling as well. Although I have to check my Big C countertransference, my sense was that this was part of my resonance, or little c countertransference [chapter 8]. As for the sadness, we refer to grief as an opportunity for reconnection to the heart [chapter 7]. I am holding this as part of my working hypothesis—that part of her appreciating herself more fully may be about her connecting to unresolved grief.
Brad	So if it's OK, maybe we can just slow down a little bit, because I was feeling into that sadness too. [*we both sit in quiet for a few moments*] So you've made attempts toward self-care, and you go through the motions, but you don't feel worthwhile to do that?	I invited her to slow down also to give myself time to practice self-inquiry, because I wasn't sure in the moment if the sadness was coming from me or I was picking it up from her, so it seemed useful to take a little time for us both to be with the sadness. Not all clients can be present to their internal states, so this gives me

SPEAKER	TRANSCRIPT	ANNOTATION
Brad *(continued)*		a glimpse into Aiyana's capacity for connection, self-reflection, self-regulation, and presence [chapter 9].
Aiyana	I get the sense that I'm not worthwhile to do that, like it's frivolous, and couldn't be good for me. No, that's not it, like it shouldn't be... [*she sits in reflection for a few moments*] I guess it doesn't feel like I imagined it to be because people talk about self-care and... [*she doesn't finish her sentence and sits in reflection again for a few moments*] There's a disconnect within me for feeling it.	As she shares her thoughts, they seem quite fragmented to me. The last part struck me as important, particularly due to my working hypothesis, that she might want something for herself—in this example, self-care—and begins to disconnect from her intention. So I will ask more about that as we continue to clarify the therapeutic contract (Pillar 1).
Brad	Let me know how this lands for you, but it sounds like the disconnect comes because you don't feel worthwhile enough? Like somehow you don't deserve to treat yourself to self-care?	I continue to ask clarifying questions (part of Pillar 1), but it's starting to feel like we may be moving into exploratory questions (Pillar 2), so I want to make sure that before I go any further I return to the initial question about what she wants for herself out of our process together (Pillar 1), which I will do next.
Aiyana	Yes, exactly, I don't deserve it.	This seems to land for her. I experience what feels like a settling.
Brad	OK, so it seems like we're getting clearer on this theme. And from this place, I'm curious what would you like for yourself out of our time together?	I revisit the contracting question (Pillar 1). I want to point out that therapy doesn't start after we've agreed to a therapeutic contract. Pillar 1 can be very organizing for many clients. And for me as the therapist, the contracting process thus far

SPEAKER	TRANSCRIPT	ANNOTATION
Brad (continued)		has given me so much useful information. As I have already named, I am starting to form a working hypothesis that holds a tentative understanding of the core dilemma—what might be getting in the way of what she most wants [chapter 2]—and that will inform my inquiry process moving forward (Pillar 2). I also want to point out that her struggle in answering my initial contracting question could be the exact situation she is dealing with—that she shuts herself down around self-care. And here she is getting "self-care" in therapy. My working hypothesis is that this might be creating a core dilemma for her.
Aiyana	I guess... [*she pauses for a moment*] Accepting that I'm worthwhile. Like, I really have a hard time doing that—accepting that I am a valuable person, to myself.	This feels very powerful to me. Sometimes in NARM we call this a *kerplunk* moment, meaning that something lands for our clients as they connect to their intention; often there's a settling, grounding, and organizing process as clients connect to something true for them in an embodied way.
Brad	What's it like as you say right now, at least the intention for that?	I'm curious how she may be relating to what I named as a kerplunk moment.
Aiyana	It felt good to say that. I have kind of an opening in my body, a little bit more open. I don't feel scared or mad at myself for saying it.	I noticed what looked to me like a grounding or settling, so it's good to have her self-report align with my observations.

SPEAKER	TRANSCRIPT	ANNOTATION
Brad	Oh, so something seems different internally for you now the second time around. I notice that you're not calling yourself selfish or thinking it's phony. There seems to be a different experience than what was happening before.	I point out that this time she did not disconnect like she did previously when she stated her intention; that in the here and now she is relating to herself differently than she was even just a few minutes ago. Here I am supporting the possibility of agency [chapter 5]. Instead of relating to herself through self-criticism, there might be something new emerging.
Aiyana	Right.	
Brad	So how would it be for us to explore together what's getting in the way of feeling worthwhile?	We often word the contract as "what's getting in the way of" what the client says they most want for themselves, as opposed to agreeing to work toward a specific goal. This keeps the process more open and doesn't force us to choose sides in an internal conflict that we may not yet be aware of. Clients may want us to choose sides, and in those cases we would want to work directly with how they believe this would help them, again without colluding with a specific strategy that they may be using. Agreeing to explore the obstacles helps reinforce the client's capacity for agency and keeps us, as therapists, in an open, receptive, and curious place in relationship to our client's internal conflict.
Aiyana	Yes, I think that'd be good. I would like to. I'd really like to look at this.	This is the consent that allows me to know we can begin our exploratory process (moving into Pillar 2). I also felt into what

SPEAKER	TRANSCRIPT	ANNOTATION
Aiyana *(continued)*		I would describe as a gentle fierceness. Almost as if right in this moment she is taking care of herself and appreciating herself just by identifying what she wants for herself. This often happens in NARM therapy— that by clarifying their intention, the client is already doing what they most want for themself, or at least the beginning stages of it.
Brad	I appreciate the energy that's coming from you as you name that. And I'd be happy to explore this with you, and how this might be getting in the way of you caring for yourself. I am also aware that you may be doing in this moment what you would like for yourself. I mean, you could look at this process so far with me as an example of you taking action to address something that's important for you. And I would define that as an act of self-care.	Notice how I explicitly agree to the therapeutic contract. This now becomes the organizing thread as we move forward. We can always continue to refine and adjust, or even change, the contract. I then reflect back my observation that she's doing in this very moment what she wants for herself, which is part of Pillar 3: Reinforcing Agency.
Aiyana	This doesn't feel like self-care for me. Because I feel like I'm pushing myself. I do hope we come to some understanding about this. But I'm kind of nervous.	She holds a different perspective on what I shared. And I notice how she's reporting anxiety right now, compared to just a few moments ago where she was feeling open. I am curious about both.
Brad	OK, so you're feeling a little bit nervous. Are you saying that the nervousness is connected to how this doesn't feel like an act of self-care?	Pillar 2: Asking Exploratory Questions. I'm curious if her nervousness may be connected to what I reflected back to her.

SPEAKER	TRANSCRIPT	ANNOTATION
Aiyana	I picture self-care like a nice massage, or really relaxed, something I really enjoy.	I am hearing the word "relaxed" in contrast to what she said before about "pushing herself." So I begin wondering if pushing herself could be a strategy that is getting in the way of giving herself the self-care she wants. And on a deeper level, if she doesn't feel worthwhile, perhaps she may not feel she deserves "good things." These reflections are all part of my working hypothesis.
Brad	So what I hear you saying is that because you're feeling anxious, that doesn't fit exactly with what you are perceiving as self-care. Although the thing that's a little bit confusing for me is that before you felt like sometimes it felt phony when you were trying to do those things.	Notice how I reference back to the dynamic she shared earlier, where even hearing herself say she wanted self-care felt phony and fake. This is an intervention designed to support her reflection on how she is relating to this desire she has for herself.
Aiyana	Yes. Right.	
Brad	So, I don't know about you, but it's possible that maybe sometimes self-care might be things that also bring up some anxiety.	I am just reflecting this back as a possibility. Personal growth— which I do view as self-care—is often very difficult and can take people into scary places.
Aiyana	Right. [*reflecting on this for a few moments*] Self-care brings up anxiety?	She says this in a quizzical tone, like she's not sure.
Brad	Before you were saying that some of the things that people talk about for self-care, they feel kind of phony to you. But then just now you were thinking about those same things for yourself.	I'm reflecting back a possible bind here: that she wants to feel more relaxed, for example, but then she feels that it's phony.

SPEAKER	TRANSCRIPT	ANNOTATION
Aiyana	Right. It's true. It feels phony, some of the self-care things feel phony.	She is starting to gain greater self-awareness of a pattern. Remember, she said at the beginning she has trouble with self-acceptance and feeling worthwhile, so it makes sense to me that if she feels that, it would feel fake or phony to give care for herself as that requires her to feel accepting and worthwhile.
Brad	Yes, and right now, does this feel phony?	Pillar 3: Reinforcing Agency. I ask her to reflect on how it feels in this moment for her to relate to doing something for herself.
Aiyana	No, because I'm really invested in it.	My working hypothesis here: Because she is invested in this for herself, perhaps that means she does in fact feel worthwhile?
Brad	Invested in … what's the "it"?	This is a good example of an intervention we refer to as drilling down [chapter 4], which is part of Pillar 2.
Aiyana	I'm invested in myself.	That's a big statement, and a shift from where she was earlier where she didn't feel worthwhile. This might be an example of a movement toward disidentification [chapters 2 and 6].
Brad	And how is it for you to say that?	Pillar 4: Reflecting Psychobiological Shifts. I noticed a sense that I might describe as strength or confidence in how she was speaking and looking to me.
Aiyana	Relaxing.	Which is part of what she said she wanted before. I also notice her taking this in, which to me is an expression of self-care.

SPEAKER	TRANSCRIPT	ANNOTATION
Brad	Relaxing.	Mirroring back to her a word that feels significant in her process. This is a simple intervention in support of the relational process [chapter 8]. This mirroring intervention gives her an opportunity to be with her experience as I am holding space with her.
Aiyana	To … feel … [*it took her some time to get her words out*] To feel like I'm somebody, like I'm competent.	Another very powerful statement.
Brad	To feel like you're somebody, like you're competent.	Again, another mirroring intervention. I don't want to over-complicate this; sometimes these simple interventions can be quite powerful.
Aiyana	Oh my God, here it comes, I'm going to cry. [*she starts softly crying*]	I don't know what's driving her tears, but for me, this feels like a reconnection to her heart. If you've lived for so many years feeling like you're not worth-while, not competent and not a somebody—all deep shame-based identifications—begin-ning to feel in your body that you are worthwhile, competent, and a somebody can be very powerful. Additionally, she is reporting her body relaxing, which often signifies physio-logical loosening that can be accompanied by emotional feelings.
Brad	Is it OK to let yourself have the tears? Because I'll tell you something, Aiyana, it doesn't look phony to me.	I know that she might not feel that her crying feels like self-care, but I am inviting the pos-sibility here that it is an act of self-appreciation and embody-ing authenticity.

SPEAKER	TRANSCRIPT	ANNOTATION
Aiyana	Yes, it feels real. [more tears]	She names what I feel inside myself, that these are very real and important tears, which could be an expression of the primary emotion of grief [chapter 7].
Brad	You used the word "competent," like you're invested in feeling competent, but, the word you used before was "worthwhile."	I'm curious how she is relating these two words. This is part of Pillar 2, drilling down [chapter 4].
Aiyana	Yes. It's like… [holding back more tears, almost a sense of her choking on them] This doesn't happen a lot in my life.	
Brad	This?	Another example of drilling down.
Aiyana	Feeling competent. [holding back tears] I'm going to really lose it now. [she starts crying more strongly]	Notice the tears come strongly as she connects to this deep feeling of competence. She didn't seem ready to take in what I had shared about feeling worthwhile, which is fine; it's an example of something I would bookmark for possible revisiting later.
Brad	Just take your time. There's no pressure.	I heard her at the beginning of the session talk about pushing herself. Part of my working hypothesis is that Aiyana may have some autonomy survival style patterns, which can include putting lots of pressure on oneself, and perhaps expecting that I have an agenda or expectations for her. So by inviting her to take her time I am reflecting that I have no agenda and am not expecting anything from her. I am just being present to her experience and don't need anything from her; I'm also inviting her to be present to her experience and not push herself either.

SPEAKER	TRANSCRIPT	ANNOTATION
Aiyana	I never let myself cry. It feels really good to cry.	When a client says something like this, it usually refers to a primary emotion. Default emotions generally are easier and more familiar for a client, whereas a primary emotion is generally more unfamiliar. Default emotions don't generally feel good to connect with; in fact, they often feel overwhelming and out of control. When a client reconnects to their primary emotions, it often feels organizing and life-affirming—or, using her words, an act of self-appreciation [chapter 7].
Brad	If it's OK, I'd like to share with you my perspective. [*she nods yes*] I'd like to share with you that from my perspective—this is an act of real self-care.	I'm responding to her saying it feels good. I am connecting it back to the things she mentioned she envisioned self-care to be, like a massage or other good feelings. This intervention is potentially supporting a new way of her relating to her own emotions.
Aiyana	Yeah, it is. [*her crying softens and she seems to relax again*] I think I just have looked at it as I have to always do the next thing to get to where I want to go. But this feels more real. To have someone be there with me. I can do it all day long in private. But it doesn't push me to be with it … I just hide it.	I'm hearing that there is something important about this process being done with me, another person, that is supporting her to take her time to be with herself in a new way. I feel touched by her simple acknowledgment of our process, which for many clients can be experienced as deeply supportive and intimate. I also am feeling into some of what feels like my own Big C countertransference. I myself have my own autonomy patterns, and I know what it is like to push myself very hard.

SPEAKER	TRANSCRIPT	ANNOTATION
Aiyana (continued)		So I am practicing self-inquiry to discern my own feelings from her experience. I am sitting both with feeling touched and reflecting on my own possible counter-transference. All of this is part of the R in NARM [chapter 8].
Brad	So you've chosen to kind of push your edge here.	Pillar 3: Reinforcing Agency [chapter 5]. I am flipping the script here. She's used the language around feeling pushed, and now I am framing it as her pushing her edge—as an act of self-care.
Aiyana	Yes.	This in itself feels like an acknowledgment of an increased sense of competence.
Brad	And how is it now that you're here?	Pillar 4: Reflecting Psychobiological Shifts [chapter 6].
Aiyana	I'm feeling competent at feeling sad over it.	I hear an honoring of her reconnection to these core parts of herself.
Brad	Yes. And the way I translate that is just being competent at being real. You don't have to do anything for anyone else, you don't have to prove anything. You don't have to work so hard. You just get to be you.	Pillar 4: Reflecting Psychobiological Shifts, specifically reflecting the possibility of disidentification. She may be able to feel worthwhile just in being herself authentically. This can be profound healing, particularly for someone who has strong autonomy survival style patterns. Additionally, this demonstrates the process of intersubjectivity, because in this moment I was feeling touched from my own sense of being human and the work I have done to accept myself, which allowed me to connect to her increasing sense of feeling worthwhile as a human.

SPEAKER	TRANSCRIPT	ANNOTATION
Aiyana	Yes. Which is really nice. [*more relaxing and settling*]	Many of these interpersonal experiences are not verbally communicated, yet it often seems they are felt by both therapist and client.
Brad	Yes.	
Aiyana	I feel like tingly right now, in my hands and in the back of my head.	Pillar 4: Reflecting Psychobiological Shifts. Sounds like there are some shifts happening physiologically for her now, which often comes with disidentification and an increasing sense of being fully human.
Brad	Does it feel OK?	I just want to make sure these sensations are OK for her to stay present with.
Aiyana	It feels good.	Since she says it feels good, I will just give her space to be with it.
Brad	Hey, maybe it's like a massage after all?	After a few moments, I make a little joke, which is a reference back to what she said earlier about what she thought of as self-care. I also have noted from our previous session that she appreciates humor.
Aiyana	It's my little soul massage. [*laughter*] Feels good.	Beautiful language here: "soul massage."
Brad	[*We sit in silence for several moments where it seems she is very relaxed and settled. And then I notice a slight shift in her.*] So how are you doing as you're giving yourself a soul massage?	I noticed something shift in her, so I want to check in. I am wondering if there might've been a movement toward disconnection after a significant few moments of connection. Tracking connection–disconnection is part of Pillar 4.

SPEAKER	TRANSCRIPT	ANNOTATION
Aiyana	I was looking outside and then started doubting myself, like, "Oh my gosh, what am I doing here?"	Now she is describing the movement toward disconnection with the beginning of self-attack through doubting or judging herself and her efforts toward self-care and deeper self-appreciation. We anticipate this disconnection will happen, and we don't try and force our clients to stay in the connection. Ultimately we are supporting the increasing capacity for clients to stay present to both sides of the connection-disconnection dynamic and learn to tolerate complexity.
Brad	If it's OK, let's try to answer the question that you asked yourself, which is: "What are you doing here?"	Pillar 2: Asking Exploratory Questions, but this time I am using her own question but asking it in a way that is intended to take the self-criticism out of it.
Aiyana	I am trying to ... [she pauses to reflect] ... No, I am working on acceptance of myself as worthwhile.	This goes directly to the root of this whole process, which is about agency, disidentification and connection to her authentic Self.
Brad	And I caught this little switch that you made from "I'm trying to" and then changed it to "I am."	Reflecting back how she corrected herself away from efforting to accepting. This agency intervention reflects how she is shifting old self-rejecting patterns and increasing self-compassion.
Aiyana	Yes.	
Brad	Does that feel different than trying?	Pillar 2 in support of Pillar 3, continuing to refine the difference here in how she's showing up with herself.

SPEAKER	TRANSCRIPT	ANNOTATION
Aiyana	Yes, because I am actively showing that I'm worthwhile.	Again, a reinforcement of agency and disidentification. She can now show up the way she most wants to that she shared with me from the beginning of the session during the contracting process.
Brad	Yes, and again, if it's OK, I'd invite you to just notice how that feels to be present with this.	Pillar 4: Reflecting Psychobiological Shifts. I was observing that strength and confidence that I observed before. Many clients will move right past these shifts, as sometimes they are very subtle, so this is an invitation to check in with her internal state to see how it is to be connected at this moment.
Aiyana	Yes, I feel it in my stomach, like a calming down. It's like a little tingle in the top of my stomach now. Normally I'm like a big ball in my stomach, constricted. But not now.	Supporting the physiological shifts as part of Pillar 4. I anticipate that it very likely will shift at some point, but I am not pushing in any way, just being present to the experience as Aiyana is present with herself in this moment.
Brad	And I want to point out that this releasing and calming comes when you're able to proclaim for yourself that "I am worthwhile."	This is an example of threading, which is part of Pillar 3: Reinforcing Agency. The calming down didn't come out of nowhere. Remember, she said she was nervous before and also pushing herself, both descriptive of sympathetic nervous system states. So she is able to shift into a more parasympathetic nervous system state that allows for calming and settling as she is able to proclaim for herself that "I am worthwhile."

SPEAKER	TRANSCRIPT	ANNOTATION
Aiyana	Right. I am really worthwhile! [*said emphatically, like she was trying it out*] Wow! It has been a long time since I've said that. I'm really trying to break out of that old pattern.	Supporting her to have time with these shifts. Now she's trying it out cognitively, by repeating this word "worthwhile" and seeing how that feels to be present with it. She realizes that she has not been treating herself like she's worthwhile for a long time, which represents a shame-based identification.
Brad	I see that, yes.	Part of Pillar 4, reinforcing that she is breaking out of this old pattern right now in real time. Many times clients dismiss or minimize this occurrence, so I want to gently remind her that this is what's happening. I felt quite moved by sharing in this process with Aiyana, and in this moment I was feeling into a sense of warmth in my heart.
Aiyana	I don't know why, but I've done a lot of things, and none of them felt fulfilled ... or noticed. But right now, I'm being noticed. That's what I'm doing.	This feels very important to me, that she is giving herself this "noticing." She is also being noticed by me in a compassionate way, which supports her to relate to herself differently than viewing herself through objectification, self-rejection, and self-hatred.
Brad	You're allowing yourself to be noticed.	Pillar 3: Reinforcing Agency through reflecting the language back in a way that highlights the new way she is relating to herself, allowing herself to be noticed by herself and me. People who don't feel worthwhile generally relate to being noticed through self-shame and self-rejection. Right now, she is using being noticed to relate to herself in a different way.

SPEAKER	TRANSCRIPT	ANNOTATION
Aiyana	Allowing myself to be ... [*she takes a moment to reflect*] Oh my! [*begins laughing*] ... to be really noticed, yes, that is amazing.	I view this as a moment of reconnection. I observed, and felt within myself, a lot of life energy surging up as she said this.
Brad	And if it's OK, I'd invite you to give yourself some time with that. Giving yourself the permission to be noticed.	Pillar 4: Reflecting Psychobiological Shifts and offering an invitation to be present to what she's experiencing. Notice that we're not pushing for our clients to experience "positive" states; we're just inviting them to be present to what is happening. I am anticipating that at some point she may shift toward disconnection, and if so, we will explore that process.
Aiyana	Yes, it feels OK. At this moment, I'm feeling it ... [*pauses*] ... that I'm really like ... [*pauses*] ... I can't say the word.	It seems to me she's feeling into something very deep and profound.
Brad	It's OK, there's no rush, just take your time.	Naming a strategy she has used and reminding her that I have no agenda for her and that she can take the time she needs with her experience.
Aiyana	That I'm really worthwhile. That I am an important person.	Sometimes in these moments, it almost feels like a rebirth. I feel it can be a very sacred process of profound transformation as we dissolve the old patterns that have been limiting us and embody a new way of feeling about ourselves. A coming home to our true and most authentic Self.
Brad	If it's OK, just continue to take your time with that.	Pillar 4: Reflecting Psychobiological Shifts by continuing to invite her to take all the time she needs with this new experience. This might be seen as the savasana phase of NARM.

SPEAKER	TRANSCRIPT	ANNOTATION
Aiyana	We've talked about that being in two worlds, and you know that is really hard. You have to leave some people, a little bit, not all the way, but they get mad at you for going to school or they get mad at you for changing. They think you've changed because you got an education, and then they don't want to talk anymore. Or the relationship just feels different than it used to because they think you're too smart now. This just came up for me. [*pauses to reflect*] … Wow, I'm having a huge breakthrough here … to really be noticed and witnessed. I'm going to sit with that.	Now she's describing the bind, or what we call the *core dilemma*. She is naming that people have reactions as she embraces increased autonomy, agency, and self-activation. There are current people in her life, but I sense that there are deeper cultural and intergenerational binds here too (often these cultural and especially intergenerational binds are unconscious and therefore go unnamed). The act of separation-individuation is a threat to a child when experiencing attachment and environmental failures, so the adaptive survival style patterns serve to inhibit our movement toward authenticity.
		This piece of feeling noticed and witnessed, to me, speaks to the new ways she is allowing herself to show up and relate to herself showing up with greater self-compassion. Also notice at the end she says, "I'm going to sit with that." For the first time, she's giving herself more space and not relating to herself with such pressure. That's another possible sign of disidentification.
Brad	So there's some people in your life, whether past or present, who have noticed you, but when they see you doing these things for yourself like getting educated and getting a career and all these things, they have a belief about you or have some kind of judgment about you? They have a reaction to you?	Pillar 2: Asking Exploratory Questions. What I am specifically curious about is: from this place of feeling more connected, how does she feel about people who may have given her the message that her authenticity is a threat? I wonder if there may be some emotion around it. This speaks to the Emotional Completion Model in NARM [chapter 7].

SPEAKER	TRANSCRIPT	ANNOTATION
Aiyana	Yes, definitely a reaction.	Acknowledging the reality of how they have been with her, as opposed to taking responsibility and blaming herself for other people's reactions—this reverses the splitting that we hold in child consciousness where we internalize others' reactions as something about us personally. This is all part of the process of shifting from child consciousness into adult consciousness.
Brad	And what do you feel about that now, about those people? Here you are, following your sense of self and what's right for you, and they have this reaction to you doing that— [*she jumps in before I finish my sentence*]	Pillar 2, continuing to ask about how she feels as she reflects on their reaction to her authenticity and self-activation.
Aiyana	I feel really clear right now, I feel super clear. I'm the same person, I'm the exact same person. So that belongs to them, not to me.	Here is a protest, an expression of healthy aggression. I could feel the clarity, strength, and confidence. This feels like another significant shift.
Brad	Yes, I invite you to just notice that "it belongs to them, not to me." [*I give her a few moments to reflect on that*] And from my perspective, to say something like that you only can say when you feel worthwhile.	Pillar 4, which includes a piece of psychoeducation here, where I am tying together this statement to the experience of feeling more worthwhile. It's in service of supporting disidentification and adult consciousness.
Aiyana	Yes, everything's brighter. Like, visually. Outside like the room just got really clear. The background … [*looking around more*] Oh my goodness, I feel really clear. I feel really worthwhile right now!	Often when clients are reconnecting to themselves in this way, they will report significant physiological shifts, and one that is common is seeing more clearly. We don't exactly know what is happening

SPEAKER	TRANSCRIPT	ANNOTATION
Aiyana (continued)		physiologically, but we have many years of anecdotal evidence within somatic psychology that describes the profound shifts in clients' eyes when these internal trauma patterns shift; and clients often report seeing more clearly or even seeing more, like taking in more of their environment. It's a joke in our trauma trainings that a long-term client will notice a painting in our office that has been there for ten years, but it's the first time they've really "seen" it.
Brad	And I noticed that it flowed easier off your tongue that time.	Pillar 4. Earlier she was saying "I feel worthwhile" timidly or even questioningly, but this time she said it confidently.
Aiyana	Right. Yes, it's nice.	In this moment, as I looked at her, she looked like she was beaming, as if she was coming alive.
Brad	It's nice. And what are you noticing internally, in your body, as you're sitting with this clear, nice feeling?	Pillar 4. This intervention is designed to support the possibility of an anchoring of this powerful experience in her body.
Aiyana	Clear. Relaxed. I am feeling worthwhile.	I am observing that she reports her internal experience with greater confidence and strength, which is quite different than how she was earlier in the session.
Brad	And last time when you were in this place, you had these thoughts of people who have been in your life who have had a reaction to you really showing up and being worthwhile and being seen and received.	This is part of Pillar 4 that is almost an anticipation of a possible disconnection. I noticed last time that the disconnection came as she was feeling worthwhile and then started thinking about these people in her life who have

SPEAKER	TRANSCRIPT	ANNOTATION
Brad *(continued)*		a reaction to her autonomy and authenticity, so I bring it up to see how she may be relating to it from this place. It's also a way of keeping connection and dis-connection in relationship. It's so easy for clients to feel that they have to choose one side, and I am bringing it up here to support the possibility she can hold both without having to choose one, and find a new way of relating to this core dilemma. I use this intervention quite often as I find that this capacity to hold dual awareness supports increasing psychobiological capacity.
Aiyana	Yes.	
Brad	And now?	
Aiyana	I feel OK. I feel comfortable, relaxed. Normally I would have that shame, but I don't have of any of that. I would normally be in my head right now and I'm totally not there. I feel good. I feel noticed. I feel important to myself. Like I'm noticing all these ways I'm with myself.	She's speaking to the integra-tion process of reconnecting back to herself and support-ing greater organization and coherency.
Brad	Again, I invite you to take all the time you need with that, with your own noticing of yourself.	Pillar 4, supporting her to be present to this process in this new way. Supporting disidentifi-cation and perhaps planting the seeds for post-traumatic growth.
Aiyana	I feel competent, happy inside.	Notice she returns to the word "competent" from the beginning of the session. We've been working this thread the entire session. This is the power of Pillar 1 in helping organize,

SPEAKER	TRANSCRIPT	ANNOTATION
Aiyana *(continued)*		frame, and support working with complex trauma patterns without moving into fragmentation or overwhelm.
Brad	So this is completely an invitation and we don't need to do this. But since you're at this place of feeling relaxed, happy, and competent inside, I'm going to make the invitation that if you want to, if you want to challenge yourself even a little bit more, you can bring up a few of these people who have had a reaction to you changing, and notice what happens for you as you reflect on them. Again, it's an invitation and if you don't feel like doing this, that's perfectly fine.	This intervention is an invitation to see how she is relating to the same dynamic that she experienced before but from a different place. It may support her movement toward increasing disidentification. It's also going to give me more information about how she is relating to herself in this moment.
Aiyana	Sounds good. I'm going to do it.	If she wouldn't want to, that's completely fine, and I would go in another direction. It's really just an invitation for self-inquiry.
Brad	OK, just do it in a way that feels right to you.	Wanting to remind her of this pattern of how she pushes herself and that she can determine for herself—based on her own sense of Self—the right way to do this reflective exercise.
Aiyana	[*she takes time to reflect*] That made me dizzy.	She is describing a physiological reaction, which I am curious about.
Brad	Made you dizzy?	Asking directly about her experience.
Aiyana	Yeah, kind of makes me dizzy. And I feel kind of squeezed inside, like in my stomach. I want to do it again.	Now she refers to the squeezing she has mentioned previously that happens in her stomach. Then she says she wants to try again, which is

SPEAKER	TRANSCRIPT	ANNOTATION
Aiyana *(continued)*		interesting—instead of running away from the dizziness, which many clients might do, she chooses to revisit it.
Brad	OK. Again, please do it in the way that works for you.	Reminding her indirectly that she doesn't have to push herself, part of an old familiar pattern.
Aiyana	Yes.	
Brad	So from this place of feeling more competent, how is it this time to reflect on these people who have had reactions to you?	As I check in, I thread back that she was feeling more competent when I offered this invitation as a platform for reflecting on these people.
Aiyana	Much better. It was nice.	I find it interesting to hear how her experience shifted.
Brad	What was different about it this time?	I am genuinely curious about what was different this time around, so I move into inquiry (Pillar 2).
Aiyana	I noticed smiles from them. Before I was seeing something different, but this time I was actually able to see smiles.	Of course, she's just envisioning these people, but whereas previously she saw them having a reaction to her, this time she's seeing smiles.
Brad	What do you think those smiles are in response to?	Pillar 2: Asking Exploratory Questions. This was not a random question. The intention was to invite a reflection of how she is feeling about herself. It's possible that she might be experiencing herself now as worthwhile and feeling more confident to show herself to others, even those who have had reactions to her in the past.
Aiyana	See, that question ... [*she stops before finishing this sentence and reflects*] The thought	I notice a quick disconnection, using a self-rejecting strategy (while she's projecting the "fake

SPEAKER	TRANSCRIPT	ANNOTATION
Aiyana (continued)	comes, "They're just fake smiling at you." That thought came back really quick.	smiling" onto them, clearly she's the one who is thinking this), but I am also aware of how conscious she was of this shift toward disconnection. To me, this demonstrates increasing psychobiological capacity (adult consciousness).
Brad	I notice how you tracked that thought coming back really quick this time. Those thoughts are often unconscious for most of us. So you caught that old thought.	Part of Pillar 4, tracking connection and disconnection, and a little bit of psychoeducation.
Aiyana	But I don't feel that now. Like I would usually tighten my stomach around these thoughts. But I don't feel that now.	I am noticing here her language is reinforcing agency. She's aware now that the tightening that she experiences somatically is related to these self-rejecting thoughts.
Brad	OK, so you just noticed it as a thought, but you didn't tighten your stomach.	Pillar 3: Reinforcing Agency. Reflecting back to how she related to her internal experience differently this time around—she didn't identify with it.
Aiyana	And then I'm thinking, no, they wouldn't do that.	This is a new way of relating to herself and her vision of those in her life. Oftentimes we are caught in projections onto those around us, and it's possible she's shifting those projections.
Brad	So if they wouldn't do that, and if they're not faking, what might they be smiling in response to?	This question, asking what they are smiling in response to, is inviting her to identify something internally about herself that they may be seeing and responding to with an authentic smile.
Aiyana	[tears softly coming again] Watching me become important to myself.	Disidentification. Instead of relating to herself as not worthwhile, now she is embracing this

SPEAKER	TRANSCRIPT	ANNOTATION
Aiyana (continued)		process of becoming important to herself. Which is what she said she wanted at the beginning of the session, an expression of self-care and self-appreciation.
Brad	That was my guess too.	Not only was it a guess, I was feeling it toward her too. I was very moved to watch her becoming important to herself. I felt a strong sense of heartfulness, which I had actually been feeling throughout the session, but it definitely became obvious in this moment [chapter 8].
Aiyana	Yes.	
Brad	How is it to take that in?	Pillar 4: Reflecting Psychobiological Shifts.
Aiyana	It feels nice. Feels like a smoothness, and feels like a smoothness coming through me. [*gesturing a flowing movement across her torso*]	Different than the constriction she described earlier.
Brad	Yes, if it's OK to take your time with that. It's very different than that stomach tightening that you've had in the past.	Notice how I am weaving in the old state of disconnection as she is presently experiencing this state of connection.
Brad	How are you doing overall?	
Aiyana	Good. Really good right now.	
Brad	Well, I don't know exactly what those people are really thinking about you. But I do know for me that I really appreciate seeing you become important to yourself.	I was speaking from my sense of heartfulness. Part of Pillar 4 can be appropriate self-disclosure by the therapist. We need to be mindful that it be authentic and done in relationship. I was feeling very touched and honored to be part of this process and wanted to share that with her.

SPEAKER	TRANSCRIPT	ANNOTATION
Aiyana	Thank you, Brad. It's been a long push ... but I feel like I've arrived.	Notice the language of the "push" that goes back to the old strategy of working hard, pressuring, pushing. But this moment of feeling that she has "arrived" is very powerful and significant.
Brad	And maybe there's a possibility that it doesn't have to be pushed so much moving forward.	I'm offering the possibility that she may be able to embody her growth without these old strategies, as she has today in our session. This reflection of a new possibility relates to her original intention of wanting to show up with greater self-care.
Aiyana	Right ... that's one of the things about the people in my life. If you're not having that struggle, like there's something's wrong with you. I don't have to have that struggle anymore. I don't have to.	This is very common from clients who have come from certain communities or cultures, that one way they have adapted is to push, pressure, work hard, and if there's not a struggle, then there's risk or danger. I have experience of that myself based on my own cultural and intergenerational trauma, so I know that first-hand. I get the sense that she may be speaking to something very big here that may relate to cultural and intergenerational trauma patterns. This runs very deep. The question for another time will be how Aiyana is able to embody deeper into her authenticity while still being able to feel connected to her family and culture in an authentic way. This relates to the 50-50 balance [chapter 2].
Brad	Yes. And I imagine that you may continue to bump up against	For future sessions with Aiyana, I imagine we will continue to

SPEAKER	TRANSCRIPT	ANNOTATION
Brad *(continued)*	that bind, especially since these people are still so actively in your life.	address these larger binds that run so deep. I also like to anticipate possible challenges that seem likely, as it allows clients to relate to the potential challenge from a place of adult consciousness where they don't have to disconnect; in fact, they often relate to this potential challenge with a sense of confidence, strength, and hope. We referred to "consensus reality" in chapter 9, which is acknowledging the reality of being an adult in a complex world. We don't want to infantilize or lie to our clients that everything is going to be perfect from here on out. Again, this intervention is designed to strengthen her feeling of competence by supporting the possibility for increasing capacity to tolerate distress.
Aiyana	Yes, probably so.	Seems to me she's responding from adult consciousness here.
Brad	So I mean, you know, this … the funny thing about this work is that on some level, it looks like a small little piece of work, but it's— [*she interrupts me with excitement*]	I'm reflecting back my sense that what she has connected to here today is significant, and it's so easy to minimize it. Like I mentioned previously, I felt as if there was a sacred quality to it, a rebirth, a coming back home to herself.
Aiyana	It's really, really, really big! [*laughter*]	I can see her taking in the significance of this.
Brad	Yes, it's really big, really big.	I start wondering if there may be another disconnection coming as I see her really sitting with the depth of connection she's presently experiencing.

SPEAKER	TRANSCRIPT	ANNOTATION
Aiyana	I feel so clear. It's almost like I've been in a fog before this. It's not like some huge life-changing event. I mean, obviously it is. I don't know, maybe I'm going back. I'm doing it, I'm starting it …	She's using similar language to what she used before about feeling "clear." Again, this is common for clients coming out of these adaptive survival style patterns to experience greater clarity after "fog." In fact, alterations in consciousness are a symptom for many people who have experienced developmental trauma. Some people refer to it as a "trance," and here Aiyana calls it a "fog." For clients with strong dissociative features, it can be experienced like a deep fog, and coming out can be powerful.
		So Aiyana begins feeling into the clarity, and then she starts feeling the internal bind again ("I'm going back. I'm doing it, I'm starting it"). The question I am holding here: What would it mean for her if this were a "life-changing event"? How would that impact the people in her life? How might it impact her relationship to her family, her community, and her culture?
Brad	You're starting what?	Pillar 2: Asking Exploratory Questions. I'm wanting to understand exactly what she's starting.
Aiyana	Feels like I'm … talking it backwards.	At this point in our session, she has become very aware of her internal process. To use her language from earlier, she is "noticing" the ways she is relating to herself, which is reflective of increasing agency.

SPEAKER	TRANSCRIPT	ANNOTATION
Brad	And again, this is the second or maybe third time you've caught that so quickly. And that's probably going to happen. Those thoughts are usually part of the process. But you're developing an ability to notice them and be with them differently than you have before.	Pillar 4, I am supporting her in tracking her shifts between connection and disconnection. I am reinforcing agency here too.
Aiyana	Yeah, I feel really good about that! So thank you for that.	She references me, and I'm happy to take some of the credit here, but as Larry likes to say, we're only the "copilot." She's the one who is fueling this transformative process.
Brad	Thank you. [*we sit in silence for a few moments as I feel things settling*] Quite a massage, huh?	I am referencing the massage joke from earlier, as a way of reinforcing that she is engaging in self-care and that comes out of her relating to herself as worthwhile. Humor, when used judiciously, can support the disidentification process. We often see clients begin taking themselves less seriously. Therapy can feel quite playful in these moments.
Aiyana	[*laughter*] Yes! My soul massage.	Reinforcing for herself that she can take care of herself and it doesn't have to be experienced as a threat.
Brad	Does this feel like an OK place for us to wrap up, or is there anything left over for you?	We're out of time, but I just want to make sure if there's anything left, she has a chance to name it. Obviously we can't get to everything in one session, and in NARM we don't put pressure on ourselves to tie everything up. But if there is something still up for her, we can bookmark it for our next session.

SPEAKER	TRANSCRIPT	ANNOTATION
Aiyana	I feel good. Thank you. I felt very natural working with this. I didn't feel any sense of you trying to take me anywhere. It felt very noninvasive. This felt very powerful—to sit here and experience that depth of feeling, and to connect to what I was seeking, it just feels really amazing.	This is nice feedback for me. The noninvasive part highlights the importance of the NARM Relational Model. It does help me as the therapist to create a certain internal and relational space that clients experience as noninvasive. Additionally, the NARM focus on contracting, inquiry, and agency supports the client experience of having the sense that they're steering the ship of the therapeutic change. I believe the time we took to contract and establish relational consent around what she wanted for herself supported her internal sense that she was driving this session. I wasn't trying to get her anywhere, make anything happen, or fix anything; I was bringing the NARM relational skills to support us both being curious, interested, and present to her intention and what might be getting in the way of her connecting to her aspirations for herself. She's naming her increasing psychobiological capacity (adult consciousness), and it does feel enlivening and empowering.
Brad	Thank you.	As we ended, I was feeling moved by the deep sense of heart connection. I was feeling into gratitude for Aiyana that I could participate in this process with her. "Thank you" doesn't begin to capture my gratitude.

CHAPTER 11

Clinical Transcript Demonstrating the NARM Organizing Principles

Rich is in his late thirties and identifies as a white, heterosexual male. He has sought out therapy to come to terms with what looks like an impending divorce. He has only been married for a few years. Throughout his adolescence and adult life, he has a history of going directly from one relationship to another, what he has referred to as "love addiction." In this session, he shares about his lifelong fear of abandonment.

Rich has been through various forms of mental health treatment as well as a 12-step program. He has also been active in various meditation and spiritual communities. He is currently struggling with advice he has been receiving that he should take at least a year off from relationships. He is eager to make a decision regarding what to do about relationships in general, and his marriage specifically.

This was the first session that I (Larry) had with Rich. It was clear to me that his previous personal work had been beneficial for him because he showed a capacity for self-awareness and insight throughout the session.

Please note: This transcript is of a real client session. The client's name and other revealing information have been changed to protect confidentiality. This session was minimally edited for clarification and to avoid repetition. Otherwise, this captures the full NARM session with this client.

SPEAKER	TRANSCRIPT	ANNOTATION
Larry	What would you like for yourself from our session today?	Asking for the client's intention as the first step of Pillar 1 [chapter 3].
Rich	I thought about it prior to the session, and two things popped up. One that is more of a preface, which is probably less of what I'd like to get out of our session but more of a statement. I know that in therapy clients get very personal and really experience a lot of emotion. And I wanted you to know that sometimes this is really uncomfortable for me, thinking of being nearly a forty-year-old-man sobbing.	Rich is not directly telling me what he wants yet but is sharing with me a fear, which seems important.
	So, really what I'd like to take a look at is that I'm married, and now separated, and probably heading for divorce. And some of the advice that's been given to me is that I should just be completely alone for a period of one year—no romance, no dating at all—and there's fear, dread, and apprehension that comes up with the thought of that. And that's really what I'd like to explore.	
Larry	OK, you said there were two things, and is there another one as well?	
Rich	Yeah, the first thing was just almost like my apprehension towards like the raw emotion that clients experience during therapy and my discomfort with that. It's like, if I am to shed tears, it sounds uncomfortable because there's probably a lot there. But the second thing I	The fear that I hear is that he is going to get emotional in the session and that it could impact the therapeutic process. As for the advice about abstaining from relationships, I'm sure whoever has given him this advice means well, but there may be something to explore

SPEAKER	TRANSCRIPT	ANNOTATION
Rich (continued)	think it would probably be more pertinent to explore, which is what I mentioned with the celibacy, no dating for a year.	about his relationship to the advice, because it frightens him. I want to stay open to what he is sharing, not take sides, and help him explore what he believes will be best for himself.
Larry	Well, and just to be clear, there's no expectation that just because other people may have shed tears that you're supposed to or anything like that. If you're feeling emotional and you're struggling with it, that's something we can explore in the course of the session. It's all ultimately your choice, whether you choose to express it outwardly or just feel it inwardly. So I just want to be clear that there is no expectation on my part about how you show up emotionally.	I am making clear that I don't put expectations on him regarding how he relates to his emotions. He gets to have his own relationship to his experience, and I will support that.
Rich	OK, I understand.	
Larry	I've heard a couple things. One is that somebody recommended that you take this year off from all relationships and sexuality and everything. And then I heard you have a kind of fear reaction to thinking about that.	While I am holding the advice he got with neutrality, the fact that he has fear about it tells me that there is something worth exploring here. This is part of the clarification process in Pillar 1.
Rich	Yeah.	
Larry	So what would be the optimal outcome of our work today—if at the end of our time you really got what you wanted, what would that be?	I am looking for whatever his intention might be. Pillar 1: Clarifying the Therapeutic Contract.
Rich	Maybe to explore what is blocking me from following through with an entire year of abstinence and no dating, what's so	He is operating under the assumption that he has to do this or that it might be a good idea. I don't take sides in this

SPEAKER	TRANSCRIPT	ANNOTATION
Rich *(continued)*	terrifying about that, and how can I get past it.	internal struggle, for or against, but I do note his perspective.
Larry	Well, there's an assumption in there that you actually want to do that. I mean, it sounded like this wasn't something that you came up with? If I understood you correctly, this was something that somebody recommended to you?	Clarifying to understand where this advice was coming from.
Rich	Yeah.	
Larry	I wouldn't want to just make that same assumption myself. As we do the exploring, perhaps you will decide if that is actually something that seems right for you or not. And then if it does seem right for you, and there's fear with it, that also could be part of the exploration that we do together.	I am clarifying the therapeutic framework. And I am adding an element that he doesn't bring up, about the assumption that this is what he should be doing, because to ignore it is to tacitly accept that the advice he is getting is correct for him. Also I am differentiating between the behaviors he is considering and what he might most want for himself internally.
Rich	OK, that makes sense. Yeah, I would like to explore if abstaining from relationships for one year is right for me, and if it is right for me, I'd like to know what's blocking me from making that leap.	He is putting the cart before the horse: first we have to explore if it is right for him and if it is something that he wants to do.
Larry	I wouldn't want to start off assuming that someone's advice is something you automatically should take. I don't have a position on it one way or the other, except that I wouldn't assume it automatically. It's your life and your decision—if you choose to or not to.	I clarify my position. I tend to challenge any and all assumptions about what is supposed to happen in the therapeutic process that a client comes in with. Otherwise, the open inquiry that we hold in NARM [chapter 4] is already being compromised.

SPEAKER	TRANSCRIPT	ANNOTATION
Rich	Makes sense.	
Larry	So did you say more than one person mentioned this to you, or was it just one person?	I am gathering information about what is influencing his assumption.
Rich	More than one person, and then reading some books. They talk about the withdrawal period and it got me thinking, "Oh, maybe I am a love addict." I seem to relate to many of those symptoms. And maybe the healthiest thing I could do would be to follow through with that advice of a certain period of abstinence. And as I reflected on that possibility, that's when a lot of anxiety came up. I don't know if I can do that—which to me only felt like more evidence of the idea that it would be good for me to try.	Separate from how he internalized this advice, I am also wondering if there is a real part of him that wants to get out of the possibly compulsive relationship pattern that he has been in.
Larry	Well, that's one possible interpretation. But there could be other elements in your reaction too. The way I work is that I don't like to make assumptions without really exploring it together.	NARM is driven by open curiosity and an inquiry process, and we don't make assumptions without exploring the details. Assumptions can be driven from child consciousness, so we want to support how a client is relating to these beliefs from the present moment.
Rich	OK, maybe we could simply explore whether or not a lengthy period of no dating would be a good decision for me or not?	
Larry	I think that may be a useful place to start, to see if you're really on board with the personal recommendations and books you read, to see if that's	This is part of the clarification process that is involved in establishing the therapeutic contract [chapter 3]. I am clarifying with him what he means

SPEAKER	TRANSCRIPT	ANNOTATION
Larry *(continued)*	really right for you. So as you've read and talked to some people, I hear you're questioning if you are a love addict. And I'm just curious about this concept and how you relate to it, maybe we could start there?	by "love addict" and how this might relate to what he's wanting for himself out of our time together.
Rich	OK, that sounds good. I think the concept is maybe primarily twofold: one is I think the discomfort that I've described simply just being single, not dating, not being in a relationship—and that kind of stands out to me a lot. And then secondly, like my wife that I'm separated from, and other women that I have dated, seem to have similar patterns where they get overwhelmed and then distance themselves, and then I draw closer. So just from my own experience and the information I have, it seems that I have a pattern to my romances, and a pattern that I'd like to break free of.	Here he mentions that he has a pattern that he would like to break free of, which seems to be grounded in his own desires rather than based on another person's advice. We may be getting closer to an intention that can orient our work together (Pillar 1).
Larry	Now I hear you talking about your relationship to relationships, or your relationship to romantic relationships in particular.	This is my way of reflecting to him that the focus of the session is now getting a little bit clearer. We're clarifying his intention.
Rich	Yeah.	
Larry	This idea of being celibate for a year, I would call that a strategy. So let's say that this strategy were to work exactly as everybody predicted and that you would hope, what would be the hopeful result of that year's abstinence?	By asking him what he would like to get out of the strategy, I am inviting a clearer intention.

SPEAKER	TRANSCRIPT	ANNOTATION
Rich	Good question! Potentially a new relationship with myself and how I behave in a relationship, as well as perhaps the type of woman that I'm generally attracted to, which as I stated gets maybe overwhelmed at a point by too much intimacy.	His narrative is becoming clearer to me now, in that it sounds like he is struggling with both fear of intimacy and a desperation to be intimate. This internal conflict is what we describe as the core dilemma around connection: our deepest desire and greatest fear [chapter 2].
Larry	So again, if we look at what you're describing right now and try to see into what is ultimately the intention that you have there, what is it that you're really wanting for yourself?	I'm helping the client clarify his own personal desire, as opposed to something he was told or read about.
Rich	I think deeper potential healing into some of the ... I don't know how to say that, like unresolved things from my own life and my own childhood perhaps that have shown up in my patterns of romance.	He is demonstrating self-reflective capacity here, even though he doesn't have a lot of clarity. That gives me a sense of the work he has done previously and his capacity for moving forward.
Larry	So if you are able to resolve these things from your childhood, then what?	It is essential that the client, to the best of their ability at that moment, identify the result they want. This intention sets the stage for the second part of Pillar 1, which is the understanding of what we are doing together, particularly oriented to what's getting in the way of the client getting what they most want. This is beginning the process of exploring the core dilemma.
Rich	I just want to have a good relationship. That's as simple as it is, really, truly precise. And it feels good to say that, like I feel a little more relaxed.	I observe that the clarification is supporting a relaxing in his body, which is a reflection of increased connection to oneself.

SPEAKER	TRANSCRIPT	ANNOTATION
Larry	And what you're describing in terms of the relaxation that you experienced was also very visible. I could see the muscles in your face relaxing and your shoulders relaxing a bit too, so it fits with what I was observing.	Often as clients get closer to something that feels meaningful to them, there is an internal shift that can be observed in relaxation or settling in the body.
Rich	Yeah, I could feel it like from my head to my toes. It's interesting.	He's describing his somatic experience, something that is quite difficult for clients to do at least initially.
Larry	And so it's useful then to see that these other things you described—like if I'm celibate for a year, then I'll have a new relationship to romantic relationships and I'll have a better one—that's what we refer to as strategies. I make this important distinction between strategies and the core intention, and sometimes, just as you've discovered, the core intention is often much simpler. What I hear you acknowledging is that your desire is really just to have the capacity for a healthy relationship.	This intervention is designed to distill out his own intention—his heart's desire—from all the advice that he has been given.
Rich	Yes.	Seems like this reflection landed for Rich.
Larry	And part of what you find helpful that you've already said is that you're aware of old patterns for yourself, that there are some things that have gotten in the way, certain choices that you've made around certain kinds of women that you're attracted to, for example. There is no guarantee about the	This is clarifying the contract of what we are going to do together, which sets up our exploration of the obstacles in the way of him having the kind of relationship he wants.

SPEAKER	TRANSCRIPT	ANNOTATION
Larry (continued)	relationship itself, but we can certainly work with what gets in the way on an emotional level, on a psychological level, of having the kind of relationship that you most want.	
Rich	Yeah, definitely, what's getting in the way of me having a healthy relationship.	He consents to our working agreement, which allows us to have a contract to orient to as we move forward. This is the Pillar 1 process.
Larry	Can you share with me an experience in relationships where you have noticed internal obstacles getting in the way of having a healthy relationship?	This is an example of how we use deconstruction of experience as part of Pillar 2 [chapter 4].
Rich	Yes. Immediately, as I think about any romantic relationship, I start to feel anxiety—like what if she leaves me?	
Larry	So as you start to get closer with someone in a relationship, then are you saying that this anxiety about being left, is that what comes up for you?	I am always trying to clarify and simplify the narrative.
Rich	Yeah, I think so. It's not present all the time, but it's when I'm in the kind of relationship I want to be in, it seems coupled with a fear that comes and goes, which is what if she leaves me.	He continues to clarify and help me better understand how he's organizing and relating to this internally.
Larry	And what are you experiencing right now, Rich, as you talk about this?	I can feel something shifting for him, so I invite his awareness to his experience. This is Pillar 4: Reflecting Psychobiological Shifts [chapter 6].

SPEAKER	TRANSCRIPT	ANNOTATION
Rich	It does feel calming in my body to name it.	Notice that as he is able to stay present with his experience, he begins to feel calmer.
Larry	I'd invite you to take a moment with that. And just to notice that as you name it, something in you starts to calm.	Pillar 4: Reflecting Psychobiological Shifts.
Rich	Yeah, definitely.	
Larry	Is there any emotion there as you start to calm, anything that you're aware of, any particular emotion?	I ask this question because I am sensing sadness starting to surface. This is what I am picking up in the resonance. But I don't name that for the client. That would be more interpretive than we tend to be in NARM. Instead, I ask from my curiosity.
Rich	A little bit of sadness. Oh, that's the feeling I've been experiencing.	Here he names the emotion for himself, which is optimal from a NARM perspective. Remember back to the beginning, where he had apprehension of sobbing and being emotional. Now he is able to begin feeling that sadness somewhat.
Larry	I'm assuming here, so please tell me if this is right or not, but what it sounds like is that as you open your heart more to somebody, then this anxiety of being left comes up. Tell me if that seems right to you.	This assumption emerges out of my working hypothesis, which is how we organize the information that our client is sharing with us. Because I am edging toward interpretation here, I ask the client if it seems right for him, as opposed to me telling him what he is feeling. I am putting pieces together that he has previously shared with me, but I am introducing a new aspect of opening his heart, so I want to make sure this resonates for him.

SPEAKER	TRANSCRIPT	ANNOTATION
Rich	Yeah, definitely.	
Larry	I know you said that you're in the process of a separation right now. Is there some ways you're experiencing now what you had feared?	I am bringing to his attention the experience in his current life that he described earlier. Part of Pillar 2 is focusing more on the client's current life, and how they are relating to their current life, as opposed to focusing primarily on history. We are curious as to their direct experience in the here and now. What is unfinished from a person's personal history tends to surface organically when we stay with a clear focus on the here and now. This is the phenomenological process of this work.
Rich	Yes.	
Larry	When you think about being left, please share any associations around that, and they don't have to make completely logical sense. When you think about those times you're getting closer to a romantic partner, I wonder if we can look more closely at the anxiety that you have identified.	This is drilling down, an intervention part of Pillar 2. I am working more and more on the level of direct experience. And inviting him to explore the anxiety.
Rich	It feels like a very overwhelming fear. I don't know how to describe it. Like an obsessive fear, it becomes the most important thing. It's like, "Oh my God, I'm about to be left," and it becomes more important than anything. It becomes a primary focus of all my attention. And it also feels almost life-threatening. It just feels like such intense fear that brings	I am hearing child consciousness and the strategies that he uses to try to manage this fear of abandonment. You can also see the direct relationship here between the unresolved fear of attachment loss from childhood and the fear of relational loss in adulthood. I notice he mentions childhood feelings and want to ask further about this.

SPEAKER	TRANSCRIPT	ANNOTATION
Rich *(continued)*	me back to childhood feelings, really intense primal fears that I'm going to be abandoned and not going to be OK.	
Larry	So I'm hearing that one of the deepest fears around this is that you're going to be abandoned and/or you're going to at least feel abandoned.	Clarifying the anxiety he's describing and seeing if I am capturing it the way he is relating to it.
Rich	Yeah.	
Larry	And then you made a connection to something, I wasn't sure exactly what, but something related to your childhood. Was it your childhood in general or something specific in your childhood that you were talking about?	Pillar 2. I am reflecting and clarifying the narrative.
Rich	Definitely my childhood. I know that there's an old feeling of terror if I'm abandoned. And I know that I was burned really badly when I was about eighteen months old and separated from my family and in a burn unit for a month. And I don't know if that was the beginning of this feeling that I'm being abandoned and like my life is over. So yeah, I remember my whole childhood, throwing a tantrum if I didn't know where my mom was, and then moving into my teenage years of dating feeling like, "Oh my God, what if she leaves me and gets sick of	It's very common in NARM that as we begin exploring the here-and-now symptoms and difficulties, unresolved themes from the past emerge organically. He is clearly beginning to come in contact with what sounds like significant developmental trauma.

SPEAKER	TRANSCRIPT	ANNOTATION
Rich *(continued)*	me." And into my adulthood and even into my marriage.	
Larry	So is there an emotion in you right now as you think about these experiences and reactions that you've had over your life?	I ask this question about emotion because I can see and feel that emotion is surfacing. This is the first step of the NARM Emotional Completion Model [chapter 7].
Rich	Yes. A sadness of how that fear has been present for most of my life, and sadness that this fear has caused me a lot of suffering.	Grief as a primary emotion often emerges as clients begin to reconnect to themselves in this way.
Larry	How does that affect your feelings towards yourself when you acknowledge the suffering that you've experienced around this fear of abandonment?	In NARM we focus on how the relationship to oneself is distorted in adapting to developmental trauma. Rather than having him regress to what sounds like significant early trauma, I explore how bringing up the theme of his suffering affects his relationship to himself in the present. Optimally, before addressing significant trauma, a certain amount of self-acceptance and compassion is already present. This compassion serves as an antidote to possible regression and counteracts the universal theme that children blame themselves on some level for whatever trauma they experience.
Rich	It brings up a negative sense of myself, like "I'm no good. I'm just going to bring that fear into the next relationship, and that	Here he is blaming himself for the difficulties he has experienced, what we introduced in chapter 2 as shame-based

SPEAKER	TRANSCRIPT	ANNOTATION
Rich *(continued)*	fear is going to be like the virus that infects the whole thing." And then it feels like, "Oh God, there's something wrong with me."	identifications. As clients begin to connect to primary emotions, self-shaming can emerge as a way of moving away from the primary emotions and reinforcing the old adaptive survival patterns.
Larry	Notice how quickly all those linked together—there was a judgment and then there was a kind of futurizing that because of this issue then you're going to mess up future relationships and you'll never "get it right."	This is an example of threading, part of Pillar 3: Reinforcing Agency [chapter 5]. Threading is like a connecting of dots—disconnected aspects of our experience—that can be experienced as very organizing for clients. The client tends to have various reactions and is not always aware of the sequential nature of those reactions. Threading tends to be organizing to the client and minimizes any tendency to fragment.
Rich	Yeah, that's definitely all there.	
Larry	But what I didn't hear is how it is to just look at the pain and the hurt that you've been carrying around and the fear that you've been carrying around about being left. If it was a friend of yours, or if you have a niece or a nephew or something like that, if it was somebody that you cared about and they were starting to realize some of what you're realizing, that they had a fear of abandonment for as long as they can remember—how would you feel towards that person?	When a person is stuck in child consciousness, they automatically blame themself. Here I am externalizing the dynamic with the anticipation that if it were anybody other than himself, he would feel compassion. This externalization process begins to build a bridge to embodied adult consciousness and to the compassion that usually comes with that. This is an example of how we may use Pillar 3: Reinforcing Agency.
Rich	I might feel a lot of sympathy. I'd feel sorry for them that it	When he thinks about this in relationship to somebody else,

SPEAKER	TRANSCRIPT	ANNOTATION
Rich (continued)	happened. And also I'd feel sad. If I was watching someone I loved, I'd feel sad to watch them experience that.	he does feel what he calls sympathy, as well as sadness. Here the grief is emerging again.
Larry	Right, sympathy and compassion is exactly what I feel as I hear *your* story. Certainly being separated for a month at eighteen months old is a hugely painful and difficult experience for a small child.	I share my personal emotional reaction. This is part of the relational and intersubjective orientation that we use in NARM [chapter 8]. I use his word, "sympathy," and add my own, "compassion." The word *sympathy* feels too mild for the kind of pain he is talking about.
Rich	Yes.	
Larry	Do you remember, or do you know from family stories, whether they were able to visit you at all or were you completely isolated?	Gathering information as part of Pillar 2.
Rich	It was a burn unit in Barcelona, they were able to look at me through glass for I think a couple hours, but there was no ability to hold me or even touch me or anything. It was all through glass.	I feel an ache in my heart as I am hearing him talk about this.
Larry	What do you experience as you talk about that now? That they could see you through glass but there could be no holding or touching?	I notice an emotional reaction in him, which I am inviting his attention to.
Rich	At first like almost right now there's like a pain, like a sadness, and also a kind of frustration too, like an anger, I feel like, "This is fucked!"	As he is talking about the different reactions, anger seems to be the dominant emotion here, and it ultimately seems to be the most useful as an antidote to collapse and depression. This is the first step of the Emotional Completion Model as

SPEAKER	TRANSCRIPT	ANNOTATION
Rich *(continued)*		he identifies and relates to his primary emotion of anger [chapter 7].
Larry	And what happens as you let yourself feel some of the anger that's there about that?	Inviting his awareness to his emotional experience.
Rich	I don't know. The first thing I thought was almost like some sort of disassociation from it, like I was talking about it like it happened to someone else. But then, I don't know, maybe a little bit feeling of relief.	What I imagine he means is that he senses there is more anger there than he is comfortable allowing so he starts disconnecting from it. It is significant to note that as he allows himself to feel some of the anger, it actually brings relief. This is Pillar 4 territory, the shifting of very deeply held and embodied adaptive survival patterns.
Larry	It makes sense that you might be feeling all of those different things. You can feel more than just one reaction at a time.	I am supporting him here to allow the complexity of emotion.
Rich	Yeah.	
Larry	Do you have any memories at all of that experience?	I am asking for memories that are likely to be constructs of things he was told by his family, given his age at the time. However close to the original reality that the constructs may or may not be, they are informing his reactions in the here and now and in his life in general.
Rich	Not really memories but feelings that feel so familiar for me.	
Larry	Like what? Can you give me an example?	It is important to be as concrete as possible here. This is a Pillar 2 intervention, drilling down.

SPEAKER	TRANSCRIPT	ANNOTATION
Rich	Just like a feeling of being small, and just freaking out if I didn't know where my mom was, just like real terror.	This narrative rings true to me. This terror might lead back to the present-day anxiety and fear he has been sharing about in regards to being in romantic relationships.
Larry	Yeah.	
Rich	And I think I can almost remember being angry too. Like, "How dare you fucking leave me there!"	Anger is useful here, as a part of the protest that he is beginning to feel.
Larry	"How dare you fucking leave me there." Can you notice any emotion that goes with that?	I invite his attention to the emotion that may be driving his reaction.
Rich	Yeah, it felt good to be connected to that emotion. It feels like in the center of my chest there's a little more strength and a little more confidence.	As anger gets integrated, clients often report feeling stronger.
Larry	And if it's OK to take a little time with that … [*Rich sits quietly for a few moments*] You're noticing a little more strength and increased confidence in the center of your chest.	Pillar 4: Reflecting Psychobiological Shifts.
Rich	Yeah. That's what it feels like, it kind of feels more adult. More strength, like I can do this, I can succeed and be OK.	What he is describing sounds and feels very important and reflects the integration process. In embodied adult consciousness, he is experiencing the increasing psychobiological capacity that is part of feeling into our adult Self. It is not uncommon to hear a client reference "growing up" in this way.
Larry	Let's look at another aspect of this. If you think about an	Notice how I am inviting him to look at the child's experience

SPEAKER	TRANSCRIPT	ANNOTATION
Larry (continued)	eighteen-month-old child who's just had a severe burn, and then this complete physical separation, and the opportunity for only a little bit of time during the day to have some visual contact with the people who are most important to you— what happens for you as you reflect on this?	while remaining in increasing adult consciousness.
Rich	Yeah, I feel more anger than anything else. This is fucked up. Like I just want to punch the wall or something like that. It feels like, "This is bullshit!"	His anger is obviously building but in a contained way, which is consistent with the NARM Emotional Completion Model, rather than "getting it all out."
Larry	Except I don't think it's the wall that you're angry at.	This ironic comment is designed to help him stay focused on what the anger is really about. This is again consistent with the emotional completion process. The desire to punch the wall is a good example of an acting-out strategy. Clearly it is not the wall he is angry at, and while most clients would know this cognitively, this intervention invites them to reflect deeper on the protest and anger.
Rich	Yeah.	
Larry	But I hear the anger.	
Rich	Yeah.	
Larry	And the protest too—you said this is fucked up, this is not right.	I remind him of what he said a few moments earlier. As the energy of this anger becomes integrated, that is what brings healing.

SPEAKER	TRANSCRIPT	ANNOTATION
Rich	Yeah.	
Larry	And just notice how that affects you to, again, to feel a little bit of that anger, a little bit of that protest.	I invite him back to the felt experience of his anger because protest was the original message to the environment, and as an adult, it is a message to himself that he doesn't deserve what he is experiencing, which is an antidote to the self-blame that children feel. This communication of the primary emotion is the second step of the Emotional Completion Model, which leads to the third step around being present with oneself and one's emotions in a new way.
Rich	Yeah, it feels good. There is a more alive feeling of the protest. It feels like this is what's right. And anger is really directed at my parents, even though I know now it wasn't their fault, but the feeling is like, "Fuck you. How could you just leave me here?"	He reports feeling more aliveness as the anger gets more integrated. This is the third step of the Emotional Completion Model. His adult understanding that it wasn't his parents' fault doesn't seem to be getting in the way of the anger/protest completion. It is not unusual for clients to go prematurely to understanding and forgiving their parents as a way of not feeling the emotions that need to be felt. That doesn't seem to be happening here. In fact, that he can hold both the adult understanding and the emotional charge at the same time is significant. Adult consciousness is capable of holding increasing complexity, even of contradictory emotions and thoughts, and reflects the resolution of splitting.

SPEAKER	TRANSCRIPT	ANNOTATION
Larry	And of course you can, from an adult place, get more understanding of the situation, but we're also trying to look at what this experience was like for you, and also what you needed to do as a small child to survive and manage for a month in this environment and with this lack of physical connection to your parents.	I explain to him exactly what I am doing. Ultimately it is not about blame, it is about renegotiating this very difficult event. There is a little bit of psychoeducation going on here as well, which is an aspect of Pillar 4. I am also reflecting with him about what a child would have to do internally in order to survive this kind of experience. What the child had to do internally reflects the adaptation that they made to survive, which they usually carry forward that adaptation into adulthood. This NARM intervention is meant to increase his awareness of his childhood experience without regressing to and reliving that experience.
Rich	That's interesting you said what I needed to do to survive and manage. It almost comes back oddly to what I said, I didn't want it to be necessarily what I wanted to get out of our time today, but what I feel is like an apprehension towards feeling too much emotion or crying or something like that. What I needed to survive was that I needed like my mom and dad to hold me. And I think eventually maybe I just kind of felt like I need to shut down and not feel this intense longing.	His insight seems quite to the point. This feels significant because it comes out of his direct experience and has the sense that it is an embodied cognition, as opposed to a disconnected cognitive insight.
Larry	My experience in working with these kinds of dynamics with other people, which is generally shutting down is the only strategy that is available to a small child. At first, they might feel anger, they might feel longing,	We use psychoeducation as part of Pillar 4. I am helping him view this childhood experience through a child's eyes, but without having him regress or relive the experience. My intention is to support him in identifying

SPEAKER	TRANSCRIPT	ANNOTATION
Larry (continued)	they might feel tremendous grief, but all of those emotions feel too dangerous. It feels like there's no resolution. And for an eighteen-month-old child, a month is an eternity. It's not like if you're a grown person and even a month would be terrible, a month of isolation, but you can still visualize a future beyond that. But an eighteen-month-old little child, who lives so much in the here and now, that month is forever. And so then they've got to find some way to deal with what feels like to them like a never-ending reality	and understanding the adaptations that he would have had to make to survive that experience, and by extension, helping him understand the struggle around relationships and fear of abandonment that he has experienced his whole life.
Rich	Yeah, it's interesting you say that because I'm having multiple associations right now. One which is the feeling of shutdown, which I already mentioned, which is like, "Ugh, I don't want to cry or feel too much emotion as we begin this." But also when you say that feeling of thirty days being as if it's an eternity, when I think of that it's like that's what I think of when I imagine being out of relationship for a year, and I tell myself that it's not that long.	Notice how he is relating to these multiple associations more from adult consciousness, not feeling so reactive or urgently needing to do something (from child consciousness).
Larry	Well, and the message that you've been getting from books and from other people, they were suggesting you have no physical contact for one year.	It is very obvious here how the well-meaning advice from books and friends has put him in a very powerful dilemma. It really helps us see why "advice" can be damaging because it is ignoring the larger context of his life. It is a behavioral attempt to deal with the symptom that he has had of being anxious when he is not in relationship.

SPEAKER	TRANSCRIPT	ANNOTATION
Larry *(continued)*		In NARM we do not weigh in for or against the advice, but instead we engage the client in an exploration, so that the client can see for themself what they need to do.
Rich	Thirty days and no contact, that feels like eternity. Naming it gives me some kind of freedom from it.	He is describing the powerful impact the psychoeducation is having on him, which is an optimal outcome. "Freedom from it" is part of the disidentification process [chapters 2 and 6].
Larry	Yeah. I invite you to notice how experiencing this freedom feels like in this moment.	Pillar 4: I reflect the shift toward increasing connection, which accompanies the freedom from the shutdown and aloneness he has felt all his life.
Rich	Again, that similar feeling—more confidence, more like relating to the man and the adult that I am, that can walk through difficulties rather than relating to that feeling of being a child, that this is overwhelming and feels like eternity. It helps me relate more to myself in the present as an adult.	So much of the NARM approach constellates around supporting the possibility of the client experiencing increasing confidence in their ability to face both the challenges of life and whatever difficult emotions come up in any given situation. What he is describing reflects more of the embodied adult consciousness.
Larry	Right. And again, that seems really significant, that part of your consciousness has been very much caught up in this whole theme of abandonment and being left. And what I hear you describing is that you're coming back to yourself more in the present moment.	This is Pillar 4: reflecting and reinforcing important psychobiological shifts.
Rich	Yeah, which is really good.	

SPEAKER	TRANSCRIPT	ANNOTATION
Larry	And I noticed a shift in your body position just then.	Reflecting the somatic shifts I am observing as part of the Pillar 4 process.
Rich	Yeah, it feels good. It feels so much better to relate to myself as an adult. And I guess from this place, if I were to take a year off, it doesn't seem so long. It doesn't feel so overwhelming.	This is what successful resolution looks like. The threat that the child experienced is reducing as Rich shifts from child consciousness into embodied adult consciousness.
Larry	Yeah. Because earlier you said life-threatening. And so from this place where you are now, where this whole dynamic doesn't feel so overwhelming, when you look back at what you said earlier in the session about this experience being life-threatening, what do you see about that from where you are right now, as an adult, a thirty-eight-year-old man?	I am helping him to distinguish what was then and what is now: child consciousness vs. embodied adult consciousness. It also reflects very different brain circuitry coming online in relationship to the old event.
Rich	It doesn't feel life-threatening. It feels like maybe still a challenge nonetheless but like an adult type of challenge.	Important new understanding and awareness are coming online as he accesses adult consciousness.
Larry	That seems like a big, big shift, Rich.	Pillar 4.
Rich	Yeah, definitely, it feels like a big shift. I hope I can maintain this space of confidence and continue relating to who I am as an adult.	Notice how he starts to effort here. Most clients, when they begin feeling positive states, want to hold on to them. It's natural that they want to, but it doesn't work that way. Whenever we try to hold on to a state, it slips away. States such as confidence, love, compassion, and forgiveness are not so easily subject to the conscious will.

SPEAKER	TRANSCRIPT	ANNOTATION
Larry	But notice that this space was available to you with just a little help from me. And in just forty-five minutes being together, you were able to access this feeling, which shows me that it's available to you. It doesn't mean you'll always feel it all the time, but you know that this is there.	In response to his comment, I am supporting confidence that this capacity is always available when we explore whatever dynamics are getting in the way.
Rich	Yeah, you're right. It was available to me, it's just like a shift in perspective.	Here he is referencing the felt-sense quality of being in embodied adult consciousness.
Larry	Yeah. A shift in perspective.	I repeat his very important comment as a way of reinforcing and anchoring its importance.
Rich	Yeah, I think so. Just kind of relating from a child perspective versus relating from an adult perspective.	
Larry	And going back to something that came up earlier in this session, we saw this pattern where as you get closer to a romantic partner and start to open your heart more, then this fear comes up stronger. So let me put that kind of side burner for a second and just ask you to think about what would a child in this isolation ward do with his heart? Particularly his heart towards the people that he loves and completely depends upon, his parents in other words, what would he do with his heart?	I am helping make a connection between a pattern in his life in general and having to spend a month in isolation as a child.
Rich	The child would just shut down and not want to feel the intense longing, I would imagine.	

SPEAKER	TRANSCRIPT	ANNOTATION
Larry	And you just used specific words that feel very important: "the intense longing." I also imagine that a child would be longing to be touched, more than I think most adults can even begin to imagine.	I have no doubt that it is very helpful for him to identify this intense longing and the early roots of that longing. Remember, he used the label "love addict" before, which did more to conceal these internal dynamics than clarify. With our exploration, he now has more information for what might have been driving these behaviors and feelings, and he has more "adult" capacity to make decisions aligned with his authentic desires.
Rich	Yeah, definitely. And just hearing it named like that is kind of intense just because it's like, "Oh, shit, that's that feeling." That intense longing, that describes the feeling that I've experienced probably my entire life.	He makes an important connection to what he has experienced most of his life.
Larry	And from that perspective we can understand again how as a child when you couldn't find your mother, how strong your reactions that you described would be.	I weave the narrative back to how he would get so anxious when he couldn't find his mother. I am taking the various fragments of the narrative and helping him thread them together into a more coherent tapestry.
Rich	Yeah.	
Larry	So just so you know, we're coming to the last few minutes of our time here together.	When we are dealing with themes of abandonment, it is important for therapists to be aware of the possible associations between ending the session and the client's early experience of abandonment.
Rich	OK.	

SPEAKER	TRANSCRIPT	ANNOTATION
Larry	But we still got a few minutes left. I just wanted you to know so that it wouldn't feel abrupt.	
Rich	I appreciate that. Yeah, it's cool just to name some of these things. There seems to be a certain strength in the aware-ness of them. Yeah, intense longing, that's something I felt. And the ability also to access this place of strength is also really powerful.	He keeps emphasizing strength, which is again part of an increasing psychobiological capacity.
Larry	It's very touching.	As part of the NARM Relational Model and Pillar 4, self-disclosure is about therapists sharing how we are being impacted by being with our clients' experience. It supports an authentic connec-tion between two humans and supports heartfulness.
Rich	I hope that if, and most likely when, I do shift back into that state of intense longing, or child state, that I can try to remember the possibility of being able to access this place of strength and confidence in my adult Self.	He is referring to using the learning of this session as a resource moving forward, not in an efforting way, but more of like a touchpoint to support his continued growth.
Larry	It can really make a difference when you know this is available to you, even in those moments when you're stuck in some old pattern. You know that this kind of strength and confidence is still there, it's not lost, it just sometimes goes missing for a little while.	Psychoeducation and a little bit of clarification on my part. In NARM we hold that these states are part of our inherent nature, part of our birthright. Access to them on the level of awareness can be diminished or lost in adapting to develop-mental trauma, but the states themselves are never lost.
Rich	Yeah, that's good to know.	

SPEAKER	TRANSCRIPT	ANNOTATION
Larry	OK, well, now I think we are getting to our time here.	
Rich	OK, beautiful. Thank you so much. I really appreciate it. And I think I got a lot out of our short time, so I'm very grateful.	
Larry	I'm glad. I appreciate you sharing this very personal piece of your experience with me. So thank you.	

Conclusion

We would like to return to the beginning of this book, in the introduction, where we invited you to reflect on your intention for reading this book. Now that you have completed it, we want to invite you to revisit your intention for how you will use what you learned in this book:

- How might you use this information to support your professional work?

  - In terms of your impact as a helping professional, what would you like to happen?

  - What is your heart's desire?

- How might you use this information to support your personal growth?

  - In terms of impact on your own life, what would you like to happen?

  - What is your heart's desire?

- What do you notice internally? We invite you to take your time to reflect on your body, emotions, thoughts, and any other internal experience.

This book is designed as a practical guide to support you in applying the NeuroAffective Relational Model for healing complex trauma. We hope that you have already begun to use these NARM principles and skills in support of your clients. We hope that this book can be a useful resource for you to return to as you bring NARM into your professional and personal life.

We know that there is a lot of information to integrate. NARM is a depth-oriented model that takes time to learn and integrate. As a "cheat

sheet," we have made available a diagram of the NARM protocol in Appendix A. As a quick takeaway, here is a reminder of the basic therapeutic model of the NARM Four Pillars:

Pillar 1: Clarifying the Therapeutic Contract

It starts with us inviting reflection: *What does our client most want for themself?*

Pillar 2: Asking Exploratory Questions

Then we invite curiosity: *What is getting in the way of what our client most wants for themself?*

Pillar 3: Reinforcing Agency

Then we support exploration: *What is our client's relationship to the patterns that are in their way of what they most want for themself?*

Pillar 4: Reflecting Psychobiological Shifts

Then we reinforce: *How is it for our client to experience the shifting of old patterns into new ways of relating to and being with themself?*

We hope that for some of you this book has inspired you to learn more. The NARM Training Institute offers four levels of professional and clinical training. These trainings are offered both in-person and online. If you are interested in training in the NeuroAffective Relational Model, please visit the website www.narmtraining.com.

We also encourage you to listen to our podcast, *Transforming Trauma*, where we introduce listeners to inspiring NARM therapists who are having profound impact on the individuals and communities they serve. We also host ongoing conversations with thought leaders in the trauma field, as part of our mission to collaborate with others in evolving and promoting the trauma-informed movement.

We are building an international community dedicated to using NARM to heal complex trauma. We are just at the beginning of our work. Our professional community consists of passionate individuals committed to healing trauma and supporting post-traumatic growth. In addition to professional training on complex trauma, we are focused on promoting education,

research, outreach, and advocacy based in our unique mentorship model. We look forward to collaborating with you in evolving the trauma-informed field and changing our world.

As we end, we would like to reflect on our intention for writing this book and how we hope you might use it moving forward. It is our hope that this book will be used by helping professionals in enhancing therapeutic effectiveness for healing complex trauma. We thought we would share an email we received from someone who attended a NARM class and began using the principles and skills that you've been introduced to in this book. What they share captures what our deepest desire is for this book.

> I just wanted to share that I have been implementing the few NARM skills that I learned and have been blown away by how different I feel and how much deeper my clients are able to go. Over the past few years I have been searching for a therapy that would bring greater depth, res- olution, ease, and presence into my work. I feel so fortunate to have been introduced to NARM. I was feeling so lost and unable to effect lasting change that I was considering going into another field. This really has been life-changing. It also gives me hope that I can work through my own developmental trauma so that I can provide a holding space for others to do the same. I am so thrilled and am really looking forward to learning as much as I possibly can from NARM.

While we will continue our focus on training NARM-informed help- ing professionals around the world, we also hope that NARM can support anyone seeking personal healing and growth. It is our intention that this work can contribute to the trauma-informed movement in support of per- sonal and collective change. Our greatest hope is that NARM can lead to increasing opportunities for connection, healing, and transformation in individuals, relationships, communities, and society.

Our vision is to bring humanity to the transformation of complex trauma. In this book, we have presented an embodied, relational, and depth- oriented model that we hope will advance greater humanization in the heal- ing process. NARM is a therapeutic approach that supports reconnection to one's lived experience, so that clients can feel more fully alive—and become more fully human. When working in this way, differences between biology,

psychology, and spirituality become blurred. The integration of body, mind, and soul becomes the catalyst for a client's ever-deepening sense of Self.

Transforming trauma is a journey. It is our heart's desire that the NeuroAffective Relational Model can support you and your clients along your journey.

> *It's important not to underestimate how subversive—and ultimately transformative—this work is. We're really challenging what we take to be our identity: a certain kind of fiction about who we are that we've identified as. This challenge is more threatening— and life-affirming—than we may consciously acknowledge.*

NARM Protocol

CURIOSITY AND PRESENCE	**Attunement**	Intention	Help client clarify intention and sense into client's distress	
		Client Intervention	Clarify the therapeutic contract — Pillar 1	
		Self-Inquiry	Notice how it feels to be with the client	
	Acceptance	Intention	Make space for client's complexity	**Step 1** Identify primary emotion
		Client Intervention	Ask exploratory questions — Pillar 2	
		Self-Inquiry	Notice the impulse to rush, fix, label, take sides	
	Reflection and Exploration	Intention	Understand how client organizes their inner experience	**Step 2** Reflect on emotion's intention
		Client Intervention	Clarify the core dilemma	
		Self-Inquiry	Lightly hold working hypothesis	
	Mindful Interventions	Intention	Hold possibility of new way of client relating to self and world	**Step 3** Support new relationship to unresolved emotional conflicts
		Client Intervention	Support increased sense of agency — Pillar 3	
		Self-Inquiry	Notice tendency to be goal-driven	
	Integration	Intention	Support client's increase in psychobiological capacity	
		Client Intervention	Reflect psychobiological shifts — Pillar 4	
		Self-Inquiry	Notice capacity to be present with and affected by client's shifts	

Right column heading: **NARM Emotional Completion Model**

NARM Personality Spectrum Worksheet

Your Name:

Date:

Choosing a client, please fill out the spectrum below.

PSYCHOBIOLOGICAL TRAITS	ORGANIZED SELF		ADAPTIVE SELF		DISORGANIZED SELF			
	Circle one along the spectrum *10 (very high) to 1 (very low)*							
1. Connection *capacity for connection to oneself and others*	10 9	8 7	6 5		4 3		2 1	
2. Separation-Individuation *capacity for differentiation, independence, and adult consciousness*	10 9	8 7	6 5		4 3		2 1	
3. Self-Regulation *capacity to regulate one's internal states*	10 9	8 7	6 5		4 3		2 1	
4. Agency *capacity to take ownership for one's life*	10 9	8 7	6 5		4 3		2 1	
5. Capacity for Intimacy/Therapeutic Alliance *capacity to experience others as a source of support*	10 9	8 7	6 5		4 3		2 1	
6. Empathy *capacity to relate to the internal world of others*	10 9	8 7	6 5		4 3		2 1	
7. Self-Awareness/Insight *capacity for inquiry and self-discovery*	10 9	8 7	6 5		4 3		2 1	

PSYCHOBIOLOGICAL TRAITS	ORGANIZED SELF				ADAPTIVE SELF		DISORGANIZED SELF			
8. Consensual Reality *capacity for experiencing life with minimal projections*	10	9	8	7	6	5	4	3	2	1
9. Self-Activation *capacity to initiate and set the course for one's life*	10	9	8	7	6	5	4	3	2	1
10. Presence *capacity to be in the here and now (present moment)*	10	9	8	7	6	5	4	3	2	1
TOTAL SCORE (out of 100) =										

Please note: The NARM Personality Spectrum is not an evidence-based diagnostic tool. It is a therapeutic tool that can support helping professionals in reflecting on their clients. The scoring range helps us recognize where clients are on the spectrum of Self-organization. This personality spectrum provides therapists with a framework for assessing where their clients are on a range from greater organization (Organized Self) to less organization/more disorganization (Adaptive Self) to significant disorganization (Disorganized Self).

Identifying the level of organization–disorganization is important as it helps therapists have a clearer sense of their clients' internal world; better understanding of their client's capacity; an accurate sense of client buy-in and prognosis; realistic expectations that inform how therapists show up in the therapeutic relationship; recognition for how interventions are being received and how they are impacting the client's process; a tool for assessing a client's process over the course of therapy; and a framework to evaluate how effective NARM might be for this specific client in supporting them in their change and growth process.

Scoring Ranges
100–70: Organized Self range

Clients in this range may have more developed, secure, and well-organized psychobiological capacities that lead to them moving through their lives with greater flexibly and resiliency. Of course these individuals will still experience challenge, distress, and symptoms, but they have a more secure base with which to recover and move forward without undue preoccupation with the past and anxiety of the future. Their coping strategies tend to be more on the healthy, mindful side—things like exercise, healthy eating, social engagement, and just a general self-care orientation. They have fewer internal obstacles that are getting in their way of growth and development, and they spend more time in adult consciousness. Their observing ego is stronger, with greater capacity for self-reflection, self-awareness, and self-insight. These clients often have greater capacity for agency, to see their part in their own challenges and suffering, as well as self-activation, cultivating greater creativity, intimacy, success, and fulfillment in multiple areas of their lives. Therapeutically, there tends to be very good prognosis for treatment. These clients are more open, engaged, and collaborative, and they engage with the therapist in the spirit of goodwill. The therapeutic process is often enriching for both client and therapist.

69–40: Adaptive Self range

Clients in this range may have more disrupted, less secure psychobiological capacities that lead to them moving through their lives experiencing frequent challenge, distress, and symptoms. These clients often experience various psychobiological symptoms and disorders. Their coping strategies tend to be more problematic, and though they may experience some sense of flexibility and resiliency, they often get in their own way of self-activation, success, and fulfillment in multiple areas of their lives. They may take themselves and their issues quite seriously and have significant internal obstacles that are getting in their way of growth and development, and they spend more time in child consciousness. They are often caught in preoccupation with the past and anxiety of the future, making it difficult for them to be

present and open. Their observing ego is weaker, with compromised capacity for self-reflection, self-awareness, and self-insight. A diminished sense of agency leads to more difficulty seeing their part in their own difficulties and suffering, and they may rely on acting-in and acting-out strategies including blame and shame. Therapeutically, at least initially, there tends to be a good to fair prognosis for treatment. These clients are more challenging, in both their capacity to use the therapeutic skills and their engagement with the therapist. The therapeutic process may at times be quite challenging and frustrating for both client and therapist.

39–10: Disorganized Self range

Clients in this range may have severe and profound psychobiological limitations that disrupt their ability to move through their lives without experiencing consistent challenge and distress. These clients often experience chronic psychobiological symptoms and syndromes, including significantly disabling psychological and medical conditions. They are often desperately seeking help while at the same time feeling frustrated and unsatisfied at receiving the help they are receiving; they often dismiss, minimize, or outright reject support. Their coping strategies are limited in general, and they tend to act in and act out, at times in ways that can be off-putting, threatening, and even dangerous for themselves and others. They tend not to experience a sense of flexibility and resiliency and may disrupt movement toward self-activation, success, and fulfillment in multiple areas of their lives. They may take themselves and their issues extremely seriously and have profound internal obstacles that are getting in their way of growth and development, often experiencing the world strongly through child consciousness. They are often unable to differentiate the present from the past, have unclear and incoherent narratives of the past, and feel uncertainty or a sense of a foreshortened future. They often do not experience resiliency or agency in their lives and may blame others for their problems. They do not experience an observing ego and have impaired capacity for self-reflection, self-awareness, and self-insight. Therapeutically, at least initially, there tends to be a fair to poor prognosis for treatment. These clients have limited capacity overall, may express resistance to using therapeutic skills

for themselves, and may engage with the therapist in a challenging, adversarial, or even threatening manner. The therapeutic process may be extremely challenging, frustrating, and troubling for both client and therapist.

One important additional note about clients in the Disorganized Self range: clients are humans, and even when they are struggling with a poor prognosis and limitations in multiple areas of their lives, we stay committed to them receiving the most optimal care. Oftentimes these clients do require more support than we alone can provide, and we work with them to assure that they are getting the support they need. We also want to remember that a client's disorganization and symptoms do not define the person. The person sitting in front of us is so much more than these symptoms and their suffering. We always meet our clients holding dual awareness—the reality of the level of their challenges (using the NARM Personality Spectrum to assess) as well as the hope for them to heal (using the NeuroAffective Relational Model to treat).

We have both worked with clients who fall in this range and who have experienced significant healing and change. We have met clients who had been rejected by countless treatment providers and yet through NARM have found deeper connection to the health and aliveness within. Because someone is experiencing more limitation in their present life does not mean anything negative about the person or about their potential for healing and growth. As human beings, we are all struggling to some degree. We hope that therapists keep in mind that the NARM Personality Spectrum is a tool for humanizing our clients' experience. We hope that this tool for identifying our clients' present capacity can help us provide more effective treatment for all our clients.

Notes

Introduction

1 Heller, L., & LaPierre, A. (2012). *Healing developmental trauma: How early trauma affects self-regulation, self-image, and the capacity for relationship.* North Atlantic Books.

2 Shedler, J. (2010). The efficacy of psychodynamic psychotherapy. *American Psychologist, 65*(2), 98–109. https://doi.org/10.1037/a0018378

3 Heller, L., & LaPierre, A. (2012). *Healing developmental trauma: How early trauma affects self-regulation, self-image, and the capacity for relationship.* North Atlantic Books (p. 28).

Chapter 1

1 American Psychiatric Association. (2013). *Diagnostic and statistical manual of mental disorders* (5th ed.).

2 Kezelman, C., & Stavropoulos, P. (2012). *'The last frontier': Practice guidelines for treatment of complex trauma and trauma informed care and service delivery.* Adults Surviving Child Abuse.

3 World Health Organization. (n.d.). *6B41 Complex post traumatic stress disorder.* Retrieved October 4, 2021, from https://icd.who.int/browse11/l-m/en#/http://id.who.int/icd/entity/585833559

4 Redford, J. (Director). (2015). *Paper tigers* [Documentary film].

5 Stevens, J. E. (2017, December 7). *The adverse childhood experiences study—the largest public health study you never heard of.* HuffPost. https://www.huffpost.com/entry/the-adverse-childhood-exp_1_b_1943647

6 Felitti, V. J., Anda, R. F., Nordenberg, D., Williamson, D. F., Spitz, A. M., Edwards, V., Koss, M. P., & Marks, J. S. (1998). Relationship of childhood abuse and household dysfunction to many of the leading causes of death in adults: The Adverse Childhood Experiences (ACE) Study. *American Journal of Preventive Medicine, 14*(4), 245–258. https://doi.org/10.1016/S0749-3797(98)00017-8

7 Centers for Disease Control and Prevention. (2020, April 3). *Adverse childhood experiences (ACEs)*. https://www.cdc.gov/violenceprevention/aces/index.html

8 For more resources on ACEs: https://www.cdc.gov/violenceprevention/aces/about.html

9 Van der Kolk, B. (2015). *The body keeps the score: Brain, mind, and body in the healing of trauma*. Penguin Books.

10 Herman, J. L. (2015). *Trauma and recovery: The aftermath of violence; from domestic abuse to political terror*. Basic Books (p. 119).

11 Bremness, A., & Polzin, W. (2014, May). Commentary: Developmental Trauma Disorder: A missed opportunity in DSM V. *Journal of the Canadian Academy of Child and Adolescent Psychiatry, 23*(2), 142–145. https://www.ncbi.nlm.nih.gov/pmc/articles/PMC4032083/

12 Adapted from: *Complex posttraumatic stress disorder*. (n.d.). Traumadissociation.com. Retrieved September 20, 2021, from http://traumadissociation.com/complexptsd

13 Heller, L., & LaPierre, A. (2012). *Healing developmental trauma: How early trauma affects self-regulation, self-image, and the capacity for relationship*. North Atlantic Books.

14 Spinazzola, J., van der Kolk, B., & Ford, J. D. (2018). When nowhere is safe: Interpersonal trauma and attachment adversity as antecedents of posttraumatic stress disorder and developmental trauma disorder. *Journal of Traumatic Stress, 31*(5), 631–642. https://doi.org/10.1002/jts.22320

15 Schore, A. N. (2016). *Affect regulation and the origin of the self: The neurobiology of emotional development*. Psychology Press.

16 Sulha. (2020, June 29). *The Israel Palestine conflict – Adar Weinreb* [Video]. YouTube. https://www.youtube.com/watch?v=1c3RkOwdG9Y.

17 Tedeschi, R. G., & Calhoun, L. G. (1996). The posttraumatic growth inventory: Measuring the positive legacy of trauma. *Journal of Traumatic Stress, 9*(3), 455–472. https://doi.org/10.1002/jts.2490090305

Chapter 2

1 Mahler, M. S., Pine, F., & Bergman, A. (2000). *The psychological birth of the human infant: Symbiosis and individuation*. Basic Books.

2 Heller, L., & LaPierre, A. (2012). *Healing developmental trauma: How early trauma affects self-regulation, self-image, and the capacity for relationship*. North Atlantic Books.

3 For more information on the Distortions of the Life Force process, please see pages 10–12 in: Heller, L., & LaPierre, A. (2012). *Healing developmental trauma: How early trauma affects self-regulation, self-image, and the capacity for relationship*. North Atlantic Books.

4 *Gabor Maté: The Roots of Healing*. Sounds True. (n.d.). Retrieved December 14, 2021, from https://www.resources.soundstrue.com/transcript/gabor-mate-the-roots -of-healing/

5 Shedler, J. (2021). The personality syndromes. In R. Feinstein (Ed.), *Personality disorders*. Oxford University Press.

Chapter 3

1 Rogers, C. R. (2016). *On becoming a person: A therapist's view of psychotherapy*. Robinson (p. 17).

2 Wallin, D. J. (2015). *Attachment in psychotherapy*. Guilford Press.

Chapter 4

1 Miller, W. (1955, May 2). Death of a genius: His fourth dimension, time, overtakes Einstein. *Life* (p. 65). https://books.google.com/books?id=dIYEAAAAMBAJ&q =%22holy+curiosity%22#v=snippet&q=%22holy%20curiosity%22&f=false

Chapter 5

1 Atwood, G. E., & Stolorow, R. D. (1993). *Structures of subjectivity: Explorations in psychoanalytic phenomenology*. Analytic Press (p. 86).

2 Bandura, A. (2001). Social cognitive theory of mass communication. *Media Psychology*, *3*(3), 265–299. https://doi.org/10.1207/S1532785XMEP0303_03

3 Mahler, M. S., Pine, F., & Bergman, A. (1985). *The psychological birth of the human infant: Symbiosis and individuation*. Maresfield Library.

4 Frankl, V. E. (2020). *Man's search for meaning*. Rider Books.

5 Mandela, N. (1995). *Long walk to freedom: The autobiography of Nelson Mandela*. Back Bay Books.

6 Perry, B. D., & Winfrey, O. (2021). *What happened to you?: Conversations on trauma, resilience and healing*. Flatiron Books.

7 Siegel, D. J. (2020). *The developing mind: How relationships and the brain interact to shape who we are*. Guilford Press.

Chapter 6

1 Malhotra, S., & Sahoo, S. (2017). Rebuilding the brain with psychotherapy. *Indian Journal of Psychiatry, 59*(4), 411–419. https://doi.org/10.4103/0019-5545.217299

2 Hollis, J. (2006). *Finding meaning in the second half of life*. Avery (p. 10).

Chapter 7

1 Damasio, A. (2008). *Descartes' error: Emotion, reason and the human brain*. Vintage Digital.

2 Bowlby, J. (1999). *Attachment and loss*. Basic Books.

3 Freud, S., & Strachey, A. (2013). *Inhibitions, symptoms and anxiety*. Martino Publishing.

4 NPR. (2015, June 10). *It's all in your head: Director Pete Docter gets emotional in 'Inside out.'* NPR. https://www.npr.org/2015/06/10/413273007/its-all-in-your-head -director-pete-docter-gets-emotional-in-inside-out

5 Kammer, B. (Executive Producer). (2020, November 24). A mother's journey into finding effulgence through the NARM process of resolving grief with Heidi Winn (No. 29) [Audio podcast episode]. In *Transforming Trauma*. NARM Training Institute. https://narmtraining.com/transformingtrauma/

Chapter 8

1 Adler, A. (2002). *The collected clinical works of Alfred Adler*. Classical Adlerian Translation Project (p. 64).

2 Tronick, E. Z., & Gianino, A. (1986). Interactive mismatch and repair: Challenges to the coping infant. *Zero to Three, 6*(3), 1–6.

3 Winnicott, D. W. (2017). *Playing and reality*. Routledge.

4 J. Krishnamurti. (1972, September 12). *You can learn only if you do not know* [Audio recording]. https://jkrishnamurti.org/content/you-can-learn-only-if-you-do-not -know-0

5 Clyborne, C. (2021, October 10). *We are [not] responsible for [figuring it all out.] The client, the contract, and our willingness to stay curious...* [Facebook comment]. Facebook. https://www.facebook.com

6 Masterson, J. F. (1983). *Countertransference and psychotherapeutic technique: Teaching seminars on psychotherapy of the borderline adult.* Brunner/Mazel (p. 55).

Chapter 9

1 Vogl, B. (n.d.). *Ecoliteracy: A path with a heart: An interview with Fritjof Capra.* Retrieved December 20, 2021, from http://www.haven.net/patterns/capra.html

2 Grant, B. F., Hasin, D. S., Stinson, F. S., Dawson, D. A., Chou, S. P., Ruan, W. J., & Pickering, R. P. (2004). Prevalence, correlates, and disability of personality disorders in the United States: Results from the National Epidemiologic Survey on Alcohol and Related Conditions. *Journal of Clinical Psychiatry, 65*(7), 948–958. https://doi.org/10.4088/jcp.v65n0711

Index

differentiation between emotions and
behaviors, 211–212
disconnection from, 196–198
fear, 198–201
fear of, 212
grief, 198, 205–208
primary, 81, 216–220
primary vs. default, 208–214
reflecting on emotion's
communication, 220–222
supporting new relationships to
unresolved emotional conflicts,
222–225
empathy
attunement, 244–245
Personality Spectrum Model,
282–283
empathy, therapists
authentic empathy, 242
reflective exercise, 234
source of therapist's emphathetic
impulse, 230–232
unmanaged empathy, 232–235, 240,
242, 269
empowerment vs. agency, 147
environmental failure, 17, 46, 47
exercises
Pillar 1: Clarifying the Therapeutic
Contract, 114–115
Pillar 2: Asking Exploratory
Questions, 139
Pillar 3: Reinforcing Agency, 166
Pillar 4: Reflecting Psychobiological
Shifts, 191
practice exercises. *See* practice
exercises
reflective exercises. *See* reflective
exercises
exploration, Relational Model,
251–253
exploratory questions. *See* Pillar 2: Asking
Exploratory Questions

F

failure to thrive, 196
fear, 198–201
vs. anxiety 198–201

attachment and relational loss,
61–63
of emotions, 212
feedback
from NARM clients, 133,
151–152, 193
from NARM students, 9-10, 237
feeling stuck with clients. *See* stuckness
feelings, avoiding, 217. *See also* emotions
Felitti, Vincent, 29, 30
fight, flight, and freeze, 43, 198
fragmentation, 45
Frankl, Viktor, 149
Freud, Sigmund, 240
futuristic memory, 199

G

Gillispie, Lisa, 51
goal-oriented statements, clarifying
therapeutic contract, 101
good-enough mothers, 246
grief, 198, 205–208
default and primary emotions,
210, 212
vs. depression, 207
reflective exercise, 207–208

H

Hanh, Thich Nhat, 258
*Healing Developmental Trauma: How
Early Trauma Affects Self-Regulation,
Self-Image, and the Capacity for
Relationship* (Heller and LaPierre),
38, 68, 167
the heart in search of itself, 206
heartfulness, 2, 169, 238, 258–259
client therapy examples, 326, 358
Heller, Laurence, 1, 167
helplessness, therapists, 229–230, 234, 249
Herman, Judith, 21, 35–36
historical trauma, 46–50
holding environment, 246
Hollis, James, 173
hopelessness, 131–132, 205
hypnotherapy, 45

About the Authors

 LAURENCE HELLER, PhD, holds a doctorate in clinical psychology. He was in private practice for forty years and is the founder/developer of the NeuroAffective Relational Model (NARM), which is taught throughout the world. His book *Healing Developmental Trauma* has been published in fifteen languages. Heller cowrote *Crash Course* about working with shock trauma as well as *Befreiung von Scham und Schuld,* written and published in German, about the theme of shame.

 BRAD KAMMER, LMFT, LPCC, is a senior trainer and training director at the NARM Training Institute. He began his career as a humanitarian aid worker in Asia, which introduced him to personal and collective trauma. He is passionate about helping resolve the widespread impact of complex trauma. Kammer's work is based on the integration of somatic psychology, interpersonal neurobiology, and wisdom from spiritual traditions and traditional cultures. He is a somatic-oriented psychotherapist in private practice, professor, producer of the *Transforming Trauma* podcast, trauma consultant, and international trainer on trauma-informed care.

For more information on NARM, please visit the NARM Training Institute: www.narmtraining.com

About North Atlantic Books

North Atlantic Books (NAB) is a 501(c)(3) nonprofit publisher committed to a bold exploration of the relationships between mind, body, spirit, culture, and nature. Founded in 1974, NAB aims to nurture a holistic view of the arts, sciences, humanities, and healing. To make a donation or to learn more about our books, authors, events, and newsletter, please visit www.northatlanticbooks.com.